A
Common
Fate

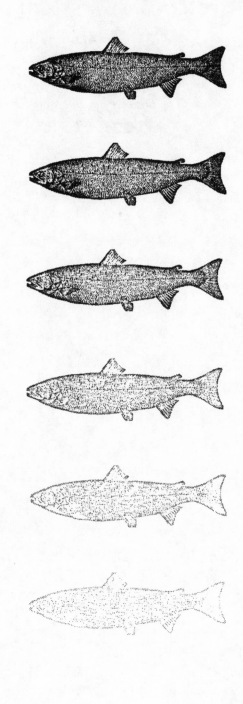

A Common Fate

ENDANGERED SALMON
AND THE PEOPLE OF
THE PACIFIC NORTHWEST

Joseph Cone

A JOHN MACRAE BOOK
HENRY HOLT AND COMPANY
NEW YORK

For Adam and
his generation

Henry Holt and Company, Inc.
Publishers since 1866
115 West 18th Street
New York, New York 10011

Henry Holt® is a registered
trademark of Henry Holt and Company, Inc.

Library of Congress Cataloging-in-Publication Data
Cone, Joseph.
A common fate: endangered salmon and the people of the Pacific
Northwest/Joseph Cone.—1st ed.
p.   cm.
"A John Macrae book."
Includes index.
1. Pacific salmon—Columbia River Watershed—Effect of habitat
modification on.   2. Endangered species—Columbia River Watershed.
3. Fishery conservation—Columbia River Watershed.   4. Ecosystem
management—Government policy—United States.   I. Title.
QL638.S2C658   1994
333.95'6—dc20   94-12020
CIP
ISBN 0-8050-2388-7

Henry Holt books are available for special
promotions and premiums. For details contact:
Director, Special Markets.

First Edition—1995

Designed by Paula R. Szafranski

Printed in the United States of America
All first editions are printed on acid-free paper.∞

1   3   5   7   9   10   8   6   4   2

Grateful acknowledgment is made for permission to reprint an excerpt from "The Grand Coulee Dam,"
words and music by Woody Guthrie, © 1958 (renewed), 1963 (renewed), and 1976 Ludlow Music, Inc.,
New York, NY. Used by permission.

Grateful acknowledgment is made to the following for information used on the endpaper maps: Willa
Nehlsen, Jack E. Williams, and James A. Lichatowich, "Pacific Salmon at the Crossroads," *Fisheries*
magazine; Philip L. Jackson and A. Jon Kimerling, *Atlas of the Pacific Northwest;* and The Wilderness
Society, *Pacific Salmon and Federal Lands: A Regional Analysis.*

CONTENTS

Acknowledgments

I have not done a scientific study of it, but it seems customary to end acknowledgments with one's spouse. I'd like to reverse that practice here and thank my wife, Tylar Merrill, for without her primary assistance this project could not have been completed. Exactly coincident with the writing of this book we've been raising a son from birth to age two. Anyone who has any experience of that event knows how it can easily take all of one's energy and interest. The continuing support Tylar has shown for my writing project within that bigger endeavor has been a constant affirmation of her care—and of her resourcefulness.

I'm indebted to many colleagues for their insights, advice, and encouragement. Chief among them are Bob Malouf and Sandy Ridlington, director and managing editor, respectively, of Oregon Sea Grant at Oregon State University. Both of them encouraged and supported the book in numerous ways from the beginning. Jim Larison, former director of communications with Oregon Sea Grant, and Bill Wick, former program director, also were important in getting the project started.

I appreciate the reviews of many of those who were sources for the book. In particular, I thank Jim Lichatowich, Michael Blumm, and Gordon Reeves for diligently reading and commenting on sizeable portions of the manuscript.

Naturally, any errors which remain are my responsibility entirely.

Friends and fellow writers John Russial, Glen Gibbons, and Richard Strickland helped sharpen my prose and my thinking; and for the insights that can come only from good conversation I'm especially grateful to Janice Gotchall, Paul Conte, Marcia Brett, and David Bayles. Bill Merrill was, as always, a merry cornucopia of information and perspective.

Several writers and researchers who specialize in salmon history and biology generously shared resources and background material with me: Court Smith, Bill Pearcy, Chris Frissell, Dan Bottom, Janet Webster, Cleve Steward, Lori Bodi, Kai Lee, Doug Markle, and Irene Martin.

For her assistance I thank Becky Hiers, with the Confederated Tribes of the Umatilla Indian Reservation, and I value the time and attention given to me by tribal officials Antone Minthorn and Louie Dick. Russell Jim of the Yakama Indian Nation generously responded to my questions about certain Indian ceremonies.

Finally, I deeply appreciate the efforts of my agent, Bob Lescher, and of my editor, Jack Macrae, for keeping the Northwest, as a territory of hope, alive in New York City and helping to share it with the rest of the country.

DENIAL AND ENGAGEMENT

If the courage is lacking now to take the steps necessary to sensible conservation, we shall have the losses and the hardships eventually anyway; with the difference that, if action is delayed, depletion will have progressed further and rehabilitation made just so much more difficult.

—WILLIS H. RICH, "THE FUTURE OF THE COLUMBIA RIVER
SALMON FISHERIES," 1940

The wind came in gusts off the slate gray ocean, surging hard as if it would charge up into the mountains. It blew rain over Highway 101, dousing the sparse morning traffic of cars, log trucks, RVs, and one government-green sedan heading south out of Florence. Inside the sedan, Gordon Reeves reached over on the seat and, eyes fixed on the rainy highway, plucked another carrot stick out of a sandwich bag. Judiciously, he took a first small bite. He was thinking, and he liked to chew things up fine.

It was only 10:30, but this was lunchtime for Reeves, and the inside of his car was his fast-food place this morning, another busy one of a busy week. He had left home and gone to his office at 7:00 A.M., then driven two hours, down the Oregon coast. He was spending more time alone in a car than he liked, but it was giving him a chance to think about what he was seeing in the forests of the Coast Range. What he was seeing worried him. Reeves, a fish researcher and ecologist with the Pacific Northwest Research Station of the U.S. Forest Service, had gotten himself what he considered an interesting,

1

and quite likely controversial, assignment. He was evaluating how successful the Forest Service and the Bureau of Land Management were in their efforts to improve conditions for salmon in the federal forests of the Northwest.

To do the evaluation, he needed to investigate an enormous amount of country, not just the Coast Range but also parts of the Cascade Mountains in Oregon and Washington and the coastal mountains of northern California. This morning in March 1988 he had driven from Corvallis, in the valley east of the Coast Range, over the coast summit.

It had begun to rain as soon as Reeves started up into the coastal hills. In good years, the Pacific Ocean dumps huge quantities of rain and snow on the mountains of the Pacific Northwest. With enough rain and certain sorts of soils, the mountain slopes spawn a multitude of streams, draining the rain off and sending it back to the ocean. Rain was necessary for salmon. It was a comforting thought as Reeves peered beyond the windshield wiper.

But it wasn't just a matter of topography and climate, not just mountains, streams, and rain. The salmon also needed certain conditions in their living space, and over millions of years they had evolved to find those conditions in the mountain forests of the Northwest. Geography was destiny for the salmon, and that destiny was relatively secure as long as the streams, mountains, and forests changed only with the slow rhythm of geological time.

The problem, Reeves knew, was that the secure time was long gone. As he drove along the coast now, he thought about how things had changed in the forests in the last hundred years and especially in the last ten years, and about how those changes affected the salmon. And he chewed his carrot sticks.

Not far out of town, the roadside cafes and the shops that rent dune buggies petered out, and the highway slipped into a tree-lined route marked by turnoffs for the national recreation area and for parks and campgrounds. Places had melodious Indian names such as Siltcoos and Tahkenitch, but most of the Indians were long gone. This stretch of the Oregon coast was the sort people thought of when they considered it still mainly wild and unpopulated. They were right about the unpopulated part, at least relatively speaking. It was not Connecticut or Virginia. But wild? Reeves knew well that that was only relative, too.

As he passed Tahkenitch Lake, the clouds hung low on the forested hillsides, wreathing their way among the trees. He nodded his head as he watched the streaming clouds. He knew he wasn't likely to see much of that effect on the lower Smith River: not enough trees.

The turnoff for the Smith, a few miles farther south, was announced by a huge International Paper Company pulp mill, squatting on the banks of the estuary, its lights on in the pallid daylight. The mill sat not far from the spot where in 1828 a band of Indians had attacked the camp of the fur trader Jedediah Smith, one of the first white travelers through the area. All fifteen men in camp were killed, though Smith himself happened to be away. When he discovered the dead men, he fled north, through uncharted mountains crisscrossed by swollen rivers and bogs. Before he finally reached the outpost of the Hudson's Bay Company at Fort Vancouver, on the Columbia River, he had endured great hardships. That was the story people tended to know. What grievances the Indians had against the animal trappers had been forgotten.

Three years later, Smith himself was killed by Comanches on another fur-trading expedition. Once he left the Northwest he never returned to the river on the Oregon coast that was named after him, commemorating the massacre. All in all, it was an inauspicious beginning for the European-American possession of the region.

As Reeves turned off the highway and onto the river road, the sour smell of paper pulp lingered in the car. It went with the territory. Most of the private lands owned by International Paper and others had been logged, and many of the hillsides looked stripped, showing only a few trees of any size. In many places the bottom land alongside the river had been turned into pasture for cattle. Here and there up one of the short ravines that notched the foothills a double-wide house trailer, a pickup truck, and a TV satellite dish announced the presence of a resident. But Reeves drove fifteen miles up the river road without seeing anyone. It was that sort of rural Oregon—where you don't see people, only their effects.

The Smith River ran mostly through Douglas County. More timber regularly came out of here than from any other county in Oregon, which meant it was also one of the top timber counties in the whole United States. For decades, Coos Bay, the port thirty miles south of the Smith River, had reigned as the largest lumber-exporting harbor in the world. Reeves knew that the timber harvest in Douglas County was prodigious; one billion board feet of raw timber per year was common in the 1970s and '80s. A board foot is an inch thick, a foot long, and a foot wide. A billion board feet of logs yielded enough lumber to frame about one hundred thousand houses of the preferred American size, two thousand square feet.

Things taken out and not put back disturbed Reeves's sense of balance, and he watched grimly as he passed the stubby hillsides. But he didn't have much say about what people did on private lands. His job was to look at what was done on the public lands.

At an intersection, he turned off the main road and up into the hills, alongside the North Fork of the Smith. This drainage would have been heavily forested once, but as Reeves ascended the winding logging road the consequences of the road's placement were clear. Most of the forest adjoining the road had been logged in the 1950s and '60s, clearcut down to stumps and brush. For about ten miles or so he drove past clearcuts and stands of small young trees. Then abruptly, past a turn in the road, the hillside returned to thick forest. By law, the National Forests were required to be managed for "multiple uses," which included fish and wildlife, water, recreation, and wilderness, as well as timber. The managers of the Siuslaw National Forest had decided to leave this part alone. Reeves slowed down, looked at his written directions, then pulled off the road and stopped.

Unbending himself from the driver's seat, he came out under a canopy of Douglas-fir trees, which diffused the rain into a drizzle. He popped the trunk, reached for a couple of duffel bags, and, standing quietly in the drizzle, began to take his clothes off.

Six feet fall, Reeves had the healthy look of a man who was outdoors much of the time and, in his late thirties, also still played sports whenever he could—in his case, squash. He liked the speed, concentration, and finesse involved in a good game of squash. He liked the challenge when things were going fast.

Down to his underpants, he took a neoprene brace and slipped it over his left knee. Years before, he had played hockey in college, but that had ended abruptly with knee troubles. The knee troubles didn't end, though. After three conventional surgeries and one arthroscopic operation, the surgeon had told him he had the knees of two different men: one a thirty-five-year-old, the other an eighty-five-year-old. Reeves wasn't interested in moving like an eighty-five-year-old, so he wore the brace and tried not to let it get in his way.

Quickly now in the chilling air, he put on long underwear and stepped into a blue rubber dry suit, squeezing his ankles through the black skintight neoprene cuffs. Fussing and breathing out hard through his nose, he forced his head through the collar. Reaching behind him, he pulled the long zipper across his shoulders and stood up straight. He should stay dry, unless the suit had holes he hadn't seen.

Reeves was one of a handful of fish researchers in the Northwest who pioneered the use of wet suits and dry suits for examining rivers. He had gone through this drill—of taking off blue jeans and sweater and putting on an underwater suit—hundreds of times, alongside logging roads from California to Alaska. Now, as he sat on the bumper, lacing up his felt-soled boots, he was eager to finish the preparations and get into some water he didn't know.

Carrying his face mask and snorkel, he clambered down to the river past a sparse clump of white-barked alder trees. He was lucky; he had to travel only a short distance upriver. With a grunt he pulled the rubber hood over his head and smoothed it around his close-cropped beard. He slipped the face mask and snorkel over the hood and stepped into the river.

At the surface, the river looked like a troubled mirror, reflecting broken bits of sky. But underneath that surface Gordon Reeves entered a different world, separate and whole. He eased himself in.

The icy current jingled past his ears as he moved quietly but firmly against it. He swam a kind of dog paddle where the water was deep enough, and braced himself and crawled on his hands and knees where it wasn't. As he moved, he disturbed some fine silt on the streambed, which rose up in brown plumes. Flecks of green from the forest tumbled by in the current. An orange newt darted by on its way over to the riverbank.

The swimming and river walking were clumsy because the streambed had very little texture, nothing to hold on to, little for Reeves to steady himself against. The bottom was smooth and uniform. Too smooth and uniform, he thought. There were no fish.

In a few minutes he came to the project, several logs placed across the creek, cabled into the bank and bottom. Moving upstream, Reeves swam up to these logs while looking at the streambed. He saw no gravel downstream of the logs. He stepped out of the stream, walked past the logs and got back in. There was no gravel above them either. Reeves stood up again and blew out his snorkel.

"That's not going to do much," he said out loud.

He shook his head slowly, and looked around. Up on the hillside, young trees were growing. But other parts of the forest system did not seem to be coming back. Where was the gravel?

Reeves didn't know. It might have all washed out in the big flood of 1964, when the torrential rains that scoured the hillsides met no resistance from the roots or the downed limbs of standing trees or the trunks of fallen trees, because there weren't enough of these left. They had been taken out in logging or cleaned away afterward. There might just not be any more gravel, at least not for a long time.

Which was a shame, Reeves thought as he looked at the logs, because they were placed in the stream at considerable cost and with considerable hope of trapping gravel. The structure had been built for the salmon because they needed gravel, but it didn't matter a damn. He hadn't seen any salmon and he doubted any would be there. Or if they passed by, they wouldn't stay very long.

Pulling his face mask off, he shuffled out of the stream and walked back to the car.

Gravel, of a certain size and quantity, is only one of the necessities salmon get from an intact forest system. During the last fifty years scientists have shown that salmon, like all other creatures, have evolved in close relationship with their physical environment. More than with most wild creatures, perhaps, this evolution has written a remarkable life history. The closer a person comes to the details of the story, the more intriguing it becomes. But even the simplest outline is appealing.

Scientists call the Pacific salmon and their close relatives the sea-run trout "anadromous." It's a perfect word for those who know Greek, but a clumsy one that most people instinctively mispronounce. The correct way is with the accent on the second syllable. Anadromous simply means "running up." The Pacific salmon (chinook, coho, chum, pink, and sockeye) and the trout (steelhead and cutthroat) all run up rivers as adults.

But that's a long way from where their story begins.

First, they are born in a river or stream, where they stay until they have become the size of a finger—"fingerlings"—or larger. Then, all in a rush of hormones and physiological changes unsurpassed by most other adolescents, their constitution is transformed. Starting out as creatures of freshwater, the juvenile salmon become creatures able to live in the salty waters of the sea. Other fish such as the Atlantic salmon and striped bass also breed in freshwater and live much of their lives in the ocean. But less than 1 percent of all fish species are anadromous like them.

It is hard to think of an exact human comparison for the fresh-to-salt metamorphosis. The magnitude of it may be conveyed, though, by imagining making a rapid change from breathing oxygen to breathing carbon monoxide.

Remarkable as it may be, the little salmon do abruptly move from a comparatively protected life in shallow, wooded streams to swimming out into the vast, mysterious ocean. Here their adventures truly begin. For as many as six years they make their way, often thousands of miles, in a dangerous world. Where the salmon go is only sketchily known, but many populations entering the ocean from the Pacific Northwest swim up to the Gulf of Alaska and then circulate with the prevailing currents out as far as the Aleutian Islands. As they swim, they feed voraciously on such creatures as small squids and shrimplike euphausiids. Gradually they grow to adulthood. Then, obeying an urge that is far older than they and not to be denied, they return to freshwater, to mate and spawn.

At this time of their lives they seem paragons of creation. Once, the

Columbia River boasted a prime summer run of salmon, dubbed commercially as the "Royal chinook." (The locals also knew them, less grandiosely, as the "June hogs.") These giant fish commonly reached four feet in length and sixty pounds, and their heads were proportionately large and fierce-looking. It was easy to attribute extraordinary qualities to these wanderers.

In the lower Columbia River they were often caught in big nets hauled in by workhorses. When caught, they resisted furiously. Their skin was a mottled bronze, and beneath it their deep orange-red muscle tasted ripe, rich, and buttery when cooked. The flesh would never again be as firm and delicious as it was when the fish entered the river for their spawning runs. In the 1880s, the fishery based on the June hogs established the reputation of Columbia salmon throughout the United States.

For all the salmon that escape the fishery—today, as then—an arduous journey often lies ahead. The spawning run takes them not just anywhere but to the streams of their own birth, often near the exact spot where they were spawned. The journey inland may encompass hundreds of miles and take weeks of effort, and was usually done without eating.

Finally, home, in a fine flurry of beating tails, the females deposit eggs in the streambed and the males release their milt in the water above, fertilizing them. Exhausted by their efforts, adult salmon die shortly thereafter, often in a matter of days. Some anadromous trout survive and can spawn again.

Of the many remarkable things that these fish do during their lives, perhaps none is more extraordinary then the run home, upriver, against the current. In their determination to get to their natal streams they will not stop trying. Again and again they throw themselves upriver over waterfalls. The leaping defines them and gives them their common name.

"Salmon" derives from the Latin verb meaning "to leap": *salire*. The English have been using the word "salmon" to describe this genus of fish since at least the thirteenth century. A chronicle of Richard the Lion-Hearted refers to "fysch," "flesche," and "salmoun." Even then, salmon was apparently considered something quite distinctive—no mere fish.

Under the best of circumstances, some salmon can leap extraordinarily high. Scientists have measured chinook salmon, for instance, jumping vertically more than seven and a half feet, and steelhead trout jumping nearly eleven feet. A person doesn't need a Ph.D. to appreciate the sight of a bright, healthy, strong chinook of, say, thirty pounds and three feet in length, exploding out of dark water and in a gleam of motion, jumping more than twice its length, up and over a waterfall.

Scientists have studied the mechanics of the leap, of course, and have determined that a salmon can get a big boost in its upward surge when conditions are just right. Not surprisingly, the ideal conditions happen to occur under short, nearly vertical waterfalls, which are common in the mountains of the Pacific Northwest. It works this way: Water falling into a pool creates a standing wave. If the salmon can time its effort so that it matches the upward thrust of the wave, the wave acts like a booster rocket, propelling the resourceful fish up and over the falls.

The wave boost is an aid, not a necessity, for the jump. Just as remarkable are the ranges of leaps; a coho salmon of twelve pounds can leap six feet up and twelve feet out, a 1:1 weight-to-extension ratio. Compare that with American track star Carl Lewis, who, at 175 pounds, jumped some twenty-eight feet to win the long-jump gold medal in the 1992 Summer Olympics. The comparison may not be altogether fair, but the best human jump is only about one-sixth that of the fish.

Going and coming; the mysterious pull of the oceanic unknown; the determination in the return to their origins; the extravagance in spawning and dying. The dramatic life history of the salmon touches on the essential poetry of life. Anyone who spends time with them becomes smitten by the story. The native peoples of the Northwest, who have spent more time with the salmon than anyone else, virtually all have legends to account for the miraculous reappearance each year of the salmon from out of the ocean. Many believed that the salmon had homes at the bottom of the sea and that the salmon's abundant return was a sign of the fish's favor. To secure that favor, certain ritual acts had to be performed, such as returning to the bones of the fish to the river.

For thousands of years, the indigenous peoples of the region have cultivated their knowledge of the fish, learning the ways of their local runs. As much as they are a crucial item of food to them, the salmon have also shaped their lives: what they think about, how they think. One recurring motif in Northwest Indian drawings of salmon is the representation of a human face within the salmon's body. The Indians see themselves as interdependent with the fish.

For certain biologists the life story of the salmon is also unusually absorbing. The relationship between the salmon and their environment can be as subtle as any in nature. That was just the worry Gordon Reeves had with the lack of gravel in the streambed on the North Fork of the Smith River.

Gravel of a certain size, Reeves knew, was critical to the spawning success of salmon. When the female builds a "redd," the nest for her eggs, she begins by hollowing out a pit in the streambed. With strong thrusts of her tail she sweeps light gravel and silt out of the way. Once the eggs—about four thousand of them in the case of a coho salmon—are deposited in the pit and the sperm spread over them, the female jostles gravel back into place over the pit, to protect the fertilized eggs.

For salmon, biologists have experimentally determined that gravel from about the size of a pea to the size of a grapefruit is best, depending on the size and species of the salmon. Not enough gravel, or gravel of the wrong size, usually means the fish will not spawn in the area, or the fertilized eggs will likely be washed away or preyed upon. The result is the same: That particular stretch of river will go unseeded with young fish. That appeared to be the case on the North Fork of the Smith River.

Gordon Reeves would have been less discouraged by the North Fork if it were the exception to what he was seeing on other forest lands. Unhappily, it was not. Many millions of public dollars were being spent on projects to improve habitats both for salmon spawning and rearing. Each has different requirements. For spawning, good conditions in streambeds are wanted. For rearing, good conditions in stream channels are necessary. To their credit, the federal agencies at least seemed aware of the need to improve habitat conditions for salmon. But the rehabilitation projects often weren't meeting expectations. Worse, until Reeves's work in 1987 and 1988, most federal projects weren't even being rigorously evaluated.

But Reeves believed that salmon's problems went beyond what could be solved through better engineering in the stream environment. In the forested areas that he knew, salmon populations were often not doing well—and had not been doing well for some time. The coho, or silver, salmon that are native to the coastal forests of Washington, Oregon, and California, for example, were suffering a decline that was at least twenty years old. One scientific study said that 10 percent of local coho populations had become extinct in the region since 1968. What was worse, the trajectory for coho didn't look like it was going anywhere but down. The conclusion was unacceptable to Reeves: The species could become extinct all along the Northwest coast.

Part of the cause, Reeves had come to believe in 1988, were degraded conditions of the lands in many forests, not just in the forest streams. Reeves was not alone in this thinking. But he had the knowledge and skill to support this interpretation and the determination to work toward a solution. For him, addressing the decline of the salmon was a professional concern. But it went beyond that to something deeply personal.

Reeves had come out of a working-class family. His father was a millwright in the Union Carbide plant in Niagara Falls, New York. The fathers of the other kids he hung around with in the 1960s also worked in factories, but young Gordie was different; in 1969 he was one of the first boys from the neighborhood to go off to college.

The State University of New York at Oswego was not a hotbed of campus protest during the next crucial years of the Vietnam War. It wasn't a Berkeley or a Columbia. But neither was it asleep, and Reeves himself woke up to politics during his time there. Long afterward he remembered his surprise when a professor canceled class in favor of an antiwar protest, saying, "Learning isn't in the classroom now. It's in the streets." For the young man from Niagara Falls who wanted to better himself through a good education, the old ideas of "education" and "responsibility" showed themselves as questions rather than as simple answers.

The world of fisheries biology that he graduated into in 1973 was also a changing one. For decades, fish and game biology was dominated by men who had grown up as fisherman and hunters and saw it as their primary role to perpetuate those experiences. The emphasis was on extracting the "interest" from nature's bank account: the surplus salmon, ducks, and deer. But after 1970 and the first Earth Day, more public attention became focused on the natural "principal" that was supposed to be generating the interest in catchable fish and shootable birds and mammals. As the plight of the bald eagle and the grizzly bear made plain, not all was well with species and the ecosystems that supported them. In 1973, Congress passed and Richard Nixon signed the Endangered Species Act.

A new generation of wildlife biologists appeared on the scene, reflecting the broader public concerns for the environment. Reeves was one of this new generation. In 1973 he began work at the Lake Ontario Environmental Laboratory, taking part in research that had not been much addressed before: the effects on fish of nuclear-power-plant discharges, heavy metals, and pesticides. The research lab in which Reeves worked discovered PCBs—then still unabbreviated as polychlorinated biphenyls—in some fish in Lake Ontario. That was quite a time; PCBs had never before been detected in fish.

Despite that and other accomplishments, or rather because of them, Reeves didn't stay long at the laboratory. He had been writing grant proposals and getting them funded, but he felt keenly that the director of the laboratory was receiving all the credit. Not only did he feel he was doing the director's job for him, he felt limited by the work he himself could do with only a bachelor of science degree. Reeves and his wife decided to move to California, where he had been accepted for graduate studies at Humboldt State University, a school in the heart of California salmon country.

During the next several years, while Reeves went to school and worked summers crewing on a commercial fishing boat, he made some extra money working on research projects. One contract, a performance audit of salmon restoration projects on federal lands in California through Alaska, was especially valuable. It opened new horizons. Having grown up in the East, he had never seen mountains and forests like these before. These were real mountains—high, huge. In some places in the forests, he could still walk through virgin stands of towering trees, where nature seemed to display all its richness, undiminished. He was deeply impressed.

As he conducted this survey in 1978 and 1979, he saw that other forest places, however, were distinctly diminished. The fish environment was in trouble in many locations, and he began to question whether well-intentioned, small-scale restoration efforts would make any difference to salmon abundance.

One time, on the central Oregon coast, he had finally persuaded the reluctant local biologist to show him one of the projects on the "completed" list, a simple project to truck in gravel to create spawning beds for chinook. At the site, however, Reeves learned that the contractor had dumped the wrong size rocks into the stream. The rocks were the size of bowling balls, which Reeves knew no chinook could move. Nevertheless, the project had been chalked up as "completed successfully." Another time, a report claimed that a salmonid restoration project had had dramatic results, increasing fish populations by about 500 percent. Intrigued, Reeves put on his diving gear and took a look for himself. He noticed that the increased fish populations weren't salmonids—salmon and trout—but shiners and dace. "We never *said* they were salmonids," the local biologist explained.

Such experiences taught Reeves how the fisheries-enhancement game was played, and he learned to be skeptical of claims of success: A lot of "paper salmon" were created. Still, Reeves didn't blame individual biologists. Most efforts were well intentioned.

This contract job for the Forest Service made Reeves realize that he wanted to direct his own research projects, for which he'd need a doctoral degree. It also put him in touch with senior fish researchers who provided him the opportunity to do just that. In 1980 he began doctoral studies under Jim Hall, of Oregon State University, and Fred Everest, of the Forest Service's Pacific Northwest Research Station, which, like the university, was located in Corvallis, Oregon.

Hall was widely known for his involvement in the first long-term study of the effects of logging on fish in a sizable area of Northwest forest. This study in the Alsea River watershed on the Oregon coast, begun in 1959, had persuasively shown what many had believed: that logging could cause primary changes to the stream environment. With trees gone and shade over a stream eliminated, water temperatures could increase. Without roots to hold it, topsoil could slide into a stream, depositing sediments that could fill up holes in the steambed gravel, suffocating newborn salmon. With logging debris decomposing in the stream, oxygen available for aquatic animals in the stream could decrease. In the Alsea these effects were implicated in a decrease in cutthroat trout populations.

When Reeves began doctoral studies in 1980, the gross effects of logging on fish were clear enough. As he considered a subject for his doctoral research, he was interested in understanding more subtle effects. At the time, for example, the Forest Service and other stream managers operated under the principle that the only important temperature changes in streams, as far as salmonids were concerned, were ones that might be lethal to them. Reeves doubted that the only effects worth taking seriously were the deadly ones, and he set out to see what the truth was. In studies he designed and con-ducted in both the laboratory and in the field, he showed that nature wasn't quite so simple. With increased temperatures in a stream, one less-valued species of fish, redside shiners, would tend to compete more successfully for food than steelhead trout. So, even though steelhead weren't killed off by a drastic temperature change, their populations still declined.

Completing his doctorate in 1984, Reeves went right to work as a fish researcher for the Forest Service. It was a deliberate choice. The National Forests might have problems, he saw, but they also provided scope and opportunity in which his efforts might make a difference.

First of all, they comprised huge areas of the Northwest. Ten million acres in Oregon, for example, were in National Forests. That was an area more than three times larger than the entire state of Connecticut. Washington and Idaho added another 14 million acres of National Forest. In addition to the forest lands, the Forest Service also managed almost as much acreage in range and other lands. Arguably the agency had more of an influence on the natural environment of the Pacific Northwest than any other single entity.

Yet, in spite of its benign, Disneyesque mascot of Smokey the Bear, the Forest Service was not primarily in the business of forest protection. The National Forests were—despite what people in some urban areas might have thought—not sisters to the National Parks. The National Forests were part of the U.S. Department of Agriculture; trees were viewed as a crop, and large-scale timber-cutting was not only permitted but encouraged. As pri-vately held lands were logged in the Northwest, the industry turned increasingly to the public lands, primarily those administered by the Forest Service.

The shift from private to public lands began in earnest in the 1950s. By the mid-1960s harvests on federal lands (including those of the Bureau of Land Management) exceeded those on private lands. So intensive and so extensive was the cutting of the National Forests that by the mid-1980s serious effects were becoming apparent. Because the best and most valuable timber was from big, old trees, the industry wanted these forest stands. A single old-growth Douglas-fir, the principal commercial tree, could yield anywhere from about two thousand board feet of lumber to several times that much. The retail value of the lumber from a single tree could range from several hundred to several thousand dollars, depending on the size and quality of the tree and on market conditions.

So sharp was the interest in the old trees that by the mid-1980s only about 10 percent of the original area of the "old-growth" forests remained (on both public and private lands), and as the trees vanished, so did some species that made their home in these forests and depended on them. The depletion of the old growth had reached such a stage that in 1987 a number of environmental groups began bringing legal action against the U.S. Fish and Wildlife Service, the Bureau of Land Management, and the Forest Service in order to protect one of the dependent creatures, a reclusive small bird—the northern spotted owl.

On the face of it, this seemed a particularly sorry situation—that government agencies responsible for conserving fish and wildlife were contributing to its decline and potential extinction. Sorry as it might be, it wasn't as if warnings hadn't been circulating for years.

Although the spotted owl was little studied by scientists before the 1960s, research at Oregon State University in the late 1960s and early '70s had established the link between the owl and old forests. In 1972 the chief of the Forest Service had duly acknowledged the relationship in a memo to the director of the U.S. Fish and Wildlife Service. By the late 1970s the timber industry and the land-management agencies all recognized that conservation of owl habitat would require a reduction of logging on the productive federal forests west of the Cascade Mountains. However, logging only increased, dramatically, in the 1980s.

As predictable and as lamentable as the plight of the owl might have seemed to some, Reeves and other ecologists recognized the bird as only a symptom of a much broader problem. Northwest forest ecosystems as a whole were in trouble.

Ronald Reagan's quip about redwood forests—"A tree's a tree; how many more do you need to look at?"—seemed a fun-house mirror distortion of the prevailing attitude toward forests in America. Forests were only trees, and trees were there to be cut; and they could be cut and regrown without significant loss to the forest. Even most forest scientists seemed to believe that. But even as worldwide public attention was becoming focused in the mid-1980s on the destruction of the tropical rain forests and the significance of that destruction for the global environment, a small group of scientists was developing parallel concerns about the uncut, old-growth rain forests of the Northwest.

Many of these researchers were based at Oregon State University's College of Forestry and the Forest Service's Pacific Northwest Research Station. By the mid-1980s, their research was challenging the old attitudes about old-growth forests. In the process, they were quietly fomenting a scientific revolution among their peers.

The conventional wisdom was that it was better to cut down trees before they become so old that they started to rot and had no value as timber. But as the big, old trees were cut down, and as nearly all the original forest lands were liquidated and dysfunctions in the forests began to crop up, scientists such as Jerry Franklin, Charles Meslow, and Chris Maser had begun to see the connections. Old, dying, dead, and rotting big trees might have declining economic value, but their ecological value seemed priceless.

Evergreen cone-bearing trees had come to dominate the Northwest over 25 million years. During the time a variety of intricate relationships had evolved among the species of these forests. The northern spotted owl, for instance, is vulnerable to being preyed upon by larger birds. Within an uncut old forest, though, the spotted owl can thrive, because it can take advantage of the tree "canopy." The dense network of tree limbs found within old-growth stands provides ideal nesting sites; the limbs also offer enough open space for a medium-sized owl to maneuver in. But the canopy is clumsier airspace for a bigger bird. In flight the spotted owl can readily capture the mice and other prey it needs without readily falling prey itself.

While most of the scientific attention was focused on the importance of old trees for the land, a few scientists were intrigued by the significance of old trees for life in the water. This happened to be the main activity of Gordon Reeves's closest colleague at the Research Station, James Sedell. Sedell, an aquatic ecologist, had delved into descriptions of coastal and valley streams written by the first explorers and the surveyors working for the armies of Great Britain and the United States. The majority of these nineteenth-century accounts noted that streams were clogged with fallen logs, over-grown with brush, and often swollen with beaver dams, making passage virtually impossible. Alexander McLeod, who led the first trapping expedition to the central Oregon coast in 1826, wrote entries in his journal that were typical of many reports. On the Alsea River, up the coast from the Smith, McLeod noted:

> Late last night the four men sent up the South Branch returned, not being able to proceed owing to the quantity of fallen trees which obstructs its navigation.

Later in the century, official reports of the U.S. secretary of war revealed that significant portions of Oregon's second-largest river, the Willamette, did not flow in a single main channel. Instead, it flowed in five channels, which "braided" together. When the river was cleared for navigation, more than five thousand trees were pulled from a fifty-mile stretch during a ten-year period. The trees were big, ranging from 5 to 9 feet across and from 90 to 120 feet in length.

Trees along and in the river, Sedell surmised, were a main structural component supporting the richness of river life. Since the Pacific salmon had evolved in such rivers, it made sense to think that the ecological character-istics of intact forests were vital to the fish's survival.

A key problem in understanding river-forest relationships was the European-American settlement of the region, which altered those relation-ships profoundly. Forests became sources of timber for construction; rivers

became pressed into service as highways. After the initial clearing of submerged trees and woody debris for navigation, many rivers were put to use
to transport felled logs. Around 1890 "splash-damming" became common.
Temporary dams were built across streams and logs were dumped in the
ponds created above them. When the pond became full of logs and water, the
barrier dam was released—often dynamited—and the torrent drove the logs
downstream.

This practice not only blocked the upstream migration of adult salmon
while the dam was in place, the subsequent log torrent regularly killed any
salmon in its way. It also scoured stream channels, removing spawning gravel
and destroying riverbank vegetation, effectively ruining the stream for the
spawning and rearing of juvenile salmon. Sedell found records of more than
160 major splash-dam sites on Oregon coastal streams. In some places splash-
damming was still being practiced in the 1950s and '60s.

As if these short-sighted practices weren't bad enough, fishery agencies,
partly in reaction to the destructiveness that they associated with logs and
partly to remove what they considered "obstructions" to fish migration,
devoted enormous efforts over many years to hauling logs and large woody
debris out of rivers and streams. Sedell found that up to 90 percent of agency
funds intended for fish habitat restoration were used for removal of jammed
debris. From the 1940s into the 1970s fishery agencies viewed wood in
streams as unnatural.

As Sedell continued his studies of old-growth forests in the early 1980s,
he came to appreciate the importance of large trees as a natural condition of
Northwest rivers, one that salmon had evolved with. The dense shading
provided by streamside trees helped keep waters cool, and litter falling from
the trees provided nutrients that worked through the food chain to the fish.
Within the streams, fallen trees, roots, and branches created protected areas
and pools in which fish could hide from predators, allowing them to survive
winter storms, spring floods, and summer droughts. As the wood itself
decomposed, it provided food and habitat for a succession of aquatic organisms that salmon fed upon.

Sedell's recognition that large wood was not a problem for salmon but a
necessity for their health was a breakthrough concept for fish researchers, com-

parable to the recognition that old trees were a necessity for spotted owls. Sedell became a man obsessed with this knowledge, exploring it, examining it, presenting it at every opportunity. Gordon Reeves became infected by it. He began to feel that what he was learning from Sedell, about forest and stream interactions, and from others at the Forest Sciences Lab, about the dynamics of old-growth forests, held the key to the survival of the region's resources.

During the summer of 1985 a district ranger on the Siskiyou National Forest, in southwestern Oregon, asked Reeves to begin some basic research on the fish populations of the principal river of his district, the Elk. The Siskiyou Forest office had scheduled the Elk watershed as a major source of timber. As far as anyone knew, the forest lands in question were not a particularly productive habitat for salmon.

The Elk flows through a section of the Oregon coast that remains comparatively undeveloped. The nearby town, Port Orford, is home to about one thousand people and probably several times that many shorebirds. A few commercial fishermen and loggers make their living in Port Orford, but otherwise it is mainly a crossroads, the sort that tourists call quaint as they drive past the seashell and kite shops close by the tiny harbor. The Elk itself needs no advertising, and many of the locals who know it want none. Clear and cold, the river shoots out of rugged and steep canyon country, where much of the forest is still uncut and the fishing hard to beat.

Reeves spent a lot of time snorkeling the Elk. Days and sometimes nights in 1985 and 1986, he lived in the river, not only the main stem but many of the tributaries that fed it. He went everywhere, from the headwaters of the Elk, twenty miles inland, down to the Pacific. He learned to understand the river from the fish's point of view—where the deep pools offered hiding places and where the riffles and insects could be found.

Besides snorkeling, Reeves also counted fish using the standard method that fish biologists used elsewhere in the country. The technique was called electrofishing. Wearing chest-high waders, he walked in the stream, carrying a metal probe. The probe put just enough electric current into the water to stun the fish, which he would gather into a net and count. They recovered in a few minutes, and he would put them back. His equipment was tailored for the Elk: A lightweight generator was mounted on a packframe; the probe could be carried in one hand, the net in the other. He wore a pair of polarizing glasses to help him spot the fish.

Moving gingerly over rocks, feeling the cool grip of the current on his legs as he paddled or walked against it, he looked up into canyons with trees cantilevered out from the slope. While he feasted his eyes, his ears heard only the regular murmurs of flowing waters. Reeves fell in love with the Elk. By the time he was finished in 1986 he had found that the Elk, far from being unproductive, was one of the most productive salmon rivers south of Alaska. In 1985 alone, he and some assistants counted an estimated quarter of a million juvenile chinook salmon leaving the forest, going downstream to the ocean.

The second remarkable finding Reeves made was that just four relatively small sections of the Elk, amounting to only about 15 percent of its extent, produced the majority of salmonids. The four sections shared similar physical characteristics. They were "flats": The terrain of the streambed had almost no slope. Riffles in the flats produced quantities of insects, which was essential food for fish. The flats spilled into overflow channels, providing additional protection for young fish. And deep pools in the flats contained large amounts of wood, which conferred all the benefits Sedell had been discovering.

Productive as they were, these four small areas were not islands that could stand alone, Reeves recognized. They depended on the cooler water from upstream that fed into them.

From his direct, in-the-water observations, Reeves drew an important conclusion. "The interconnectedness of the system," he wrote in his research report, "requires that the [Elk River] basin be managed as a whole and not just as individual isolated reaches." The flats in particular, he warned, were vulnerable to the increased deposits of sediment that would frequently follow road-building and logging in the Siskiyou Mountains. The Siskiyous commonly have mushy geology—steep slopes and erosive soils. Sediments could raise water temperatures, widen channels, fill in pools, and smother juvenile fish.

Of the prime areas that Reeves surveyed those two years, the single most productive was the North Fork of the Elk. Flowing through a dramatic, steep canyon lined with tan oak, madrone, and towering fir trees, the North Fork seemed like one place anyone would want to preserve for its natural beauty alone. Given its productivity for fish, and given Reeves's warning about how vulnerable the flats could be to logging and about the need to manage the basin as a whole, it came as a shock when he learned that the Siskiyou National Forest had plans to allow logging of two sizable areas in the North Fork drainage. The two sales were planned to yield 7 million board feet of timber.

While the logging plans were going forward in 1987, funding from the Siskiyou Forest office for Reeves's fisheries studies was drying up. It did not seem to be a coincidence. Fishing interests and logging interests were heading for a fight.

No one called him off the research, however, and he, Sedell, and their boss, Fred Everest, found money to continue the riverine studies. They wanted to do something no one had attempted before: a full fishery analysis of the entire Elk River basin, considering it as a discrete and unified natural section. It was an intellectual challenge, a practical, even physical challenge; and it might prove very informative. Still, it seemed clear that the local National Forest office wasn't keen to hear what the fish biologists had to tell them. People asked Reeves how he could continue if the Forest Service didn't want him.

He had a pat reply. He *was* the Forest Service. He had identified the Elk as an area of interest.

It wasn't long before Reeves's studies of the Elk River came to the attention of conservationists, who promptly used them for their own purposes. In 1988, conservationists succeeded in convincing Congress to include part of the Elk as a national Wild and Scenic River. In 1989, a local group, the Friends of Elk River, developed an alternative to the official Forest Service management plan for the river. They proposed reducing timber harvests in the Elk watershed by 70 percent, mainly to protect salmon.

As the Elk seemed to be in danger of slipping out of their control, some officials in the Forest Service now began to think of Reeves as an irritant, not a "team player." The Forest Service didn't value too much independence among the troops. Officials there acted like those in any big hierarchy, only more so, because the service had a public trust, and to keep the public's trust, the company line said that dissent looked bad.

Many field biologists, working out of ranger districts, were in a position to know about depleted stocks of fish and wildlife. But local biologists concerned about the welfare of fish were going against the current in an agency that placed a higher priority on timber-cutting. Research station biologists, like Reeves, had more latitude to ask questions and more authority to follow through on what they learned. But they could get ignored or denied, too.

Reeves didn't see himself as a partisan, an advocate of preestablished positions. He thought of himself as a scientist. Sure, he was a man with a Ph.D. in a technical field, but that wasn't what being a scientist meant to him. He wore the title, the degree, and the government job lightly. His beard and his Birkenstock sandals represented an independent turn of mind. Explaining himself, he would tell about the first time, in the late 1970s, that he saw a bumper sticker that made him laugh with recognition: "Question Authority." It was a good working principle for a scientist.

A scientists wasn't a know-it-all with a fancy vocabulary. A scientist, he thought, was a professional who asked questions of nature and reported the answers he found. It was not his job to be concerned with institutional constraints that would compromise the questions.

For Reeves, though, the constraints after he discovered answers—such as the proposed logging in the North Fork of the Elk—were increasingly frustrating. He was frustrated because he recognized that a great many people were affected by the failure of the agency to change its behavior toward fish and rivers. Because streams weren't treated as his knowledge told him they should be and the salmon were not doing well, people who made their living fishing might soon be looking for other work. The people who caught fish for recreation would be out of fish, too; and the people who just liked to know that the fish were there—who liked to go to see them spawn in the rivers and know that life in the wild was going on—they, too, would be losers.

But the greater loss would have little to do with these concerns. Reeves saw in the salmon a portent of the natural world they occupied—the world he also occupied and his two young sons would inherit. He had a word for what he saw happening to the environments he studied: They were "simplified." To an ecologist, an environment that is simplified is no longer diverse, rich with a variety of life. That sort of world held no anticipation for him.

In 1988 Reeves was frustrated. But he was not defeated. He had a new role in which he could perhaps exert more influence on behalf of the fish and their world than he could as a Forest Service biologist. He was the president-elect of the large statewide chapter of a national organization of biologists, and in that capacity he decided to engage in a little consciousness-raising.

The American Fisheries Society was a well-established scientific organization, whose origins went back to 1870. Its early members had persuaded Congress to form the first federal agency responsible for fisheries. Ever since, most American fish biologists and fisheries managers, especially those working for state and federal agencies, have been members of the society. Among other activities, the society publishes research and keeps members abreast of developments in their profession.

The Oregon chapter, one of the largest in the national organization, had about four hundred members in 1988. The highlight of the year is the annual meeting, a time to renew professional contacts and friendships, drink beer, and talk about fishing. The Oregon chapter traditionally wrapped the socializing inside two days of serious-minded conference, in which members gave prepared talks on issues of current interest. A topic might be the status of the Warner Lake chub, or new techniques in marking fish, or diseases in fish hatcheries, that sort of thing. In addition, the chapter's offices decided on a theme for the program and invited a group of distinguished speakers to address it. That was where Gordon Reeves saw his opportunity.

The situation he was personally encountering on the North Fork of the Elk, and the circumstances in many other places that he was aware of, led him to an inescapable conclusion about the management of America's natural resources. However well intentioned fishery managers might be, resources were undeniably in trouble. Perhaps conditions seemed not so desperate on this or that river or lake, at the moment; but you had to be a fool or blind, Reeves believed, to miss the trends—the economic, political, and social forces arrayed against wild creatures, especially the salmon. It was a rare biologist, even a rare manager, who was unaware of the alarming long-term prospects.

One problem, Reeves had come to believe, was that the institutions they all worked for seemed incapable of fundamental change. Agency officials worried about shifting political priorities that might affect agency budgets, and field staff busied themselves with technical activities that were driven by the prevailing political and economic priorities. Little time or attention was generally left over for the larger and more troubling questions of values. Avoidance of these questions had the effect, intended or not, of supporting the status quo. At the end of 1988, the last year of the Reagan administration, awaiting the start of the Bush presidency, Reeves felt strongly that responsible resource management, not special interests, needed to be moved to the fore.

In the 1940s, the ecologist Aldo Leopold had proposed a "land ethic," which put natural-resource decisions on a firm, non–special interest footing. A natural-resource decision is "right when it tends to preserve the integrity, stability and beauty of the biotic community," Leopold had written. "It is wrong when it tends otherwise." Every wildlife biologist was familiar with the writings of Leopold, a former Forest Service supervisor. Yet these were not the values of most resource-management institutions, and environmental conditions had only worsened since Leopold's time. The 1970s and '80s saw the emergence of a more radical environmental ethic. Reeves, like many of his fellow biologists, was familiar with this "deep ecology" movement, which suggested that the very premise of natural-resource management was suspect.

The "radicals" rejected the prevailing notion that nature was for human uses alone. Stewardship, they reasoned, no matter how benign, assumed that humans had a right to control nature. The deep ecologists, following the lead of the Norwegian philosopher Arne Naess, argued that nature had rights of its own, which were primary. Rivers had a right to be rivers, salmon had a right to be salmon, trees had a right to be trees, just as they were, without human interference.

It wasn't long before groups such as Earth First! put the ethics of deep ecology into militant action. Earth First!'s motto was "No Compromise in the Defense of Mother Earth." As the 1980s wore on and the environmental losses mounted, the rhetoric of such activists became increasingly aggrieved. "When you look closely at the unholy assault the industrial state is mounting against the public's wildlands, against natural diversity . . . it forces you to consider any and all means of resisting the destruction." The founder of Earth First!, Dave Forman, wrote this in 1987.

A radical critique might have been in circulation, but as Reeves looked toward the annual AFS chapter meeting for 1989, he was wary. He had learned as a younger man how people working in institutions seemed to develop an extraordinary capacity for denying the truth of their circumstances.

His father had been a rebel and had paid for it; that was the message Reeves took from his father's short life. Working at Union Carbide, the elder Reeves was a lifelong advocate for unions in a nonunionized workplace. It seemed every time the union came around to organize, management gave everyone raises.

"Hell, why do we need a union?" his friends on the shop floor would ask.

"Because it gives you a voice," his father would say. "I don't want to be just a number. When I drop dead in here, I don't want them to cart me out and just put someone else in."

Reeves remembered as a teenager his father taking him and his brother to the plant. He told his sons he never wanted them to work as he did.

"But whatever you do," he had said, "don't be beaten down by the system."

As it happened, one day Reeves's father broke a rib and punctured a lung on the job. He was just given two aspirins and sent back to work. Later, a blood clot in the lung developed into pneumonia, and the senior Reeves died. Union Carbide admitted no wrongdoing and was not required to make any payments to his widow.

Gordon was in his early twenties then. The experience taught him a lesson about people and institutions that he never forgot. He knew it was important for the speakers at the 1989 AFS meeting to be knowledgeable and professionally credible, if they were going to influence the members and begin the slow process of changing institutional behavior.

The talks by the speakers invited by Reeves and his colleague Dan Bottom were to focus on the responsibilities to future generations and to ecosystems, responsibilities to the public and to the organizations they represented.

As president-elect Reeves rose to welcome the full house, he was nervous. A little speech impediment made some consonants sound a bit thick, but that wasn't what made him anxious. He had prepared the conference carefully and had done what he could to be certain the invited speakers offered thoughts that met the challenge of the subject. Now it was up to the speakers.

David Bella, a professor at Oregon State University, identified a chronic problem in organizational decision-making, what he called the "systemic distortion" of information. He had studied how and why technical concerns were stifled going up the NASA chain of command, the reasons the space shuttle *Challenger* had lifted off despite the fears of lower-level engineers about the safety of the shuttle's O-rings.

Bella's enthusiasm for his material seemed to carry his listeners with him, and heads began to nod in recognition when he noted that the *Challenger* disaster was not some fluke but a result of the normal way organizations work. They tend to place first priority on their own survival, Bella said, even if that means trouble for whatever or whomever they're supposed to protect. Organizations selectively produce and sustain information favorable to them, which frequently means looking out for those at the top of the pyramid.

"Favorable assessments, which do not disrupt organizational systems, have survival value," Bella said, his voice charged with irony. "Contrary assessments tend to be systematically filtered out.

"The cumulative outcome is systemic distortion of information."

If this sounded familiar to AFS members, Bella implied, they should begin to call offenders to task.

The professor brought the insights of the seasoned systems analyst to fisheries management and gave his listeners some novel perspectives on their own circumstances. Another speaker, Jim Lichatowich, delivered a hard dose of all-too-familiar workplace reality. Lichatowich had been assistant chief of fisheries for the Oregon Department of Fish and Wildlife for five years, but had quit a year before over policy differences with higher-ups in the department. When a leader quits over a matter of principle, others who had been following him think hard about their values.

Lichatowich was a relatively short, solidly built man, an ex-Marine. As he took the podium, he promised to highlight some workaday myths about managing natural resources.

Fishery managers once believed that both a fish agency and the fish resource could be protected by quiet inaction, he said. If the powerful Oregon timber lobby didn't like a new fishery regulation, for example, the state fish agency would avoid the issue by not enforcing the regulation. But such cowardice didn't help the fish in the past, Lichatowich argued, and the agencies had been slow to challenge the special interests since. Society had changed, however, and Lichatowich claimed there were new expectations.

"As natural-resource managers and professionals, we have an important connection to future generations," he said. "Our decisions will strongly affect the quality of life of our descendants—a big responsibility.

"In carrying out that responsibility, we need to remember that we are fortunate to live in a pluralistic democracy.

"To me," said Lichatowich, sticking his jaw out, "that means disagreeing with your neighbor is OK, disagreeing with the president's policies is OK, and even disagreeing with your boss is OK."

Disagreement was part of true progress. Individuals needed to be alert to the subtle forces that tended to dampen disagreement; they need to be wary of institutional pressures to be "team players."

"The word 'team' in 'team player' is misleading," he said. "A team is a group of individuals with different points of view, different skills, or different experiences brought together to achieve a common goal—a goal whose achievement needs the individual contributions of the team *members*.

"The *different* contributions of the team members are important. Contrast that with team players—the individuals who wait until decisions are made and then conform their thinking to fit.

"The team player believes that an agency decision not only directs what work he or she does but overrides his or her need to think independently."

He looked at them wryly. Come on, the expression said. Let's get it right.

The ballroom erupted in emotional applause. Everybody knew exactly what Lichatowich was talking about.

He wanted to conclude by describing for them the world as defined by two different, opposing economic systems. Capitalism and Marxism were not Lichatowich's opposites. His were the *industrial* economy and the *natural* economy. The industrial economy was "linear" and "extractive." The natural economy was "cyclic" and "renewable."

"A decision may make perfect sense from the standpoint of the industrial economic system," he pointed out, "and be a disaster to the natural economic system." But because environmental decisions are typically made from only the industrial economic standpoint, dissent is crucial if one is concerned about responsible management of natural resources.

"Our challenge," he said, raising his voice and squaring his shoulders, "is to be sure that administrators, commissions, and the public understand the issues and consequences. That way they can make the most informed choices, for us and for our descendants."

Lichatowich stopped, and the applause was immediate and loud. Gordon Reeves finally relaxed. The speakers seemed to be tapping some common reservoir of pent-up frustration. The release felt good.

Later, at the banquet, members kept coming up to Reeves and to other speakers at the head table, wanting to continue the talk about ethics.

Reeves was very pleased. The issues that he believed everybody thought about—individual responsibility and honest resource management—were no longer under wraps. It was a good start. The right subject, environmental responsibility, had been engaged. Now, with the right opportunity, responsible actions might flow from newly liberated thoughts.

One appealing definition of the Northwest is "anyplace the salmon can go." The definition is chauvinistic when it's applied to Oregon, Washington, and Idaho, as it often is within the region. Pacific salmon are found in the North Pacific all the way up the coast from southern California through British Columbia and Alaska, and around into the Russian Far East, Korea, and Japan.

But even when the definition is limited to the three American states usually thought of as the Northwest, the range of the salmon is vast and diverse. The salmon inhabit not just the coastal forests or the forests of the Cascade Mountains but also the plateau country of eastern Oregon, the rolling hills of southeastern Washington, and the high mountains of the Salmon River in Idaho. By the 1970s that area was a tangled net of legal jurisdictions. A single fish spawned in a forest in Idaho would pass through some forty state and national jurisdictions on its migration to and from the sea.

The U.S. Forest Service and the Bureau of Land Management had a significant effect on the well-being of salmon through their management of federal lands. But numerous other agencies of the state and federal governments affected the salmon through their management of public resources. Some believed that the salmon would benefit from a single agency that had both the responsibility to plan for the fish throughout the region and the authority to carry out the plan. Without such a mandate, the salmon were overlooked, or worse, hemmed in at every turn by old alliances and old enmities.

For the people who cared about salmon, it was appealing to think that a new institution might unravel the snarled nets of competing bureaucracies, or perhaps just cut through them. In the beginning high hopes were placed in the Northwest Power Planning Council.

The federal law that established the council, the Pacific Northwest Electric Power Planning and Conservation Act of 1980, was one of the last hurrahs of Jimmy Carter's administration. The law appeared to offer an innovative, progressive solution to the problems of a new era of energy use in the Northwest, an era expected to be marked by increasing demands for both electricity and social accountability.

One key innovation of the law was that conservation of energy would be considered a resource, just like gas, coal, or hydropower. The oil embargo of 1973 had made many Americans realize how dependent they were on foreign sources of energy, and the Northwest Power Act set out to foster greater energy independence.

Consistent with this idea of self-determination, the act gave the public the right to be involved in planning its energy future. Effective planning, the act recognized, needed to take not only the production of energy but also its social consequences into account.

In this light, the needs of salmon—dramatically affected by development of the hydroelectric system—would be addressed.

Energy planning, public involvement, and equitable treatment for salmon —these three key elements were intended to correct imbalances that had arisen over the years as the Northwest had become industrialized.

By the late 1970s, it was clear to many in the Northwest that energy planning in the region needed to be redefined. During the preceding decade, the electric utility industry and the federal agency that marketed electric power, the Bonneville Power Administration, had planned for a massive building program of nuclear power plants. These powerful institutions had thought to implement the program without much public involvement, but opposition rapidly mounted over the plants' nuclear hazards, the damage they were causing to streams and rivers during construction, and their cost.

Cost overruns on just one of the five proposed reactors of the Washington Public Power Supply System, the Satsop nuclear power plant on Washington's Chehalis River, had risen more than 1,750 percent, to more than $7 billion. Overall the cost of constructing all five WPPSS plants rose to $24 billion. The funding for the projected five nuclear plants became very shaky, and critics began pronouncing the WPPSS acronym "whoops." "Whoops" was right, as it turned out, for in 1982 the project collapsed in cost overruns, precipitating the largest municipal bond default in U.S. history. Only one of the plants was completed.

The 1980 Northwest Power Act, then, seemed positively prescient in reducing the utility industry's role in the region's energy planning and in placing policy-making into the hands of the Power Planning Council. The council would be appointed by the governors of the states of Oregon, Washington, Idaho, and Montana. The law seemed as responsive to the needs of the public for its time as the construction of the hydropower system itself had seemed during the New Deal, two generations before. President Franklin

Roosevelt had come into office then with a vision, and what he considered a mandate, for publicly controlled electric power.

The Wall Street Crash of 1929 had brought down the private utility industry, which had been organized under holding companies whose value had become grossly inflated in the years leading up to the Crash. By the early 1930s power sales slumped as factories closed. Development of new electric generating capacity came to a standstill. The Depression began. Roosevelt saw the opportunity to create jobs, industrialize, and populate the Northwest through developing the hydroelectic capacity of the Columbia River Basin. He hit these themes in a speech in Portland during the 1932 presidential campaign.

"This vast water power can be of incalculable value to this whole section of the country," Roosevelt said. "It means cheap manufacturing production, economy and comfort on the farm, and in the household."

With Roosevelt elected, in 1933 work on Grand Coulee and Bonneville, the first federal dams and powerhouses, began. Enthusiasm was high for public power, and songwriter Woody Guthrie extolled its virtues in his ballad "The Grand Coulee Dam":

> *Uncle Sam took up the challenge*
> *In the year of Thirty-Three*
> *For the farmer and the factory*
> *and for all of you and me,*
> *He said, "Roll along, Columbia,*
> *You can ramble to the sea*
> *But River, while you're rambling,*
> *You can do some work for me."*

By 1975, when the hydropower development of the river was essentially complete, eighteen giant dams spanned the main stem of the Columbia River and the Snake River, its largest tributary. They turned the basin into the greatest producer of hydropower and transformed the entire region's economy. The Northwest had become, in many ways, the region that Roosevelt willed.

But the dams had also turned the mighty Columbia into a series of slack-water pools, making a bitter jest out of Woody Guthrie's "Roll along, Columbia." The water of the Columbia was regulated and manipulated by intrastate, interstate, and international agreements, from the headwaters in British Columbia to the mouth at Astoria, Oregon. More bitter still to some people was how industrialization of the river had damaged the river's salmon populations. By 1930 the salmon had already been severely depleted by decades of hard fishing. Fifty years later they had dwindled to less than one-quarter of their historic abundance.

After the dams were constructed they were the major cause of the salmon's steep decline. They cut the salmon off from their spawning areas altogether in huge areas. Grand Coulee Dam on the Columbia in north central Washington, and Hells Canyon Dam on the Snake, along the Oregon-Idaho border, were built without means of getting the fish over them. Together they eliminated more than one-third of all the salmon habitat in the entire Columbia-Snake basin.

Permanent blockage to migration was one extreme. But wherever the dams were placed they added impediments in the way of migration. The salmon had always run the gauntlet going out to sea and coming back. Juveniles going downriver had to escape predatory birds and larger fishes; adults returning to spawn had to elude sea lions, seals, and fishermen. For the juveniles gliding downstream and the adults charging upstream the dams were just one more hazard.

The hard engineering constraints of the dams could be alleviated somewhat if their operators made mechanical modifications and provided water to aid the fish's transit through the powerhouses. But running water for fish meant, in practice, losing the money that would come from using it to generate electricity. The loss was particularly felt in years when the runoff in the river was lower than normal. The utilities naturally wanted the water for power, not fish. But in dry years the fish also needed the water the most.

After a particularly bad year for fish in 1977—the snowpack in the mountains of the Columbia Basin hit a hundred-year low, and the springtime snowmelt into the river was inadequate—fish advocates clamored for change in river operations. The National Marine Fisheries Service, the federal agency responsible for salmon, began to consider bringing petitions under the federal Endangered Species Act for certain populations of Snake River salmon. Partly in response, Congress attempted to accommodate the concerns of the Fisheries Service as it developed the new Northwest Power Act. As it happened, the chair of the House Subcommittee on Energy and Power, Congressman John Dingell of Michigan, was an avid fisherman who admired the salmon. He led the fight for provisions in the legislation to right the old imbalances between fish and power.

To a significant extent, it looked as if the salmon advocates were successful. The Power Act described a new regime not merely for the development and conservation of energy resources in the Northwest. The law also called on the power council "to protect, mitigate, and enhance the fish and wildlife, including related spawning grounds and habitat, of the Columbia River and its tributaries, particularly anadromous fish, which are of significant importance to the social and economic well-being of the Pacific Northwest and the Nation."

"No longer will fish and wildlife be given a secondary status" in management of the Columbia River, said Dingell, explaining the bill to his colleagues in the House of Representatives.

Such were the hopes placed in the salmon-rebuilding potential of the law that the Fisheries Service bowed to the urgings of the new Reagan Office of Management and Budget and quietly suspended its endangered species deliberations.

So, in 1980 and 1981, as the Reagan era began, the Northwest embarked on an experiment in governance that called for equality between industry and the environment. For a certain type of individual—idealistic, ambitious, energetic—the Northwest Power Planning Council looked like the vehicle that would lead a whole region to a better future, one more rational, better planned, and environmentally sensitive. Such a future appealed to Willa Nehlsen.

Nehlsen was thirty-four when she arrived at the council in 1984. She came with all the right qualifications; she was bright, energetic, idealistic. She had been raised in southern California and had earned both her undergraduate and doctoral degrees from the University of California at Santa Cruz. She would say, with a laugh that was meant to leaven the solid truth of it, that she had gotten to be a rebel there in the late 1960s. In school, she had planned to become a social worker. But in 1970, with the first Earth Day, she had been carried away by the environmental movement.

She went on for her Ph.D. in botany, spending years studying development in a moss. The moss wasn't so much the thing, she would say. What she learned from the experience were the research skills and methods, the ability to look closely. From the moss, she broadened her view to aquatic environments in her next jobs, conducting research in Chesapeake Bay and then in the Columbia River estuary. When an opportunity for a staff position at the Power Planning Council arose, it seemed the "inevitable next step upriver," as she joked. But it also put her in step with the social-worker part of herself. She still wanted to help. The salmon certainly seemed to need it.

Starting at the council as a biologist and planner, Nehlsen quickly appreciated the scale of the council's challenge. To begin, the physical area under the council's consideration was immense. The Columbia Basin encompasses an area roughly the size of France, some 259,000 square miles. The basin is comprised of some thirty "sub-basins," embracing most of the physical environments known on Earth, including glacier, desert, temperate rain forest, and ocean coast. The institutional context in which the council worked was just about as varied and complex: four Northwest states, each with its own political identity and leadership; numerous state agencies with their individual jurisdictions; federal agencies; sovereign Indian governments; and agreements with Canada.

As Nehlsen made her way at the council, she came to the attention of Kai Lee, one of the council members from Washington, then a professor of environmental studies and political science at the University of Washington. Lee worried that council scientists might go stale in their intellectual interests, and he looked for opportunities for them to continue their professional development. As Lee was chairman of the council's fish and wildlife committee and Nehlsen was the committee's new staff member, he suggested they both go to a university seminar concerning a relatively new field called "conservation biology."

Lee was concerned that council policies designed to rehabilitate salmon might have unexpected effects elsewhere in the Columbia ecosystem. He recognized that it would be helpful to have an appreciation of conservation biology, which seeks to understand how biological communities become endangered and how they may best be sustained.

The seminar affected Nehlsen profoundly. Meeting the leaders in a new and exciting field convinced her that biological planning wasn't all she wanted to do at the council; she wanted to be able to influence the way the council framed its understanding of the biological issues. When not long afterward the salmon research coordinator left the council, she applied for the position and got it.

The role suited Nehlsen well, as she had a knack for looking not only at the recognized problems, the ones with the flashing lights, but around their edges to see a bigger picture looming in the shadows. Lee sensed that talent, and in 1987 he asked her to look into a question that had been troubling him.

It had been a decade since the fisheries agencies had raised the possibility of salmon as endangered species, and independently, without much data to go on, Lee had begun to fret. He reasoned that the actions of fisheries managers in the intervening years would likely have put disproportionate pressure on some of the many populations of salmon in the Columbia and Snake system. Among other things, he worried that it was often impossible to direct the openings and closings of the fishing season so that only one population would be caught. Usually a number of populations were running in from the ocean at the same time, and less robust populations would be caught right along with more numerous ones. The problem was that the weaker populations might not withstand the fishing pressure, especially if the fishing seasons were repeated year after year.

In 1986 Lee had begun asking state fisheries agency staff to tell him which of the populations in the system was the proverbial canary in the mine shaft, the one whose demise said that major trouble was on the way. When he heard nothing, he turned to Nehlsen to research the status of the Snake River salmon populations. Were any of them at risk of extinction?

For two months Nehlsen scoured the available scientific data, the population assessments produced by the state fisheries agencies of Oregon, Idaho, and Washington. What she found troubled her deeply. She prepared a report, and in July 1987 she presented her findings at a public meeting of the council in Post Falls, Idaho.

Standing at a conference table, Nehlsen did not betray the anxiety she was feeling. She looked as she usually did, calm and self-possessed. There was something reassuringly straightforward about her simple pageboy haircut, her classic Dutch-blond looks.

None of the council members was a trained biologist, so she began by showing them a series of slides to give them a bit of background. First was a map of the Snake River, showing an area that included southern and central Idaho and parts of eastern Oregon and Washington. Where the border between the states wavered from a straight north-south line, there was the Snake.

Her analysis focused on stocks of salmon, she explained. A stock is defined as a population of fish from one stream that generally does not interbreed with fish from other populations. It was important to focus on the status of stocks because each, in its differences, had adapted itself to the particular stream it inhabited. Over perhaps hundreds or thousands of years they had evolved to meet the requirements of their particular native habitat.

A chinook, that is, wasn't just a chinook, some interchangeable unit like a red 1987 Ford Mustang. A chinook from Alaska would have different adaptations from a chinook that spawned in the Sacramento River in California or in the Snake River in Idaho. And a chinook that ran upriver in the spring to the Snake would be different from one that entered the river in the fall. And even two different fall chinook stocks bound for the Snake but spawning in different tributaries, one in a forested area, the other in range lands, would likely be different. Fish of one stock would rarely do well transplanted somewhere else. The species as a whole was built of local stocks, so if species survival was the goal, the smartest approach was to ensure that local fish survived where they were.

"To retain the adaptation to its habitat that a stock has achieved over these thousands of years of evolution, a stock needs to have many varieties of genes," Nehlsen continued. Now came the nut of her presentation.

To preserve this genetic variation, she said, geneticists calculated that a salmon stock needed to have from four hundred to one thousand spawning adults, depending on the stock's particular circumstances. Since individual adults produced thousands of fertilized eggs, it might seem that a stock should have little trouble in maintaining populations of only hundreds. But salmon were uniquely vulnerable to a different group of dangers at each stage in their lives, from the river to the ocean and back. Only a handful of eggs from a redd would survive to become adults returning from the ocean. If the total number of adults escaping the fishery—the "escapement"—fell below the range of four hundred to one thousand individuals, trouble was likely.

Nehlsen now projected a chart.

"Let's look at the conclusions of this analysis," she said. "In surveying the stocks of the Snake River basin, I've found that about twenty-two of them have escapements of below one thousand."

She paused a beat.

"There may be among these stocks some that are in serious trouble."

The room became strangely quiet. A few people shifted uncomfortably in their seats. After a moment one council member asked Nehlsen to say how quickly action needed to be taken.

She pointed out that the sockeye population in Idaho's Redfish Lake was less than one hundred. The two Idaho council members exchanged troubled glances.

Nehlsen paused again.

"I didn't talk yet about the coho in the Grande Ronde," she said.

What happened to these fish in a tributary of the Snake was a disturbing story, she said. The stock had been identified in 1981 as a possible candidate for the endangered species list, and measures were suggested to prevent its extinction. But "for various reasons, there was not an endangered species listing on this stock."

"It disappeared very abruptly."

Again, an edgy silence cut the hearing room. It lasted while people considered the news: The Grande Ronde coho was the last of that species native to the lower Snake River. Now they were gone.

Council member Lee, for one, took the news hard.

"I had hoped that the passage of the Northwest Power Act meant that no stocks of fish would go extinct after 1980," he said. "It is a sad thing to hear that the Grande Ronde stocks may have slipped through our fingers while we were busy trying to get things together.

"I certainly hope that we don't have any other populations that slip through our fingers."

In the back of the room, a stout man in a business suit betrayed a dour expression. Al Wright had heard enough, and he raised his hand to speak. Wright was the executive director of the Pacific Northwest Utilities Conference Committee, which represented the electric utilities and other major customers of federal hydropower.

"I honestly was not going to say anything, but I just can't help myself now," said Wright, rising.

"You have not witnessed the extinction of the Snake River coho run. You have witnessed the final success of the eradication program of the Snake River coho run, and that's an important issue you need to address."

True, the coho had been depleted following dam construction on the Snake, Wright conceded. But in the early 1980s, some utilities proposed to spend money to restore or replace some of the coho runs in the upper Columbia, and the management agencies turned them down, he said.

"What you're seeing today is basically a total ignoring of the Snake River coho until they became extinct. In the six years of your fish and wildlife program, you haven't heard one word about this issue.

"They could have been protected," Wright continued, indignantly. "They could have been saved.

"You were never asked anywhere at any time to do that," he said. With that, he sat down, still indignant.

The indictment stung some of them, but Nehlsen stood in a momentary state of shock. If Wright was correct, the extinction of the Snake River coho hadn't been an oversight. Dams had certainly hurt them, even crippled them; but neglect by exactly the ones who should have cared and acted, the state and federal fish managers, had apparently sealed their fate.

As Nehlsen stepped away from the conference table, she was visibly upset. No one—no fisheries agency, no environmentalist, no investigative news reporter, no one—had done anything about the Snake River coho, and now they were gone forever, as if they had never existed. Today she had pointed to twenty-two other stocks, some of them, such as the Redfish Lake sockeye, quite likely also in real danger of extinction.

But the Columbia spanned a huge area, and it wasn't even the whole area of the Northwest. What about all the coastal salmon, from California through the Olympic Peninsula? What condition were all these populations in? Who would do anything about *them?* Was American society so indifferent to the life around it?

Word about the Snake River survey circulated quickly. Not long after the council meeting, Nehlsen received a call from a fellow biologist, Jack Williams, a highly regarded endangered-species specialist with the U.S. Fish and Wildlife Service. Nehlsen had taken a class in fish management from him earlier that year at Stanford University. It was one of those classes for professional people known as "short courses," but Nehlsen had had the time to meet and get to know Williams. They shared many interests, and now Williams, as head of the Endangered Species Committee of the American Fisheries Society, had thought of her for a special task. He had come to the conclusion that a review of West Coast anadromous salmonids were needed. He asked Nehlsen if she would be willing to expand her assessment of stocks to the entire West Coast. She would lead, but he would help her.

She recognized that the information would be valuable to the power council, but she also realized that the assessment would have to be done on her own time. Nevertheless she thought it should be done. After only a moment, she said yes.

Williams laid out the plan. The main part of the report would just list the stocks and their status. Jack would handle California, which he knew; Willa would do the rest. She knew fish biologists in Oregon and some in Washington; together they would see what help they could get in British Columbia and Alaska. He was finishing a review of the status of North American freshwater fish—"resident" fish—and based on that experience he thought they should plan for the salmonid review to take a couple of years, just to be on the safe side. In 1989 they should be done.

Nehlsen drew up a preliminary list of biologists and started calling, whenever she could spare some time from her council staff work. She found that it wasn't as simple as calling up, getting a set of figures that just happened to be all ready, saying thank you, and going on the the next call. At first she was worried that some biologists would take offense at a call asking them to identify depleted or declining populations of salmon and steelhead. They might feel it was a criticism of their management. Sometimes the voices on the other end of the line indeed were hesitant; the information they provided might put them or their bosses in a bad light. But generally the biologists were cooperative, once they recognized this was an AFS project and its purpose was constructive. Most professionals shared her concerns.

But many frankly did not know whether the fish populations they dealt with were in danger of extinction. Nehlsen found herself needing to call back, and developing long "to-do" lists of leads to follow and answers to track down. One call would often lead to three more. She soon realized the 1989 deadline would be blown.

Complicating her own shortage of time for the unexpectedly larger task were changes in Williams's schedule. He had been named the fisheries program manager with the Bureau of Land Management back in Washington, D.C., and he had, if possible, even less time than Nehlsen. To help share the work they recruited Jim Lichatowich, who was then working for an Indian tribe in Washington state. Lichatowich knew Washington biologists, but he possessed even more valuable knowledge. He understood the biology of salmon as well as anyone in the region.

Nehlsen plugged along through 1988 and 1989. Even if the 1989 publication deadline was going to be missed, she had another commitment she wanted to honor: She had been invited to describe the project at the Oregon AFS chapter's annual meeting in February 1990.

When the meeting date arrived, Nehlsen joined her colleagues at a resort in the Cascade Mountains. The mood at the conference was decidedly engaged. The theme, "Sustainable Management of Natural Resources: Issues and Strategies for the 1990s," had been chosen in part by president Gordon Reeves as a continuation and development of the discussions begun at the meeting the year before. Reeves and other officers wanted to move the organization beyond contemplating responsibilities to planning some specific actions.

David Bella, the university professor who had warned them the year before about the distortion of information that occurs in organizational systems, was back with a blunter message.

"Oregon's reputation as an environmental leader, gained in the 1970s, is no longer valid," Bella said, challenging the group.

As those who made decisions about the state's environment, the members of the AFS were complicit in its degradation, Bella said. He listed the problems surrounding environmental decision-making: A focus on short-term gains, the persistent influence of special interests, and self-serving organizational posturing led the list. But the rushed schedules so common to technical work only worsened decision-making, he explained, because little time was left for discussion and debate of research findings. Finally, AFS members were blinded by a "misguided assumption that technology will rescue us from any problems that might arise because of our negligence."

"We should be honest about our failures and do something about them," Bella urged.

The other featured speakers continued the opportunities for self-criticism. The chapter members heard questions about the ability of scientists, policy makers, and the public to understand one another. They heard doubts about the realistic prospects for sustainable resource use in a consumption-oriented society. They heard bitter doubts about the honest prospects for natural-resource sustainability as long as local, national, and global population growth went unchecked. There could have been few Pollyannas in the meeting when the keynote speakers finished.

As Nehlsen prepared to speak on the second day of the conference, her habitual thoroughness made her conscious of the deficiencies of the endangered-salmon survey. The project had been scaled back. She, Williams, and Lichatowich hadn't been able to get enough cooperation from biologists in British Columbia or Alaska, and the information the three of them had obtained from the rest of the Northwest was incomplete and not thoroughly reviewed, as they had planned. Nevertheless, she felt that what they had was worth sharing.

She and Williams and Lichatowich called their report "Pacific Salmon at the Crossroads: Declining Anadromous Fish Runs of the West Coast."

Two hundred or so biologists crammed into a small room and overflowed into the corridor outside to hear what she had to say. She spoke softly and with a practiced scientist's diffidence to fact. To the listeners, her quiet, plain manner made her only more believable.

Pacific salmon and steelhead populations are clearly at a crossroads, she said. The ranges of many populations were curtailed, and some runs were already extinct. Others were depleted and in danger of extinction.

For the information of the biologists she named those runs in the most immediate danger: winter steelhead in southern California; chinook salmon and summer steelhead in northern California; coho, chum, and fall chinook salmon on the Oregon coast; coho, sockeye, and spring chinook on the Washington coast; Columbia River coho and spring chinook; and chinook and sockeye salmon in the Idaho portion of the Snake River drainage.

Not a person in the room or in the hallway was left unaffected by what Nehlsen said. The situation was serious. On their watch the salmon were declining; some were dangerously close to becoming extinct; others had already slipped over the edge into oblivion.

How much time did biologists have to correct the situation?

Who could tell? Nehlsen knew no more than they. But she believed the general decline could still be reversed.

When she finished her presentation, biologists flocked to her, offering additional information. For the rest of the conference, people kept drawing her aside, promising new data, offering encouragement. She was stunned by the interest. She welcomed it, for she felt she had been carrying all the burden of the salmon herself. Now she felt the study begin to take on a life of its own.

Still she worried. Concern on its own wasn't going to accomplish enough. A research paper would be completed and it would say that fish that had inhabited the Northwest for millions of years were going extinct. That didn't seem quite enough. The organizations for which she and the others worked did not seem ready to take up the burden of this research, to chart a new direction at the crossroads. The political appointees at the top of the Forest Service were not about to cause more complications for themselves by calling attention to potential new endangered species inhabiting their lands. The spotted owl was headache enough. The Power Planning Council was in the midst of a system-wide planning process, through which it would consider the status of salmon. But the council members, as appointees of the four Northwest governors, likewise were not eager, collectively, to press the cause of potentially endangered species. And the Fisheries Service was also not inclined, in 1990, to stick its neck out.

The question was, who would champion the salmon?

In February 1990, Gordon Reeves and Willa Nehlsen were brought into a little group that could.

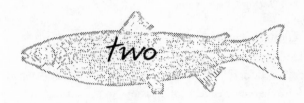

CONFLICT

Living wild species are like a library of books still unread. Our heedless destruction of them is akin to burning that library without ever having read its books. . . .

Preventing the extinction of our fellow creatures is neither frivolity nor foolish environmental excess; it is the means by which we keep intact the great storehouse of natural treasures that make the progress of medicine, agriculture, science, and human life itself possible.

—CONGRESSMAN JOHN DINGELL, IN THE FOREWORD OF
*THE ENDANGERED SPECIES ACT: A GUIDE TO ITS PROTECTIONS
AND IMPLEMENTATION,* 1989

In Oregon, if you wanted to get things done, Portland was the place. Granted, it wasn't the state capital. Salem was where the statue of the axe-toting pioneer topped the cupola of the capitol building. But even in the 1990s the state legislature met in Salem only once every two years, and for half a year at that. Salem had really never become the center of influence, only of government. Something stronger than laws had dictated what the state's major city would be.

Like that of many other major cities, Portland's dominance was geographical, originally, and the primordial force propelling that dominance was water. Portland grew up at the confluence of Oregon's two main rivers, the Willamette and the Columbia. The Willamette linked the city to the most habitable part of the state, the western valley, while the Columbia linked Portland to the rest of the far-flung Northwest. By 1890 Portland was already the state's largest city and the center of commerce and influence. As influence tends to beget more influence, in 1990 it was even more securely the state's leading city.

Among the 430,000 souls working out their destinies in Portland were a number of individuals who would probably have preferred the opportunities presented by the natural environment of one hundred years earlier to those of the 1990s. But they were game for a challenge. Oregon, and necessarily, Portland, had no lack of environmental organizations. On a per capita basis, western Oregon had probably as many environmental organizations as any place in the world. As 1990 began, two of these organizations were ready to act to save the salmon. Andy Kerr and Bill Bakke were their conservation leaders.

In a sense it all began with a single phone call, in the fall of 1989.

A former staff member with Kerr at the Oregon Natural Resources Council had come over to see him. Nancy Duhnkrack—Ned, her friends called her—had a proposal. She was taking some time off from her high-powered downtown law firm to have a baby, and in the meantime she wanted to volunteer, do some *pro bono* legal work, for ONRC. Kerr knew the chance was too good to pass up.

Duhnkrack was as smart as they come, a *summa cum laude* graduate of Portland's Lewis and Clark College Law School. She was committed and had connections; she'd been on the board of directors of other conservation organizations, including American Rivers, who were allies of ONRC. Plus, she and Kerr had been buddies since the late seventies when they were staff members of the Oregon Wilderness Coalition. They remembered those years of their early twenties as heady pedal-to-the-metal days, rebellion in the air, new realities to be created—before everybody got married and became at least, as they now joked, *semi*respectable. This was before the radical-sounding Wilderness Coalition became the Resources Council and moved its main office from the university town of Eugene up to Portland. Kerr didn't have to think about whether he'd like to have Ned working with him again. He only wondered about how best to use her skills.

Kerr wasn't a *summa cum laude* J.D. from anywhere, not even a B.A. from anywhere. He just had his 1973 high school diploma from Creswell High

School, which he kept framed on his office wall. Kerr came from a mill town and construction family, and he didn't mind anyone knowing his roots. The framed high school diploma *was* Kerr; it was the glove-in-the-face, the challenge to a duel. He was as smart as anybody with a list of degrees and usually twice as shrewd.

Just one of his unexpected hobbies was that he studied military history. He knew enough about tactics to know what a weapon surprise can be. In a few moments it was obvious to him what to do with Duhnkrack. Kerr didn't know as much about the salmon as he'd like, but what he knew made him angry.

He told his old friend about a field trip he made out to eastern Oregon, a visit to one of their old stomping grounds where he had watched as the state fish agency planned to trap every last one of a decimated salmon run. They were going to put the fish into a hatchery and spawn them there because they were afraid of losing the run altogether. To him, the business at a hatchery was so unnatural, so technological; they killed the adults first and then quickly slit open a female's belly and spilled her eggs into a bucket. Then they milked a just-dead male's sperm into the same bucket and sloshed it around. They called *this* spawning.

As repellent as it was to him, the artificial spawning itself was not what mainly upset Kerr. It was the perceived need to do it with all of the salmon, because the run had fallen to such a low level. The more he thought about it, the more angry he felt and the more guilty.

For most of the last half of the 1980s Kerr had been so caught up in battles over the last remaining old-growth forests in the Northwest that he had lost touch with the salmon. He had hoped—"stupidly," he said now—that the Oregon Department of Fish and Wildlife would be looking out for the fish, or the Power Planning Council would. But the word he was hearing more and more, he told Duhnkrack, was that some stocks were becoming extinct. The two of them could help try to prevent that. They could file petitions to protect the fish under the federal Endangered Species Act.

Kerr had learned about the strength of the ESA, as both friends and foes called it, by using it. Kerr's organization had joined in a lawsuit the year before to force the U.S. Fish and Wildlife Service to list the northern spotted owl. Kerr was confident the bird would be listed. The ESA was his kind of law. On paper, it was tough and unequivocal. It said that a petition was to be judged on its scientific merits, not on its economic consequences. Protecting the spotted owl or the salmon was strictly a question of biology, and the costs to society were not to be taken into account until after a biological determination was made.

Both Kerr and Duhnkrack knew that for that reason, the ESA frightened and angered people who might be affected. Kerr would not worry about that now. He thought it was wrong to be afraid to use the law because there might be a backlash. The ESA was the gloved fist of the environmental movement, the hand on the strong broom of renewal sweeping aside what he liked to call "the forces of darkness" and the gray bureaucrats who didn't want to "do the right thing."

Quickly, Kerr and Duhnkrack agreed in principle. In the world of political strategy, though, Kerr needed to take another step. He needed to call Bill Bakke, across town.

Kerr and Bakke, the leader of the conservation group Oregon Trout, were also old fellow travelers. For a time Bakke was on the staff of the Wilderness Coalition, too, but he had split off to form his own organization, to focus on fish. Now Kerr had a simple message for him.

Bill, we're both worried about the salmon, he said. Now it's time to do something. If Oregon Trout doesn't file petitions under the Endangered Species Act, ONRC will.

Let's shake things up, he said.

Kerr's surprise call had the desired effect; Bakke didn't want to give this one away to anybody. He called Oregon Trout's lawyer, Rick Braun, for advice. Braun was also a Lewis and Clark Law School grad, and, like Duhnkrack, was giving himself a break from money work to help a cause he was committed to. Over the phone Bakke and Braun agreed that any important decision had to be made under the right circumstances.

So, out in the suburbs, at the Hillsdale Pub, the two of them had a couple of beers and talked over a sobering decision. They realized that for the next several months, and perhaps years, a decision to petition would put them in the deepest bureaucratic cesspools they could imagine. It was going to mean nights at the office and days at public meetings listening to lots of uptight

White Guys in Ties. Before it was over, they suspected that a lot of people would lie to them; people they didn't know might even threaten them; their families would be annoyed at them; and they'd wonder, certainly, if it was worth it. But it was a decision they couldn't avoid. They couldn't sit around and knowingly watch the salmon become extinct. And they wouldn't take a backseat.

Oregon Trout would lead the development of the petitions under the Endangered Species Act. As the leader of Oregon Trout, Bill Bakke would step forward as the salmon's champion.

It takes a certain sort of man to speak up for a fish. For some people it would never make any sense. For others it needed no explaining. For Bakke it almost didn't seem a matter of choice.

Bakke's passion was fish and fishing—flyfishing for salmon and steelhead in the streams that vein the slopes of the Cascade Mountains. Here, if you want to catch big fish you learn to wait and watch and maneuver deftly on slippery footing, often in conditions others avoid—the morning chill, the fog, and the rain. After the fish are caught, more and more often—if you were Bakke—you let them go. The idea wasn't to take the lives of other creatures wantonly; the challenge was in the pursuit, not the kill.

He went to college in the sixties, but what he'd talk about was that he started the experimental college program at Portland State. He held odd jobs in the seventies, the best of which was modeling for a Portland outdoor clothing designer, Columbia Sportswear. He was an imposing guy, six feet three inches tall, solidly built, with a full blond beard, ruddy complexion, and glinting eyes. But you wouldn't expect to see him in the pages of *Esquire:* not those kind of looks. Columbia just wanted him to be outdoors, to fish. So he put on nice new fishing vests, slouchy hats, and big-pocketed jackets, and had his picture taken. It was tough duty.

He did what he needed to do to make a living in those days, but all he was really interested in was salmon and trout. Everything about the salmon intrigued him—for instance, the way runs came out of the ocean into different rivers at different times, fitting, as he thought of it, like keys in locks.

They were apparently able to distinguish the odors of their native stream and guide themselves by smell once they were in contact with the river's water. But scientists still didn't know how they traveled hundreds or thousands of miles out in the ocean and then knew when to come home, much less how they knew where, along many miles of coast, the tiny door to home would be. Some research suggested that they used the earth's magnetic field or electrical fields to guide themselves home. But no one knew for sure. There were still mysteries.

Then there was the fishing. For Bakke no other activity could compare to it: the reading of the current, the riffles, the telltale signs of deeper pools. Knowing where the fish might be and what to offer to entice them; these were skills you learned only through experience. It was a standing meditation, the water gurgling around your legs, the sun overhead silvering the ripples, the green leaves shivering as a breeze passed through. Then the lightness and finesse of your cast upon the water. The fly setting down quietly, as if it were alive.

This was pure pleasure.

Bakke could stand in the water all day, stand up to his knees, up to his chest, saying nothing to anybody, just smoking his favorite pipe, the one with the chewed-down stem taped to the bowl. The smoke would wreathe away from his head while slowly, methodically, his right arm would tick back and forth, back and forth, the rod light in his hand, the line whistling, the fly dropping just so.

For a long time the pleasure was enough.

But then one late afternoon on the Wind River in southern Washington, something happened to pull him down, down below the rhythmic surface of his motions. He listened to the river's flow and rippling and eddying. He watched its movement continually renew itself in light and shadow, light and shadow. And suddenly he knew the river was alive.

It was a being, as surely as he was, and it had something important to tell him. He looked around and he felt it all at once, a feeling almost like crying. The place was so beautiful.

He stood there for a long time, and the thought that had been drifting by in the current, always there, always waiting, rose to the surface.

He had been fishing the Wind since he was a boy. But he saw now, as if for the first time, the cut banks of the stream, eroding. Turning his head, he heard clearly the sound of the highway in the distance: the trailer rigs, the traffic. He listened for a moment, and he *knew,* knew as certainly as if what was happening to the river was happening inside of him.

The place was doomed.

It would never be as beautiful, as wild, as he had known it.

Wildness wasn't something you could make, once it was gone. And when it was gone the colors of experience bled. The intensity, the clarity went away.

Standing in the Wind River, Bakke asked himself, Was there nothing he could do?

Bakke turned his interest and self-taught knowledge of fish and fisheries into jobs with conservation groups, doing research. He began spending time at government hearings, reading turgid documents, visiting government offices, all kinds of agencies, anything to do with fish, trying to figure out what and who was setting the policy that guided the management of salmon. His reputation for thoroughness and tenacity began in the early 1970s. It was the Watergate era, and he did Watergate-style fact-finding in the waste-baskets and Dumpsters of bureaucrats.

He lived on the cheap. For a time he lived in a single-room house, and when it was cold he ate meals out in his car because it had his only heater. He didn't care. He'd rather be outside anyway.

By the mid-1970s he was already convinced that, unless something changed in the way the salmon and trout of the Northwest were managed, their long-term prospects were bleak.

The key, in Bakke's mind, was wildness. In the 1960s and '70s the state and federal agencies had thrown in the towel, Bakke thought. The agencies contained good scientists who worried about the fish and their world, and whom he cultivated for information. But more and more it became clear that the agency administrators had decided it was no use fighting to preserve the salmon as they always had been in the Northwest, as fish that spawned in the wild. The Northwest had become too developed for that.

From 1930 to 1980 the population of Oregon had doubled, and Washington's had more than doubled. Salmon now had to share their ancestral streams with people who built roads alongside them, dumped pollutants into them, grazed cattle in them, pumped water out of them, and secured their rights to these activities under a system of water law that recognized only human use of water.

If a growing human population was going to have fish to catch, most people seemed to think the fish would have to be spawned in captivity, in salmon hatcheries. Once the juveniles were raised up to the right point, they could be released from the hatcheries and sent out to sea.

The dominance of the hatchery idea was hard to fight. Seemingly everybody was happy with it. To the extent that hatcheries compensated for the loss of productive natural habitat, those who were causing that loss of habitat were happy to see them. The Army Corps of Engineers and the Bureau of Reclamation, who had built and operated most of the dams of the main stem of the Columbia and Snake Rivers, were happy. The utilities and the other industries that received the power generated at the dams were happy. The timber industry, whose road-building and logging practices could degrade the habitat for wild fish, was happy.

Such institutions liked hatcheries, but nearly all the public did, too. No one really thought about the effects on fish and streams of highway development and suburban sprawl, of shopping malls, of parking lots where farmland used to be. It was the rare homeowner who considered that the herbicides and fertilizers he applied to his lawn might ultimately turn up in his local stream, causing trouble for fish. Post–World War II society wanted to believe in the omnipotence of American technology—hatcheries as much as fertilizer, abundant, worry-free fish as much as abundant, worry-free atomic energy, "too cheap to meter."

For their part, commercial fishermen demanded salmon hatcheries. The third-generation Finn fisherman who lived in Astoria and ran his gill-net boat near the mouth of the Columbia, and the Makah Indian who trolled off the northwest tip of Washington each had his own compelling financial reasons. Fishermen of every kind clamored for as many fish as possible. Sportsmen (and women, and children) in Oregon City, Oregon, and Ilwaco, Washington, and Lewiston, Idaho, wanted to be able to catch some salmon, too, for food and for fun. The licenses and fees paid by commercial and sport fishermen supported the fish agencies. The agencies gave them what they wanted, as epitomized by the common practice of stocking trout and salmon in lakes and streams, even ones the fish had never naturally inhabited.

Fish biologists had another reason for favoring hatcheries: professional training. Turning to hatcheries to replace production lost when natural habitat was compromised was not new. Artificial propagation was deeply ingrained in the profession of fish biology and a part of the curriculum in virtually every university fisheries program.

The American Fisheries Society itself had been founded as the American Fish Culturists' Association, in 1870. At the time, the interest in hatchery-rearing—fish "culture"—had arisen in response to the decline of salmon and trout in many lakes and streams of the Northeast. The early members of the American Fish Culturists' Association promoted artificial production of fish first of all as a way of compensating for this loss. But fish culture, as a kind of animal domestication, also carried assumptions rooted deep in civilization. Not only would the number of animals be increased through artificial propagation, the quality of them would be improved over their wild-spawning cousins. Nature itself, through artifice, would be improved! As the American translator of the first European *Complete Treatise on Artificial Fish-Breeding* wrote in 1854:

> The discovery of artificial fish-culture, in a word, claims to show how, at little care and little cost, barren or impoverished streams may be stocked to an unlimited extent with the rarest and most valuable breeds of fish, from eggs artificially procured, impregnated and hatched.

Spurred on by a kind of moral fervor, fish culturists were instrumental in urging the newly established U.S. Commission on Fish and Fisheries to promote fish hatcheries. In 1872 Congress appropriated $15,000 to introduce and artificially propagate shad, salmon, and other valuable food fish throughout the country.

The first hatchery in the Columbia Basin was established on the Clackamas River, west of Portland, in 1876, by salmon cannery operators. Mainly through the efforts of Livingston Stone, a member of the U.S. Fish Commission, a number of government hatcheries were built in the 1890s. Stone, a former Unitarian minister and one of the founders of the American Fish Culturists' Association and the American Fisheries Society, was a central figure in fisheries practices in the Northwest. He saw to the placement of hatcheries on a dozen tributaries of the Columbia River in Oregon and Washington.

By the 1930s many of these first hatcheries were no longer in operation, as poor returns of adult fish had called their effectiveness into question. But the erection of the main-stem dams on the Columbia sent fish managers reeling as they watched huge spawning areas blocked by the dams. Grand Coulee Dam blocked more than one thousand miles of the upper Columbia River. The managers saw hatcheries as their only hope for producing enough fish to satisfy society's expectations—or rather their perceptions of society's expectations.

In 1938 Congress passed the Mitchell Act, which eventually led to the construction or modernization of forty hatcheries and other fish-rearing facilities. The first of these opened in 1949, eleven years after Bonneville Dam was built. During the next three decades an increasing proportion of the juvenile fish that migrated to the sea from the Pacific Northwest was raised in hatcheries, not in rivers. In the 1960s and early '70s, hatcheries seemed successful. Improved food rations and better health practices at hatcheries contributed to several years of good adult returns. Faith in hatcheries had become a kind of religion, promising salvation for salmon.

Bakke, however, saw hatcheries as a Faustian bargain. Everyone else, both the public and the experts, might say hatcheries were the answer, but Bakke would shake his head. He would smile and give his "I'm no expert, just a simple, stubborn Norwegian" look. He went on believing that since nature had always made the fish another way, it was probably the right way. Society was gambling the future on a temporary and artificial paradise.

By the mid-1970s, Bakke became a self-appointed advocate for wild fish in the Northwest, a voice crying in the wilderness. Wildness was being lost. The loss was hard to explain, almost pointless to explain if you had had no contact with the wild. But that was part of the sadness. Those who did not know how the rivers and the forests had been before would never realize how great a thing they had lost, and how their lives had been diminished for want of it.

He wrote a conservation section for a nationally circulated fishing magazine, *Salmon Trout Steelheader,* and his views began to gain some attention. He had found his themes and his tone by 1976, when he addressed a gathering of scientists, fish managers, and conservationists in a symposium sponsored in part by the National Marine Fisheries Service.

Habitat destruction was bad enough, Bakke told this group. But the hatchery cure looked to be worse than the disease.

"The unhappy hybrids that are breeding because of the mindless introduction of hatchery fish," he warned, spelled only one result:

"The wild fish are doomed."

Bakke continued, "What is a wild run to us, anyway? Is our deep feeling mere sentiment, or is there something unique and irreplaceable about it? Is the surviving wild run related to our yearning for echoes of the wild land and the wild peaks and the wilderness we have lost?"

He challenged his listeners with a practical problem.

"If we cannot determine what the benefits [of wild fish] are, and establish management policies to protect those benefits, then we should perhaps forget about wild fish and be honest with ourselves."

By the early 1980s, Bakke's predictions of a widespread salmon disaster seemed to be coming true. Although Columbia River hatcheries continued to release increasing numbers of young fish—161 million in 1982—fewer adults returned. Some scientists began to ask whether the ocean was capable of supporting so many salmon. At another symposium in 1983, Bakke reminded listeners of the stark changes one hundred years had brought to Northwest salmon populations.

In 1883 the Columbia River was the world's greatest producer of chinook salmon, 43 million pounds being harvested in that year, all of them wild fish. But in 1983 no fishing at all was permitted on the upriver portion of the spring and summer chinook runs. Those runs had composed the bulk of the commercial harvest one hundred years before.

From such evidence Bakke was beginning to draw a bitter inference.

"It appears that the ultimate regulation of the fisheries isn't scientific management of the resources, but extinction of the runs."

To Bakke, advocating for wild fish and deploring hatcheries went beyond a sentiment for wildness and a suspicion about technology. His concern was grounded in his reading of salmon biology.

Salmonid fishes had inhabited the Northwest for about 50 million years, while the species of salmon known today have been present for about 5 million years. Their proliferation throughout the region seemed to have coincided with a period of movement of the giant crustal plates of the earth. During this episode of "continental drift," the isthmus of Panama had closed, decreasing the flow of warm waters from the equator and helping to make the northeast Pacific Ocean cooler and more biologically productive. The increased abundance of ocean food sources favored the anadromous salmonids, which were already adapted for saltwater survival. Anadromy has its costs in the stress of salt regulation, in the increased energy needed to migrate, in the physical risks associated with oceanic migration. But apparently the benefits of obtaining increased food supplies dramatically outweighed those costs in the northeast Pacific and the northwestern region of North America.

Bakke recognized that the remarkable historic abundance of salmon in the Pacific Northwest was the result of their ability to adapt to local conditions. Future abundance would depend on perpetuating the genetic diversity of locally adapted, wild-spawning fish.

The need to manage for wild stock abundance should not have been news to fish managers, he believed. Bakke had no formal professional training in fish biology, but he knew that the very first publication of the Oregon Fish Commission, in 1939, had laid out the theory. Willis Rich, a professor of biology from Stanford University and the commission's first director of research, had written that salmon conservation "is based upon the theory that the several species [that is, chinook, coho, and so on] each consists of a large number of independent local populations."

"The practical conservationist must apply his measures [so] that each [population] may be maintained at the most productive level."

Once the importance of wild stocks was recognized, the situation at the end of the 1980s revealed itself as even worse than it first seemed. One hundred years earlier, the annual run of salmon into the Columbia River numbered an estimated 10 million to 16 million fish. In 1990 the run had dwindled to about 1.1 million, at least a 90 percent collapse overall. But the 90 percent decrease masked a greater loss. Nearly all of the modern runs were made up of hatchery fish. Wild-spawning populations, Bakke calculated, were at only 3 percent of their historic abundance.

Hatchery fish, moreover, didn't simply replace wild fish, however poorly. They also displaced them. Scientific studies in the 1970s and '80s were beginning to show clearly that hatchery fish posed a threat to wild fish. Once released from the hatchery they directly competed with the wild fish for food, preyed on them, and introduced hatchery-borne diseases. Artificially raised fish also tended to increase the fishing pressure on wild fish, because managers set harvests based on the abundances of the more numerous raised fish. Finally, the hatchery-bred adults that survived to spawn with wild salmon tended to dilute the genetic diversity of the wild populations.

Without wild fish, Bakke was convinced, there would be no guarantee of salmon in the long term. But the attention of the managers seemed only on the short term, on ensuring fish for the next few years' harvest. To Bakke, hatcheries didn't even make sense on a financial basis. Oregon spent about $15 million annually on fish hatcheries, but no one did the simple division to find out what the effective cost was per individual adult salmon. Bakke did, and discovered that, depending on species and run, the costs per fish were on the order of ten to twenty-five dollars. Some stocks cost significantly more, up to hundreds of dollars per fish. People were paying several times over: for the loss of the wild fish, for the loss of their habitat, and then for the unsustainable costs of the hatchery fish. It made Bakke almost physically sick.

Preserving things went deep in his personality. It applied to the most personal actions. Pretty much every night, wherever he was, he wrote in a diary. He began keeping one in 1960, when he was fifteen, and gradually they filled a shelf in his study: nice, standard clothbound books, black hardbound artists' chapbooks, and one oversized, handmade, leatherbound one. In them he committed often-lengthy accounts of fishing trips and the conditions he found on the rivers he fished. He wrote of other things, too; descriptions of people and places, personal and political situations; his first wife, his second wife, his children. Interspersed among the pages of writing were carefully crafted watercolor and pen-and-ink drawings, often of a fish or a particular design for a fly, or the view from a fishing spot. Because he illustrated the books, they were usually of unlined paper. Even so, he had no trouble writing in straight lines. His penmanship was fine, precise, regular; it was a practiced, unrushed hand.

He was basically conservative in his politics, too, in the old-fashioned sense. He preferred to work within a system, to make it accommodate change.

Acting on that premise in 1978, Bakke worked with a friend on the Oregon Fish and Wildlife Commission and persuaded the commission to adopt a wild fish policy for the state. The intent of the policy was to give first and highest consideration to the protection and enhancement of wild stocks. The commission adopted the policy, but Bakke learned after a couple of years that adopting a policy was one thing, and having the department enact it was something else. He became painfully aware that he could not rely on the established institutions, either those in the environmental community or those in government, to carry his concerns. He set about developing his own organization, starting Oregon Trout in 1983 with some friends. They pushed grassroots membership and the development of an activist agenda. The organization grew rapidly.

Meanwhile, Bakke kept one eye on the Power Planning Council. Like many others, he was willing to give the council a chance to work, but as the years passed, he became increasingly dissatisfied with its lack of attention to wild fish. In 1986 he fired off a letter to an Oregon council member, warning that the council's salmon program is "silent on threatened and endangered species." Bakke requested a formal statement from the council describing how its program "satisfied the goals that would have been implemented under the ESA" if the Fisheries Service had listed certain upriver salmon stocks, rather than deferring to the council. Bakke received no reply.

A year later, Willa Nehlsen's report to the council on the twenty-two

Snake River stocks confirmed for him that ESA petitions would be needed. So when Andy Kerr called and gave him the ultimatum, Bakke really had no doubts about the need to petition. But he wanted the petitioning to succeed. He wanted to not just make a splash, not just rock the boat, but restore the salmon. The goal must be kept in focus.

In the late fall of 1989, Bakke and Rick Braun met with Ned Duhnkrack for a strategy session. Also at the meeting was yet another sharp young lawyer from Lewis and Clark, Dan Rohlf, who was associated with the Northwest Environmental Defense Center at the law school. Rohlf, a Stanford Law grad, had just finished writing a book on the Endangered Species Act.

The first order of business was to choose which stocks to petition for. Although all of this core group of petitioners were Oregonians, they had no question about limiting the petitions to "Oregon" salmon. Chinook salmon destined for the Snake River in Idaho and its tributaries in Oregon and Washington seemed obvious candidates. The same year as Nehlsen's review, members of the Idaho chapter of the American Fisheries Society had stepped up their monitoring of the chinook runs. Chapter officers sent a letter to Rollie Schmitten, the Northwest regional director of the Fisheries Service, telling him the chapter intended to file ESA petitions for chinook if substantial improvement didn't occur.

At meetings in the fall of 1989, the chinook committee of the Idaho AFS, chaired by Cleve Steward, a fisheries doctoral student, reassessed the chapter's position on a chinook petition. A drought was continuing in Idaho, and the year's run had been dismal. Members were leaning toward petitioning. When Bakke heard about the Idaho AFS discussions, he got in touch with Steward. It would be clumsy to jump out ahead of the Idaho chapter and much better for both organizations if they coordinated their efforts. Talking to Steward, Bakke learned more about the status of stocks, which the Idaho AFS had continued to monitor. Those discussions cinched the petitions for chinook.

But Bakke wanted to make a broader case. The plight of the upriver stocks fingered the hydroelectric dams as a big problem. Of equal importance, in

Bakke's mind, was the loss of spawning habitat and the troubles associated with hatcheries. To make that case, ideally, he wanted to choose a run that was unaffected by the dams but was victimized by habitat loss and hatcheries. That would mean choosing a run on the lower Columbia River below Bonneville, the first dam. The wild coho of the Columbia were in desperate shape, as far as anyone could tell. So the ticket became downriver coho, upriver chinook. Ned Duhnkrack started to draft the petitions.

She had never written an endangered-species petition before, and she quickly began to appreciate that the task was not at all routine. There was a format, more or less: an introduction, a discussion of the taxonomy of the species, a discussion of its status and the factors that led to the decline, and a conclusion. The legal framework was actually the easy part. Duhnkrack and the others knew that the petitions would sink or swim on their biological accuracy. The Fisheries Service had ninety days to review the petitions to see if they were biologically sound, so being right in their assertions was crucial.

The petitions were for *wild-spawning* stocks—no question—because they were in danger of extinction, and also because all salmon, including the hatchery-raised populations, ultimately depended on the wild fish. The Snake River wild chinook were clearly in bad shape. But the question was, should they petition for certain specifically named local populations or lump them together?

Since Willa Nehlsen was expert on the status of the Snake River stocks, Duhnkrack asked her advice. Every wild chinook stock in the Snake was declining, so Nehlsen saw no reason not to lump them together. The one distinction that needed to be made between various chinook runs was based on the season of their spawning run. Duhnkrack adjusted her approach and began preparing slightly different petitions for the spring, summer, and fall chinook, and for the coho.

While Duhnkrack drafted the language of the petitions, Bakke gave his attention to the politics. His one overriding concern was that the petitions be both credible and effective. Mulling it over, he developed a two-step strategy.

He attended the Oregon AFS meeting in February 1990, just as he did most years. As he sat in the meeting room listening to David Bella and the others on the sustainability of natural resources, and as he thought back to the speeches the year before on environmental ethics by Bella and Jim Lichatowich and the others, he reassured himself that the chapter leaders could be enlisted in the petitions.

At a break he approached Gordon Reeves with a request. The Oregon Trout board of directors had authorized him to prepare petitions under the ESA, Bakke told Reeves. Would Oregon AFS review the petitions to ensure their technical accuracy?

Reeves knew where he stood on the question personally, but he gave Bakke a bureaucratic answer. The chapter had committees assigned to certain tasks, and Reeves, as president, would refer the request for review to the natural production committee. The cochairs of the committee were Willa Nehlsen and Dave Buchanan, an experienced research biologist and former colleague of Lichatowich.

With the AFS review of the petitions now moving forward, Bakke turned to the second step of his strategy. Biological credibility was only half the battle. If he wanted people to listen, he believed it wouldn't do any good to put them on the defensive.

He wanted to avoid the confrontational approach environmentalists had taken with the spotted owl and the Northwest forest crisis. They had used the courts to protect the forests and the owl by appealing timber sales on public forest lands and by petitioning for the owl under the ESA. The approach had certainly worked, in that it had given owls and their habitat on federal lands a reprieve. But it had also thrown the region into an uproar and had allowed certain politicians and most of the timber industry to paint the environmentalists as elitists, blind to the timber industry's significant contribution to the regional economy and insensitive to the needs of its workers. From Bakke's point of view, what was worse was that as of 1990, the confrontation between environmentalists and the timber industry had become so emotional that the opponents had stopped listening to one another. Positions became fixed. No one would budge. The public discussion of the issue congealed into mental sludge—slogans such as "jobs versus owls" and "the environment versus the economy"—and it seemed that it would take time and some outside wonder worker before any real progress would occur.

For the owl, environmentalists might argue that such gridlock wasn't such a bad strategy; at least the owl's habitat wasn't being eradicated. For the salmon, however, maintaining the status quo would be a disaster, Bakke thought. The salmon needed constructive actions, not just an uncertain delay of destructive ones. So Bakke was wary of Andy Kerr. He had been the point man in the environmentalists' spotted-owl strategy. Kerr didn't seem to mind angering opponents; in fact, he would say it was often necessary. "Our job as environmentalists is to make the political crisis commensurate with the biological crisis," Kerr said at one meeting. "It's not like we're making things up or blowing things out of proportion. Our job is to add the *true* proportion to the political debate."

"Environmentalists may be hell to live with, but they make great ancestors." That was another of his zingers. It was an interesting one coming from the complex Kerr, who held an uneasy mixture of pride and loathing for his own ancestors, who were Oregon pioneers. His great-great-grandfather, Levi Scott, had come to Oregon on the first wagon train in 1843 and founded the town of Scottsburg in the Coast Range. Scott helped open up the Umpqua River for commerce, and he helped blaze the Applegate Trail, which linked the coast with the interior. So Kerr, the environmentalist, had his own demons to fight and his own way of doing it, and Bakke didn't fault him. But they both knew that the success of the salmon petitions hinged on Bakke's knowledge and contacts, and Bakke was determined they were going to do these ESA petitions his way.

If Kerr was the perennial bad boy, the bad cop, Bakke was the habitual good cop. Once Bakke had involved the Oregon AFS in reviewing the petitions, he sent a letter to the director of the Oregon Department of Fish and Wildlife and to nineteen other agencies and Indian tribes. He also sent copies to members of Oregon's congressional delegation and to economic interests. The letter said, in part, "Management has failed to provide the stewardship necessary to perpetuate the health of these populations. Because we have failed to provide good management, we are delivered to the extreme measures represented by the Endangered Species Act.

"We view petitioning under the ESA as an extreme, last-chance opportunity to restore populations that are threatened with extinction."

Under the circumstances, he couldn't have sounded more moderate. But as important as what the letter said, Bakke felt, was that it was sent at all. This was his way. No blindsiding. All affected parties knew what was going on. The plight of the salmon was a social and public problem, and he believed that it was right—"honorable" was a word he used—to show other people appropriate consideration.

While he was apprising potential opponents and other affected parties, Bakke was also busy trying to cement other pieces of his alliance. In early March he wrote Ed Chaney, the leading Idaho salmon conservationist, asking for his views on the merits of the petitions and whether his organization would join in. Chaney had been fighting for Idaho salmon for twenty-five years, writing pamphlets, circulating position papers, being a philosophical gadfly from his perch in Eagle, Idaho. His reply to Bakke was less a personal or even a professional letter between colleagues than it was an acerbic review of the history and what they were up against.

The main problem Idaho fish faced, Chaney reminded Bakke, was inadequate springtime flows of water in the main stem of the river. High flows used to come naturally with the spring runoff, but those flows were bottled up by the reservoirs behind dams. Without good flows the downriver-migrating juveniles had trouble getting to the sea.

By the end of his seven-page letter, Chaney had talked himself out of his old bias against petitions, a bias based on his concern that an ESA listing alone wouldn't save the fish. That bias reflected an attitude deeply ingrained in the rural West, where involving the government usually meant more regulations that everyone disliked and that many looked for ways to ignore. Chaney now thought there was no "realistic alternative."

The Idaho chapter of the AFS had come to the same conclusion. At its annual meeting in March 1990 the chapter voted to petition for the Snake River chinook. Idaho's 1989 spring chinook run was only one-third as large as the previous year's, while the summer chinook were down by half. The tempo of contact between Idaho and Oregon, between Cleve Steward from the Idaho AFS and Bakke, Reeves, and the other Oregonians, now quickened. In mid-March a conference call among ten of the ringleaders recognized the inevitable. The Oregon leaders of the petition efforts needed to meet all at once, face-to-face.

Twenty-five of them met in early April in a conference room at Oregon State University. The context of the meeting had changed dramatically in the intervening month. In early April, one of the Indian tribes in Idaho, the Shoshone-Bannocks, had filed a petition with the Fisheries Service to list wild Snake River sockeye as threatened or endangered under the ESA. Ever since Nehlsen's 1987 survey, the plight of the sockeye had been common knowledge. Now those who met in Oregon had the example of the Shoshone-Bannocks to strengthen their resolve and sense of urgency.

To open the meeting, Reeves explained the procedures the Oregon chapter would follow in developing its position on the petitions. Then Bakke described the petitions. A member of the natural production committee presented data on Snake River chinook populations. A representative of the Fisheries Service explained ESA procedures. With this background established, Bakke asked the chapter to sign on to the petitions, then and there.

No one had quite thought it through—the quality of the data, the potential risks to AFS of the chapter's involvement. Some worried that if the Fisheries Service rejected a petition because the data or the petition itself weren't good, the chapter would be embarrassed, its credibility shaken. Other participants were concerned that by cosigning the petition, the chapter would be disqualified from providing technical information during the actual ESA review. Still others spoke of concerns that the chapter didn't have the resources and time to fulfill the responsibilities of a cosigner.

No one spoke against the petitions, but as a group they weren't ready to sign. Reeves let their concerns stay afloat; to him, the natural production committee was not the proper level of the organization to make the decision anyway. That job should fall to the executive committee, of which he was a member. There were no set rules on how such an issue should be decided by an AFS chapter, but he was confident it ought to go through channels to the top. A thorough review should come before.

By the end of the meeting, Bakke hadn't obtained exactly what he wanted. But the natural production committee members had voted to consider supporting or cosigning the petitions, pending their review by a technical team. That team would be composed of Willa Nehlsen and three other biologists.

For the next month this team worked with Bakke and Duhnkrack to complete the petitions. When the members were satisfied, the team recommended the chapter executive committee sign the petitions. In May the executive committee met. Reeves chaired the meeting, but for the most part he and the six others around the table said little. They read the petitions carefully, passing pages from one to the other, checking the recommendations of the technical team, making a final edit.

At the end Reeves called for a vote. He had checked the organizational bylaws and they did not say the executive committee could not vote on behalf of the membership in such an issue. The national AFS executive committee had also encouraged Oregon to sign the petitions. To Reeves and his colleagues, the issue was too important—and now the arguments were too compelling—to let the petitions go without their support. Without debate, they voted to add the Oregon chapter of the AFS to the petitioners seeking to protect the lower Columbia coho and the Snake River chinook.

On May 30, Bakke, Reeves, Kerr, and Rohlf gathered in a borrowed downtown Portland office and made their intentions official. Sitting together at a conference table in front of a group of reporters and television camera operators, they explained why they were filing the petitions. They showed the population charts for the runs of spring, summer, and fall chinook, and the lower Columbia coho. The statistics for any one of them were sobering. Summer chinook adults, for instance, had numbered thirty thousand as late as the 1960s, but had dropped below a few thousand beginning in 1979. The reporters didn't even have to look at the numbers; just the slope of the lines told the story. All of them were going rapidly to zero.

On the evening news thousands of people tuned in to hear Bakke say, "It is clear that dramatic action is required to save these fish from the plunge toward extinction."

The camera cut to Kerr, who had his chance to say what he thought was at stake.

"Saving the salmon will not be cheap, but we have no choice," he said. "For if we don't save the salmon, I think we have less chance to save ourselves as a species."

It had not been easy for them to do it, but a collection of citizen groups and individuals had done what no government agency, elected official, or editorial writer had even called for. The representatives of Oregon Trout, the Oregon and Idaho chapters of the American Fisheries Society, the Oregon Natural Resources Council, the Northwest Environmental Defense Center, and American Rivers had taken a big step to preserve and restore a remnant of the primordial Northwest.

The announcement of the petitions was like a rock thrown into a pond. The event called attention to itself, while its repercussions would likely go beyond what anybody could see.

Bakke knew how he felt. He was relieved the preparatory work was over. But he was unsure what to expect from the public, the politicians, and the other interests. Although he didn't know what the people of the region might have thought, collectively, about the announcement, he did allow himself a small hope. The salmon were not spotted owls. Most people in the Northwest had never seen a spotted owl and knew it only as an indicator of a problem. The salmon, on the other hand, were visible companions in a way of life, reminders of a natural abundance that had preceded them and perhaps had drawn them there. The salmon were food, too, and many people enjoyed eating them. Some relied on catching them to supplement their diets. The hope Bakke held was that even more important than their value as food was the sense of privilege their abundance conveyed. Who had seen a salmon charging upriver and not felt the thrill of being alive, the satisfaction of knowing that this was a good place to live?

What people in the Northwest might have thought about salmon becoming extinct was hard to tell. But partly it had to be a shock, a splash in the face with icewater, Bakke figured. The salmon were telling people that the vaunted Northwest environment was becoming no different from anyplace else on the planet. Newspapers and magazines might bemoan the loss of species as the tropical rain forests of Brazil or Indonesia were cut down. But much the same was happening in Oregon and California and Washington and Idaho, for reasons not far removed from those in the tropics.

Endangered species were a worldwide trend: Many well-informed Americans knew this in 1990 just as well as Bakke did. E. O. Wilson, the distinguished Harvard biologist, had helped put some scale on the problem. Five times before in the 4 billion years of Earth history, mass extinctions of species had occurred, associated with major climate changes. According to Wilson and other biologists, Earth was again in the throes of a major mass extinction, but this time climate wasn't responsible. Humans were.

The total number of species on the planet was not known, though Wilson estimated the range as 10 million to 100 million. What he could say with more certainty was that at least 27,000 species were disappearing forever every year.

He noted he was often asked: "If enough species are extinguished, will the ecosystems collapse, and will the extinction of most other species follow soon afterward?"

His answer was cold comfort.

"The only answer anyone can give is: possibly. By the time we find out, however, it might be too late. One planet, one experiment."

These kinds of numbers, these kinds of consequences, were almost beyond human comprehension. Four billion years, 27,000 species, what did they mean to modern Americans, who were inclined to identify themselves most strongly with others of their own family with whom they had personal contact? Four human generations, perhaps five; one hundred years the outside duration of deep interest. Now these humans were being told that something that had not happened naturally in 65 million years, a period longer than even their existence as a species, was happening again, and it was both caused by them and needed their immediate response. What were the chances that they could understand the dimensions of the problem, make adjustments to their behavior, and act in time?

The challenge was unprecedented. The endangered species crisis, as laid out by Wilson, was the defining example of *the* modern problem. If the crisis was not addressed now, not only were the consequences unknown. Nothing might be able to be done about undesirable consequences later.

Such a dilemma and such a responsibility seemed to many people to cry out for deep personal reflection.

Robert Bly, the spiritual father of a new "men's movement," saw environmental degradation broadly as one symptom of a civilization that had lost a proper role for men, leaving them with dark souls and a fiendish will to degrade life.

"The dark side of men is clear," Bly wrote in *Iron John,* published in 1990.

> Their mad exploitation of earth resources, devaluation and hu-miliation of women, and obsession with tribal warfare is unde-niable. We have defective mythologies that ignore masculine depth of feeling . . . teach obedience to the wrong powers, work to keep men boys, and entangle both men and women in systems of industrial domination.

In that same year, of Bly's book and of the endangered-salmon petitions, Gary Synder's *The Practice of the Wild* was published. Snyder, nature poet and practitioner of Zen Buddhism, examined extinction of species and called it truly unacceptable.

> The extinction of a species, each one a pilgrim of four billion years of evolution, is an irreversible loss. The ending of the lines of so many creatures with whom we have traveled this far is an occasion of profound sorrow and grief. Death can be accepted and to some degree transformed. But the loss of lineages and all their future young is not something to accept . . . "Death is one thing, an end to *birth* is something else."

But the earth and its creatures didn't need our attention as much as something else did, Snyder wrote.

> Our immediate business, and our quarrel, is with ourselves . . . Human beings themselves are at risk . . . We are in danger of losing our souls. We are ignorant of our own nature and confused about what it means to be a human being.

The poets and the deep ecologists might have been of one mind on the matter. Perhaps even most Americans, in their heart of hearts, would agree that the culture's obsession with material possessions, its indifference to the past and future, was somehow profoundly misguided. But for Bakke and others who were trying to change the direction of society quickly, before it ran over other beings powerless to get out of the way, the appeal usually had to be to human self-interest.

Sometimes the appeal could work nicely. As environmentalists sought to argue the virtues of protecting old-growth conifer forests, they were fortunate to discover the Pacific yew tree. Typically cut down, burned, and wasted during commercial clear-cutting of forests, the scraggly yew earned new respect when, in the late 1980s, a drug made from its bark was shown to be somewhat effective against ovarian cancer. Each year some thirteen thousand women die from this cancer in the United States, so the yew-bark drug, called taxol, was a particularly welcome find. The National Cancer Institute described taxol as one of the most important anticancer drugs developed during the decade.

The yew provided a textbook example of the unexpected value of over-looked species. As Congress had said when it was drafting the Endangered Species Act, the reason for preserving species is simple. "They are potential resources. They are keys to puzzles which we cannot solve, and may provide answers to questions which we have not yet learned to ask." The extract of the yew tree was only the latest answer found in nature to a medical question. One-third of pharmaceutical prescriptions given annually in the United States are based on natural substances or synthetics derived from them.

Unlike the yew tree, however, salmon had no arcane medicinal value, at least none anyone knew about. They certainly had a material value as food and a commercial value to fishermen as a food commodity, but Bakke and the other petitioners did not want to push too hard on the economic rationale for saving the fish. Some commercial fisherman still made good livings on salmon caught in the Northwest. But the Northwest catch, from a market perspective, was superfluous in 1990, a drop in the bucket. Four-fifths of all salmon in North America came from Alaska, which had fourteen thousand streams and lakes that were home to anadromous salmonids. Since 1980, the salmon catch there had exceeded an astounding 96 million fish annually, and in 1990 the catch was heading for double that number.

Bakke could walk into his local fish market and buy, if he wanted to, ocean-caught wild sockeye salmon from Alaska at generally lower prices than locally caught salmon. He could also buy chinook salmon grown to harvest in floating pens on Vancouver Island or white-fleshed Atlantic salmon grown the same way in Norway's fjords. Wild-capture fishing in the Northwest wasn't necessary anymore for salmon supply. Salmon were an international food commodity; "producers" acted in a global marketplace. Bakke recognized that economic arguments would be tilted against salmon protection, and it was not his strong suit. Plenty of other people would be willing to argue the economic merits.

Oregon Senator Bob Packwood was one of the first. Shortly after the petitions were filed in June, Packwood, a member of the Senate Commerce Committee, called a hearing in Oregon. The commerce committee would have some jurisdiction because the Fisheries Service, which would handle the petitions, was a division of the National Oceanic and Atmospheric Administration, which was under the Department of Commerce. The hearing took place in Astoria in June. A variety of interests were invited to state their views; the petitioners were expected to explain their actions.

Gordon Reeves cited E. O. Wilson as he argued that the decline of native salmon runs in the Columbia basin was a "local manifestation of what scientists have termed a planetary environmental crisis." That crisis, Reeves continued, "is evidenced by rates of extinction unprecedented within the last sixty-five million years."

After giving Packwood the body count of how bad the Columbia and Snake situation was, he tried to point a better direction for managers. "The abundance and diversity of native stocks of salmon and steelhead in the Columbia River basin have been reduced to a fraction of predevelopment levels.

"This decline is an indicator of a general decline in the health and integrity of the Columbia River system."

To restore the system and the salmon, Reeves advocated "integrated management of the entire Columbia basin, and maintenance of diverse, naturally spawning populations."

While Reeves sounded cool and professional in his presentation, Andy

Kerr didn't flinch from dwelling on the bad news when he had his chance before the senator.

"The salmon runs are a critical indicator of the quality of life of the Pacific Northwest," Kerr said.

"At the top of the aquatic food chain, the salmon reflects the condition of our streams, which reflect the condition of our environment, which reflects our own condition.

"We can learn much from the spotted owl experience," he went on, attempting to preempt the expected argument.

"Let us avoid denial that the salmon are in trouble and get on to reversing that fact. Let us not misread or mischaracterize economic change for economic decline or disaster. Let us avoid the one-sided economics which recognizes only the cost of species protection, ignoring both the benefits of conservation and the costs of extinction."

In his closing, he knew the advantage of striking an upbeat note.

"The wild salmon runs," Kerr concluded, "are sacred to most Northwesterners, even if their ancestors were born on other continents. They are a legacy that we must pass on to our children."

Cogent in defense of their actions as they might be, Reeves and Kerr were clearly in the minority of the fifty speakers who registered their views with Packwood during the hearing. In general, the speakers were upset and fearful. Packwood was sympathetic to them.

The event impressed on Reeves that the public spotlight wasn't where he wanted to be; he could contribute more working behind the scenes. Besides, he had research to do. Finding time even for that was hard, given the pressure of other Forest Service actions. On the Elk River, July 1990 brought Reeves into closer involvement with the two slated timber sales that would affect local salmon populations. He had professional concerns to register.

Willa Nehlsen, meanwhile, was being shaken in the waves rippling out from the announcement of the petitions. Ever since 1987, her involvement in the survey of stocks at risk had put her at odds with some members of the Power Planning Council and some of the council's constituents. When she presented the survey findings at the Oregon AFS meeting in February 1990, the response from many fisheries colleagues was positive. But now that she had a manuscript in circulation, those who were critical of her could be more open, too.

With the regional stock assessment, she felt she was just following up something in which she had a strong interest—and in which the council might be expected to have a strong interest, too. She would not say it out loud, but she felt her efforts were an achievement; she was bringing attention to a serious problem. And she thought that by keeping up on developments in the Northwest, she would be useful to the council when it became involved in responding to petitions.

What she didn't expect was the council's response to her AFS activities. In the spring, after the first presentation of the "Crossroads" paper, she was advised that she needed to make it clear when she was speaking as a member of the AFS endangered species committee and when she was speaking as a staff member of the council. She was also warned not to involve herself in recommending actions the council might take to address the stocks at risk. Policy-making was the elected council members' proper role, not hers.

She felt misunderstood, but she wanted to show that she was clear about what she needed to do. On her office wall, in plain sight of anyone who chose to look, she posted a reminder.

> *Do not pretend to represent the council when in fact you are representing yourself or the AFS.*

When the sockeye and then the chinook and coho petitions were filed, these strictures were not all she had to accept. The council went further, sequestering her from council discussions of the petitions. They explained their concern that involvement by her would seem as if they had prejudged the petitions. It sounded plausible, as long as a good deal of importance was placed on appearances. Nehlsen was told she could continue to work on everything except items related to the petitions.

She was deeply disappointed in the council. Her heart and soul were committed to the survival of the fish, but now she was being told to stand back. She was deeply disappointed but not terribly surprised. Her years of experience as a biologist had only underscored an innate skepticism about human institutions, what Bakke liked to call "Nordic fatalism." She had less loyalty to those institutions than she had to nature, and she knew that her preference had consequences.

By summer 1990 she had made a categorical decision about her commitments to the council. She would direct her efforts to helping the council understand and plan for fish conservation over the long term, which clearly seemed to depend upon preserving the genetic variability of existing populations, allowing them to adapt to changes in the environment. Moreover, she knew that genetic variability was the key to long-term productivity. Everyone wanted the fish to be productive. No one, however, had really come to grips with the fundamental issue of how best to maintain the genetic diversity of the region's salmonids. Nehlsen assembled a team of geneticists, the best people from around the country, and asked them to synthesize their understanding of salmon genetics and make it understandable to the policy makers. A lot of policy would rest on clarifying both *if* and *how* wild fish were genetically important.

Meanwhile, she would work on finishing the "Crossroads" paper. If she accomplished those two things, that would be plenty, and she would have put her skills to good use. She would gladly leave the public debates to people better suited and better situated for them. She had grown to have confidence in Bakke.

For his part, Bakke had spent the period before the petitions were filed and right afterward working to gain the confidence of his potential adversaries. After his letters in February, he followed up with courtesy calls to people who would see him. The main thing he wanted to show was that he was somebody they could talk with, or as he joked with his own staff, he wasn't "some kind of *eco-terrorist* and they didn't have to come unglued about me."

In his one-on-ones with the corporate executive directors and their public affairs people, Bakke's diplomatic abilities were put to the test. One of these sessions was at the corporate headquarters of the Direct Service Industries, the front group for the region's powerful aluminum manufacturers, companies such as ALCOA, Kaiser Aluminum, and Reynolds Metals. On the afternoon of the meeting, top managers of the DSI companies and a couple of well-paid fisheries consultants sat around a big polished table in an eighth-story suite. Everyone was making a point of being cordial.

Bakke stood at the front, working his way through a slide show, making the case that the issue was complex and it was to everyone's interest to keep the problem-solving broad.

"The reason I got involved in the petitions," he said, "wasn't the dams. It was fish management and the inability of the states to protect habitat."

"It's not my intent to beat up on dams and power users," he told the executives. He was not going to make out that they were solely responsible for the problems of the fish. Besides, to be arguing against hydropower *per se* would be an awkward position. What would environmentalists prefer—coal-fired power plants . . . nuclear power plants?

"We've got to make sure this stays a large issue," Bakke told the industry executives, "and you aren't the only ones paying the bill."

That message played well with the executives. What's more, they could sense that Bakke was sincere. Keeping the issue broad might indeed serve everyone's interests. As he left the suite with the leather chairs, there were handshakes all around.

Back home, when he sat back in his favorite chair, the handsome but banged-up Morris chair that he had bought second-hand for seven dollars when in college, Bakke was not unhappy with the way the petitions were being greeted. The utilities could have played the same role the wood products industry had during the forest crisis, he figured. They could have collectively blown a fuse. That they didn't was partly due to the influence of Al Wright, the utility executive. Wright didn't like the situation, but he knew his people would need to be involved.

More significantly, the businesslike tone was encouraged by Oregon's most influential political figure, the state's senior U.S. senator, Mark Hatfield. In the realm of politics relating to Oregon's natural resources, Bob Packwood might erupt in sparks. But the sixty-eight-year-old Hatfield was too seasoned for that. More than any other single individual, Hatfield could influence the response to the emerging salmon crisis. Not only was he the senior Northwest senator, he was also the ranking Republican member of the powerful Senate Appropriations Committee. He quickly determined to use his influence.

Hatfield was the longest-tenured figure in Oregon politics. First elected to the state legislature in 1951 while a college professor, he had subsequently been the secretary of state and then governor for two terms, from 1959 to 1967. His youthful good looks and charm contributed to his appeal as a national candidate, and the Oregon Republican was considered by Richard Nixon as a running mate in 1968, while Hatfield was making his first Senate bid. He would have seemed a good counterbalance for Nixon, but the two men went their own ways and Hatfield was elected to the Senate. In 1990 Hatfield had had an unbroken political career of thirty-nine years.

To Americans who might have been aware of him as a national political figure, salmon—or more broadly, natural-resource issues—were probably not Hatfield's claim to recognition. For most people Hatfield's public visibility was linked to his stance on the Vietnam War, which he opposed vocally starting in 1966, while he was Oregon governor. This was a time when opposition to the war from elected officials was rare. Hatfield's fellow Oregonian, U.S. Senator Wayne Morse, however, had led the way by being one of two senators to vote against the Gulf of Tonkin resolution in 1964.

Hatfield opposed the Vietnam War for several reasons, but the root was surely personal. At twenty-three he had been among the first U.S. servicemen to enter Hiroshima after the atomic bomb devastated the city, and the experience had profoundly shaken him. In the Vietnam conflict, he was able to see beyond the Johnson and Nixon administrations' characterization of the war and empathize with its victims. He recognized that the Vietnamese were struggling for self-determination, not communism.

"They are fighting in the name of social, economic and political justice," he wrote, "and although we may believe their view of 'justice' false and devilish, it is a vision for which they are ready to die."

The continuation of American involvement in Vietnam's civil war, the brutalization of the Vietnamese in the process, and the initial failure of his measures to change the course of American policy pushed Hatfield to see a decay of values in American public life. Opponents of the war from Abbie Hoffman to Jane Fonda to the millions of students on hundreds of college campuses were keenly aware of the same malaise. What distinguished Hatfield was the combination of his position and his response.

"Our material possessions, our wisdom, our education are all things that we must share with other people," Hatfield said in a speech in 1967, "because we are all our brother's keeper. I would much rather be a keeper than a destroyer, and that to me is what America is doing today, destroying people."

Hatfield's continued opposition to the war, and his vindication at the American withdrawal, endeared him to many people as that rare politician, a man of independence and firm moral principle. What fewer drew from his message, though, was the importance of his evangelical Christian faith. As Hatfield wrote in 1976, "Power and prestige could not be the goals which gave my life a sense of direction or purpose . . . The purpose of my life is to be faithful to Jesus Christ, to follow his way, and to be molded according to the imprint of his life."

This orientation figured prominently in his thinking about not only such matters as the proper conduct toward Vietnam's people but also the proper conduct toward America's natural resources. "We are not the owners of creation," Hatfield wrote in 1976, "but rather its stewards, entrusted with its temporary use."

"We each must live and act in ways that demonstrate loving stewardship of the whole of creation for all of humanity."

Such views gave many young environmentalists hope that Hatfield would be their champion in the Senate as he had been their champion during the war. Indeed, Hatfield supported some significant pieces of environmental legislation during the 1970s and '80s. These included a strengthened Endangered Species Act in 1973 and an Oregon Forest Wilderness Bill in 1984, which set aside nearly 1 million acres in the state. But as Hatfield aged in office and environmental partisans increased their demands even as they saw the environment suffer more, some found that Hatfield was no longer their champion. Part of the problem was that they hadn't looked closely into Hatfield's allegiance to the "stewardship" concept.

Stewardship meant use. Nature was to be used by man, "wisely," as Hatfield liked to say. He conceived of himself in the mold of those other moderate Republicans, Gifford Pinchot, the founder of the U.S. Forest Service, and President Theodore Roosevelt, Pinchot's friend and fellow East Coast brahmin. These men were "conservationists." To conserve implied use. "Environmentalist," on the other hand, implied a philosophy that made Hatfield wary: preservationism. To him the idea of *not* using the environment for human purposes was a form of extremism. It was not God's way.

In Genesis, had not God given Man dominion over the birds of the air, the beasts of the field, and the fish of the sea? Hatfield had sworn himself to serve God.

A collision between environmentalists and Hatfield seemed inevitable on those terms alone. After the Oregon Forest Wilderness Bill of 1984, Oregon environmentalists came back to Hatfield, working under the assumption that they would add to the designated wilderness with another bill during the next six years. Hatfield flatly rejected the notion.

For some, like Andy Kerr, the political falling-out-of-bed with Hatfield brought bruises and a rude awakening. Antagonism grew quickly between the two men, coming to a climax in 1988, when the senator authored certain riders to the Department of the Interior's appropriations bill. The riders had the crucial effect of limiting the ability of the public to review some forest management decisions.

Kerr and other environmental leaders berated the riders on matters of practice as well as principle. One rider allowed logging in an area considered necessary for salmon spawning, while in the process effectively overturning an injunction obtained by environmentalists. Another prevented judicial review of logging in an area proposed for national park status by environ-mentalists. A third sought to preclude many sorts of legal challenges to Forest Service and Bureau of Land Management timber sale programs.

These riders were a bitter postscript for those who believed in an enlight-ened Hatfield, the one who had written that "contemplation and the pres-ervation of nature go hand in hand. Our tendency to abuse and ruin the created world mirrors our disregard for spiritual reality, both within our-selves and throughout the earth."

In a letter to Oregonians, Hatfield offered as explanation that the riders "strike a balance . . . by ensuring that timber dependent communities are not shut down while at the same time allowing the judicious management of our national forests that preserves environmental protections."

Environmentalists shook their heads at Hatfield's idea of balance. The man some had called St. Mark now became demonized. All communication between the influential Oregon Natural Resources Council and the powerful senator broke down.

As spotted-owl lawsuits were filed, Hatfield felt the forests slip further out of his legislative control. This was not a feeling he liked. Privately, Hatfield was outraged at what he considered the environmentalists' narrowness, their lack of balance, given what he had done for them.

Bill Bakke knew this history, and as he considered his strategy in the late winter of 1990, he saw no advantage in an uninformed and hostile senator. He decided to let Hatfield know of the petition plans at the same time as the others. It wasn't special treatment, in Bakke's mind; and Bakke wasn't asking Hatfield's permission. Nothing like that. It was just courtesy.

When Bakke called, Hatfield was surprised at the proposed petitions. He thought that the funding that he had helped ensure over the years, as governor and as senator, particularly for hatchery programs, would have prevented anything serious like an endangered species problem. And he had put faith in the Northwest Power Act, that it would prevent such a thing.

But he listened to Bakke carefully, and he thanked him for the advance warning. Always the politician, it gave him time to prepare an agenda. He checked with the National Marine Fisheries Service and the Oregon Department of Fish and Wildlife, asking them to conduct a preliminary review of the status of the chinook, coho, and sockeye runs that would be under petition. And he called a hearing.

The hearing, in Portland on June 30, looked to be important. The governors of the four Northwestern states came to testify, as did representatives of the Power Planning Council, industrial interests, environmentalists, government agencies, and a list of others. The lineup looked to be important, but the situation was too new. For the most part what Hatfield heard was a massive throat-clearing. He learned one main thing of substance from it.

The Fisheries Service and the ODFW told him that, indeed, runs of

Columbia salmon were in trouble. To Hatfield, that meant action—preemptive action—was called for.

"I want to be very direct about what lies before us," the senator intoned. "A decision to list even one of those salmon runs could send an economic and social tidal wave throughout this region."

If the Endangered Species Act were put into effect to help the salmon, Hatfield worried aloud, economic and social harm might be suffered by the hydropower industry, by farmers who depended on the Columbia for irrigation, by the shipping industry and their customers who used the Columbia as a highway, by fishermen, and by many others.

"The issue will come right down on our heads," he said.

He sounded like a genuinely worried man, and after the hearing was over, and in the first weeks of summer following it, Hatfield and his staff mulled over how best to keep the sky from falling. What they came up with wasn't exactly a novelty in public affairs, but it did suit Hatfield, and it did appear to make sense. Hatfield proposed to convene a "regional salmon management planning meeting." It was supposed to address the problem and to try to find a timely solution.

He didn't call it a "summit," although that's how it quickly became labeled. Perhaps he was sensitive about the widely touted "timber summit" he had convened the year before, which had not been successful. Perhaps also Hatfield, the former political science professor, demurred because his gathering was not to be at all like one of the Cold War summit meetings between American and Soviet leaders. This "summit" was clearly not going to be ceremonial, with everything essentially worked out in advance. It also would not be over in one session. It would no doubt involve several working sessions over a period of weeks or months. Nevertheless, "summit" it would be in the most important sense: The people with the responsibility and authority to take action would be at the table.

As the summer of 1990 was coming to a close, Hatfield's staff had coordinated with staff at the Power Planning Council; two preliminary organizational meetings had been held with key participants; and an organization had been hired to conduct the summit discussions. This was a group of professional facilitators who called themselves the Mediation Institute. The first summit meeting was set for mid-October.

In the final days before the meeting, the individuals who would be participating spent some time preparing themselves. Hatfield polished his opening remarks. The speech had begun to take on added importance for him because he wasn't just Oregon's senator, he was a candidate for reelection, and he was facing the strongest challenge of his political career.

Harry Lonsdale, a maverick liberal businessman, had been gaining sympathy with the voters by linking Hatfield's pro-business votes on environmental issues with the senator's allegedly cozy relationships with certain industrial polluters. Lonsdale championed campaign finance reform, and he argued pointedly for a ban on the export of raw logs, a practice favored by political action committees of the timber industry, which supported Hatfield. Polls placed Lonsdale within a few percentage points of unseating the four-term incumbent. Coming into the first summit meeting, Hatfield very much wanted to look like the consensus builder, the statesman, an advocate for both the environment and the economy.

As he, too, prepared for the meeting, the burden of history also hung heavily on Bakke, though in a different way. In his library at home he had collected the obscure writings of men who were known only to a few, and in spare moments he had been rereading the proposals of some earlier salmon observers. One Bakke read was Livingston Stone.

"Nothing can stop the growth and development of the country, which are fatal to the salmon," Stone had written in 1892. "Provide some refuge for the salmon, and provide it quickly, before complications arise which may make it impracticable, or at least very difficult. Now is the time. Delays are dangerous."

Delays are dangerous. Bakke could only wince at that one.

For the Northwest to have ignored a warning one hundred years before was one thing, but for leaders to have ignored a similar warning only thirty years ago gave him a stronger feeling, as he read again a poor photocopy of the Oregon State Game Commission *Bulletin* for October 1959.

"I believe it is especially critical that we stake out a claim for an anadro-

mous fish sanctuary in the Snake River basin," Ross Leffler had told a
gathering of Western states fish commissioners that year. Leffler, the head
of the U.S. Fish and Wildlife Service, had picked up Stone's idea of a
salmon park.

This federal official argued that if a solution for upriver fish passage past
dams could not be found, then "certain river basins of the Pacific Northwest
should be dedicated to the conservation and development of fish and wildlife
resources as their highest and best use."

Dedicated. Bakke went back to the word, thinking bitterly about missed
opportunities.

The first summit meeting was held in the Multnomah Falls Room in
Portland's Downtown Red Lion Inn. Multnomah Falls itself is a majestic
high waterfall, not far from Portland, along the mountainous section of the
Columbia River Gorge. It is one of those scenic places much favored by the
operators of commercial tour buses and by Portland families taking out-of-
state visitors sightseeing. *"How beautiful! Oregon sure is a lovely state"* is the
expected response.

The falls' namesake is one of those hotel-chain meeting rooms that tries to
compensate the people meeting in it by being named after a scenic attraction.
In the early afternoon of Tuesday, October 17, 1990, an artificial fig tree sat
by itself in the far corner of the Multnomah Falls Room, while knots of
well-groomed men in suits and ties unraveled into the room, finding places
for themselves to sit.

A few moved to take their places around a group of tables arranged in a
hexagon, where some other men were already sitting, quietly talking among
themselves. In one corner were representatives of Columbia and Snake River
Indian tribes, wearing Western jackets and string ties or beadwork. Down
the table, one obvious environmentalist was wearing a plaid shirt. Others
near him, perhaps seeking to be less obvious, were wearing suit jackets and
ties, which made them look eerily like the gentlemen in the other corner,
most of whom were now turned in their seats, talking to correctly dressed
younger men sitting behind them in a second row. These were the executives

and the agency heads, at the table, and their lawyers, backing them up. The lawyers smiled easily, with the look of men whose meters were running, whatever happened.

Bill Bakke came in, looking a bit stiff, and sat down, saying hello to the men on his left and right. Finally twenty-four men and one woman were seated at the table. Alana Knaster from the Mediation Institute quickly introduced herself, and then Mark Hatfield, looking rather solemn, entered with an aide at his side.

Hatfield, his hair silver, his manner fatherly, sat down, took out his biofocals, and read from a prepared statement.

"I see many familiar faces representing environmental groups, energy interests, the federal agencies, and others with whom I have worked closely over the years," he began.

"I am sure each of you realizes that we are embarking today upon an historic mission which will define the very direction upon which this region will proceed for years to come. The future of the salmon runs, the ability to sustain our current economic base, and our ability to plan for future growth will hinge on the outcome of this process *and* the ongoing endangered species listing process.

"Whether you have realized it or not, you are being entrusted with the preservation of our unique way of life in the Pacific Northwest for generations to come.

"Unlike decisions which are made often by bureaucrats in Washington, D.C., I have great confidence in this 'pre-decisional' process. Why? Because it provides a forum whereby management decisions can be made *for* the Northwest *in* the Northwest *by* people who live in the Northwest.

"This is our opportunity to shape and define our own destiny—not abrogate that responsibility to individuals outside our region who do not understand the importance of the Columbia River and its resources to all our lives."

Hatfield paused, looked over the top of his bifocals, then continued.

"If you fail in this endeavor, this problem is likely to end up in our nation's capital. That is the worst place to look for a solution.

"No less than six cabinet-level agencies would be involved and over twenty committees and subcommittees of the House and Senate would claim some jurisdiction over the issue.

"We must not let this happen."

Respectful applause, as serious as the speech, met the senator when he was done. To look around the room, the effect of the speech seemed mainly to increase the number of worried expressions. *Solve it yourselves or take the consequences of others solving it for you.* It was not a happy choice.

Hatfield adjusted his hearing aid and turned to listen as the twenty-five at the table now formally introduced themselves. He knew most of them, and many just gave their name and affiliation and thanked Hatfield for their being invited to the table.

The representatives of the Indian tribes were led by Ted Strong, the executive director of the Columbia River Inter-tribal Fish Commission. Few Americans might appreciate the fact, but the tribes had rights as sovereign peoples guaranteed to them by treaties with the federal government. Most of the Columbia and Snake River tribes had signed treaties in the 1850s that reserved to them the right to hunt and fish as they always had done.

The utility industry, too, saw itself as the carrier of rights and responsibilities.

As the provider of 70 percent of all the power consumed in the Northwest, the Bonneville Power Administration had been a dominant force in the development of the region ever since the New Deal. The BPA generated an enormous amount of revenue, some $2 billion per year. But as a division of the federal government's Department of Energy, the BPA was not an independent giant. It changed tone with presidential administrations, and the advent of the Northwest Power Planning Council in 1980 had diminished its power-brokering authority. But its influence was hard to overestimate.

The BPA was represented at the table by its administrator, Jim Jura.

The customers of the BPA, the public and private utilities, and the Direct Service Industries, were represented by Al Wright.

And so it went, around the table, to the petitioners and the other conservationists from Trout Unlimited, Friends of the Earth, and other groups; to the federal agencies such as the U.S. Forest Service, Bureau of Land Management, and Army Corps of Engineers; to the representatives of the

Northwest governors. Everyone had a stack of chips, large or small, which they hoped no one else would see, except when they wanted them to. Everyone showed a poker face.

When they were done, Hatfield thanked them all for their participation, and he left. He had a political campaign to conduct.

Knaster, the mediator, set right down to work. She distributed a six-page outline of "suggested ground rule considerations." Item A read, "The purpose of these negotiations is to develop an integrated, comprehensive plan to ensure the future viability of critical salmon species in the Columbia River Basin."

How does this sound? Knaster asked.

For a moment it was quiet in the Multnomah Falls Room, just the sound of the air-conditioning and some people rustling papers. Jim Jura said he would like to see them develop a comprehensive plan that the National Marine Fisheries Service would take into account as the agency developed its opinion on the merits of a listing.

As Bill Bakke listened to this, he heard the idea that a recovery plan developed at the summit might persuade the Fisheries Service that it didn't need to grant the salmon formal protection under the Endangered Species Act.

Bakke had been waiting for this. His brow thickened, his jaw jutted forward, and for all the world he looked like a bear. "That's not why I'm here," he said, fairly growling. "Oregon Trout and the other petitioners filed their request for salmon protection because they wanted the agency with the expertise to evaluate the petitions on their merits.

"We want a recovery plan, just as the rest of you *say* you do. Only we don't think we'll get one that will work, unless the fish receive protection under the law.

"We don't want that law circumvented."

With that, the battle lines were drawn. Embrace the law, or attempt to beat it.

On that October day it was not at all clear that the summit participants could succeed in what the Power Planning Council had failed to achieve in the previous ten years, and what no one had been able to do in the fifty years since the first dams were built on the Columbia and river management disputes began in earnest.

Was it possible that these twenty-five regional leaders could put differences to the side and agree on some common environmental good, setting perhaps a national, even an international precedent?

CRISIS

All right then, what did {immigrants to America} come for? For lots of reasons. Perhaps least of all in search of freedom of any sort: positive freedom, that is.

They came largely to get away—*that most simple of motives. To get away. Away from what? In the long run, away from themselves. Away from everything. That's why most people have come to America, and still do come. To get away from everything they are and have been.*

"Henceforth be masterless."

—D. H. LAWRENCE, STUDIES IN CLASSIC AMERICAN LITERATURE, 1924

What were the agendas of the other summit players? That question occupied Bakke as the meetings continued during the fall of 1990.

He was accustomed to sleeping only six hours a night, but for several weeks he slept even less than usual while he puzzled it out, waiting for people to make their moves. It was a bit like fishing. It was best if you made no unnecessary noise, stayed alert, and were ready to react if you saw some movement.

Actually he felt pretty good. The very fact the summit was under way meant that the decline of the salmon had been elevated in public discussion. In many ways, he knew, the summit was an unprecedented public forum. Perhaps nowhere else in the world but the United States would such a controversial environmental problem be deliberated in such an open way. And while hundreds of other petitions to protect endangered species had been made, at no time in the contentious sixteen-year history of the law had all the interested parties been brought together to try to work out an agreement to recover the species before the crisis reached the shouting stage. In the summit, the salmon were receiving a hearing before the people who could take significant steps to help them.

After the first meeting and the sparring Bakke had done there, the second meeting featured backpedaling, feinting, and dodging by most of the participants. But by the third one, scheduled for Boise in late November 1990, the Bonneville Power Administration was ready to lead with a jab.

The power-marketing agency was expected to fund a major portion of whatever measures the summit members decided upon, so managers of the agency apparently decided to make a virtue out of necessity. They tried to preempt requests by making a proposal of their own. Two weeks before the Boise meeting, the BPA announced a proposal to spend $1.5 billion during the following ten years to reverse the salmon decline, especially that of wild salmon.

It sounded like a lot of money, and the components of the plan—the "Columbia Basin Accord"—also seemed designed to impress. They filled some sixty pages. But when Bakke read the "accord" closely, the biological provisions mainly sounded like the same old story. The BPA proposal didn't adequately address his concerns for wild fish, saying little about the habitat and hatchery improvements that he believed had to be major parts of any solution. Instead, it focused primarily on tinkering with the water flows in the spring to move Snake River salmon downriver.

The proposal seemed to emphasize the "accord" idea itself, a "new, long-term agreement among key parties in the Pacific Northwest." It looked as if the BPA wanted to establish a new institutional superstructure that would put itself over the Power Planning Council. Considered that way, the $1.5 billion looked like window dressing. Bakke knew the BPA claimed they had spent just about the same amount on fish from 1980 to 1990, so the "new" commitment was really nothing new. The cynicism would have made him angry, if he let himself get angry about such deceptions.

Bakke wouldn't endorse the BPA proposal at Boise, but he didn't like being in a position of only deflecting a blow. He called up Rick Braun and asked him to help plot a response.

The two of them made an interesting team, a rather entertaining one to watch. Braun was a short guy with a thick mustache who bristled with ideas. Bakke was a big guy wreathed in a blond beard and pipe smoke, who seemed to be saving his.

Braun was as quick with his tongue as was Andy Kerr, but had the smoothness and professional credentials that afforded him opportunities that Kerr, or even Bakke, couldn't get. The credentials weren't just parchment in a frame; Braun had a trial lawyer's knack for strategy, and he was deft. Plus, he liked Bakke, admired his particular blend of idealism and pragmatism, liked him enough to serve on the board of directors of Oregon Trout and otherwise donate a year of his life to their common cause. Braun disliked what he called "sanctimonious environmentalists," the ones who were forever holier than thou. In Braun's political judgment, that attitude went nowhere.

To the two of them, it still looked like the verbiage of the first and second summit meetings hadn't really amounted to much. The economic interests were still trying to frame the summit as an end run on the Endangered Species Act. Oregon Trout would have none of that. Deciding to expose what they felt was the BPA's hidden agenda, Bakke and Braun planned to counterattack at Boise.

Idaho's capital wasn't their idea of an exciting town, and the first day's meeting, given over mainly to the BPA proposal, bored them. But on the second morning of the meeting, Bakke and Braun decided it was their turn. They released a prepared statement. *Any* plan developed by the summit was not going to take the place of the evaluation being conducted by the Fisheries Service, they said.

"Oregon Trout will not support and will affirmatively resist the use of such a plan to avoid a biologically supportable decision to list the petitioned stock.

"Such use of a plan does not comply with the law."

That was that: short, simple, blunt. They answered some questions from reporters, and then Bakke and Braun just flew home to Portland to await the reaction.

When the airport limousine dropped them off at the Benson Hotel downtown, they picked up a copy of the day's *Oregonian*. "Battle On for Wild Fish, Group Tells NW Summit" read the headline. Alongside the story was a mug shot of the BPA's Jack Robertson, a deputy administrator, and his reaction to the Oregon Trout position paper.

"I believed the purpose of this summit was to come up with a regional consensus on recovery . . . that would avoid a listing," Robertson said.

Bakke and Braun looked at each other. OK, so Robertson gets good exposure and contradicts them. Well, what about Hatfield?

Standing together in the hotel lobby, they quickly skimmed down the column and turned the page to find the rest of the story. There was the reply from Hatfield's office. A spokesman said the senator "did not intend" the summit "as a way to avoid a listing."

They both stopped reading.

"Not . . . avoid a listing."

They had done it.

It seemed that they had done it! To them, it looked as if they had counterpunched their adversaries and scored a technical knockout ruling from the big-time referee. Slapping each other on the back, they ambled over to the Benson bar and drank scotch and laughed until they just about cried, they were so happy. They felt good about how they were maneuvering.

Maybe it was the news accounts, maybe it was just in the air, but word seemed to be getting around Portland that salmon might have a chance, after all.

Funny things began to happen to Bakke, just walking down the street. Not long after the Boise meeting he and a friend were talking and walking down one of the downtown streets, not paying much attention to the street traffic or to the light-rail train bearing down on them. A shrill blast of the horn, a scream of brakes, and the train came to an abrupt stop right alongside them. The driver's window flew open and a man stuck his head out.

"You're doing a great job for the fish, Bill. Keep it up," he called out. And just as quickly as he had appeared, the driver stuck his head back in, slammed the window shut, and the train rolled on.

Bakke stood on the curb, his pipe bobbing in his teeth while he broke into a big grin.

The salmon fight, nevertheless, was only begun; the Boise knockdown was just the end of a round. At the next summit meeting the industrial interests came out with a new combination. This time, their maneuvering happened in private, out of the view of most participants and reporters, at one of the task group meetings. It happened around a long conference table in a tight meeting room in the Portland offices of the BPA. It was a week before Christmas, but none of the fourteen lawyers representing the various interests was showing much glee. They sat talking stiffly of their clients, of "being proactive," of "considering hypotheticals." By and by the lawyers for the aluminum industry and the utilities, Jeff Ring and Barbara Craig, introduced the idea of a deal.

The conversation began in hypotheticals played out to Dan Rohlf, representing Idaho fish conservationists, and to Rick Braun.

Rohlf listened to Ring and heard, between the lines, *We can cut all the future unpleasantness off right here, and save my clients a lot of money and time if we reach a settlement now.*

"Is there a result that would allow you not to litigate the lack of a listing?" Ring asked.

"Let me see if I understand this," said Rohlf, and he paraphrased Ring. He understood it perfectly well: Sign an agreement before the Fisheries Service finished its ESA reviews and agree not to appeal the agreement later.

"Oh no, we can't do that," said Rohlf. "We don't see that NMFS has the authority to circumvent the listing process."

"Well, what would make you happy?" Ring asked.

Rohlf sat back. This *was* cheeky. It was just as if they were proposing an out-of-court settlement in a liability case.

"The fish are our bottom line," Rohlf replied. "We're happy to the extent that the fish runs are healthy."

The two of them gave each other their nicest professional smiles.

Braun was watching this exchange closely, and Rohlf was doing fine, but maybe he was missing something.

"We aren't saying that a recovery plan developed here should not be implemented," Braun cut in. Thrust and parry was fine, but Braun worried about getting sandbagged. It was just a hunch, but he had this suspicion that if the fish interests didn't accept an offer to set terms and not sue later, their opponents might use it to say that the conservationists were not really interested in coming to an agreement. They were only interested in being "spoilers."

"Let me see if I get this straight," said Braun, and he asked the task group mediator to summarize his notes so far.

"Well," said the mediator, "it sounds as if they"—the utilities—"knew there would be no litigation they would be more forthcoming about terms."

"Wait a minute," said Ring. "I thought this was just a discussion, that there was no official minutes of this meeting . . . that this was not a matter of the public record."

Braun smiled. "Oh?" he said. "I thought it *was.*"

For the next few minutes, the two of them went around on this, and as they did, Rohlf and Craig got drawn into it, too, and a couple of the other lawyers, as if the *officialness* of the deal discussion was the issue . . . and pretty soon the exchanges came to feel more like an unseemly tag-team wrestling match, people sweating and slapping, than a more subtle form of pugilism. By the end of it, the deal had gotten thrown out of the ring like something oafish and disreputable enough that it would likely not clamber back in again.

Ring looked chagrined. Braun continued to smile. The discussion in the tight conference room drifted to other topics.

Later that afternoon at cocktail hour, Bakke listened with growing amusement as Braun recounted what had happened.

"Look," said Braun, "the point was even if we signed something, which we weren't about to do, it wouldn't mean peace. There are other environmental groups, people not even at the table, like Andy Kerr. They aren't going to roll over."

He took a swallow of beer and wiped his mustache.

"The industry lawyers, said, 'We want certainty.' "

"And I said, 'But you don't get certainty. Let's live without it.' "

Bakke laughed out loud. He liked the justice of it. The power interests had had their way with fish for so long, they had forgotten how the other half lived.

There was always talk of finding the "balance" in the negotiations, and to the industry that seemed always to mean that the balancing began right now, with the chips everyone had *then*. But the fish advocates saw the time frame differently. The fish had already given; they were just about "balanced" out of existence. Giving more wasn't going to help them, and Bakke was not about to get suckered into some deal.

The burly environmentalist sat back with his beer, thinking strategy.

As the representatives to the salmon summit continued to meet through the winter, shuffling two steps forward, two steps back, another process was being pushed straight ahead. The National Marine Fisheries Service had no choice about its responsibilities; the Endangered Species Act required the agency to review the status of the species that had been petitioned for.

The agency's Northwest regional office conducted most of the review, which effectively depended on the resolution of one conceptual and one practical problem. Both were big. In the normal course of work for an agency that had become chronically shorthanded during the Reagan-Bush years, either problem might have taken years to resolve. Under the circumstances the Fisheries Service had months.

The conceptual problem was a function of the law itself; the definition of "species" was not as clear as the agency wanted it to be. "Species," as defined in the law, included not only the classical taxonomic level of species, that is, *chinook* salmon or *coho* salmon: separate groups of organisms that breed only with their own kind. For purposes of the law, "species" also meant "any subspecies of fish or wildlife or plants," *or* "any distinct population segment of any species of vertebrate fish or wildlife which interbreeds when mature."

The salmon petitioners had recognized that their petitions for wild populations of Snake River chinook and lower Columbia River coho depended on that latter clause. If the ESA applied solely to the taxonomic level of "species"—all chinook or coho—the petitioners would not have had a case. But they argued that the petitioned populations qualified for protection under the laws as "distinct population segments"—important local subsets of the universe of chinook and coho. From the petitioners' point of view, the language of the law and salmon biology were finely suited to each other.

If the intent of the law was indeed to preserve salmon "species" in the big, taxonomic sense of chinook and coho, then the only way to do this was by ensuring the continued existence of the genetic variation found in locally adapted populations. The species was nothing more than the aggregate of the distinct populations.

As much in agreement as the biology and law might appear, the language of the ESA did not provide the Fisheries Service with a biological definition of "distinct population segment." But the ESA did require a listing decision to be made "solely on the basis of the best scientific and commercial data available." Agency officials decided that meeting this requirement meant defining "distinct population segment" biologically.

This concern was something new. The Fisheries Service had recently dealt with another salmon listing, on the Sacramento River in California. The biological situation there was dismal. The winter run of chinook had declined from 100,000 spawners in 1969 to only about 400 in 1989, largely as a result of the operation of the Central Valley Project, which siphoned water out of the Sacramento for agribusiness. The Fisheries Service had declared the winter chinook "threatened" in 1989—without troubling to define "distinct population segment."

But the agency now wanted more clarity, so in the winter of 1990 a team of researchers based in Seattle was duly grappling with the definition.

Meanwhile, the second problem, the practical one, remained: What, indeed, was the status of these petitioned populations? To find the most up-to-date answer, the Fisheries Service drew on the local expertise of the state fish agencies. And it also requested the results of new surveys conducted in the field.

How biologists determine a population's status may not be obvious. At certain times of the year, hundreds of thousands of juvenile coho, for instance, might be occupying streams and rivers of the lower Columbia. At other times, thousands of maturing adult coho might be circulating out in the ocean. However, the critical number is how many adults come back to spawn and perpetuate their race. To obtain that information, there's a time-honored, labor-intensive method: Biologists with the Oregon Department of Fish and Wildlife and the Washington Department of Fisheries get right in and walk up the tributaries, counting fish.

Doing spawning surveys is not glamorous work, and the demands are more physical than professional or even bureaucratic, so the job often falls to a young fish biologist, perhaps one who is hired only for the season. In December 1990, a young biologist named Chris Allori had been hired to count coho salmon in part of the lower Columbia region for the ODFW.

Most days Allori was gone from home early in the morning, busy covering his territory. One particular sunny, crisp morning found Allori driving the green ODFW pickup up a logging road into the Coast Range south of Astoria. The area was new for Allori, and he looked around happily as he drove. He liked working outdoors; in fact, there was nothing he liked better than walking around in a quiet and peaceful forest, seeing fish. He didn't envy the older biologists who worked in offices. Outside was where the fish were. It was too easy to lose touch with the fish in all the politics.

The background of his surveys intrigued him. He knew that surveys conducted locally since about 1950 by Oregon fish agencies showed a steep decline in the abundance of spawners. On a group of ten supposedly representative, "index" streams, the surveys showed a decline of spawners from about thirty fish per mile in the 1950s and '60s to less than one fish per mile in the late '80s.

Cullaby Creek had not been one of those index streams, and Allori knew that his boss, Bob Buckman, the district biologist, believed that Cullaby would be a good place for wild coho. The creek was connected to the Columbia right near the sea, so that the fish that came from the ocean had fewer chances of being caught by fishermen. Eighty percent or more of all the salmon destined for the lower Columbia tributaries were caught. The adults had certainly been present there in years past, as revealed in one spawning survey from 1952 archived in the district office. Allori had looked over this document, a hand-drawn map and four neatly typed pages. The "Running Account of the Stream" listed the fish the biologist had seen and their location relative to a reference point.

The first entry began at "zero yards" and read "4 live adult silvers (coho); actively spawning in 'gravel like shale'; raising clouds of mud with each spawning effort."

The report went on for two full pages. The final count was 120 live coho spawners. All had been seen in about two miles of stream.

Thinking about that report, as Allori drove the pickup alongside Cullaby Creek he was inclined to be optimistic. About ten miles in from the Columbia, he stopped the pickup and got out. He pulled on chest-high waders, put on a pair of polarizing glasses, and walked down into the stream.

With his glasses he could look beneath the surface of the creek to see any salmon that might be hiding in a pool or snagged, dead, in the submerged rootweb of a tree. It was important to count every fish, and Allori scanned the stream and the streambank constantly as he began to walk.

No sooner was Allori knee-deep in the water than Buckman's predictions about the stream made sense. At close quarters it appeared mostly undisturbed. He surprised a couple of ducks, who splashed up out of the stream just ahead of him. A few minutes later, a great blue heron silently rose out of tall bear grass and glided away.

The banks were crowded down to the edge with dense thickets of the bear grass, sword fern, and great tangles of blackberry and nettles. He moved quickly in the water, considering he was walking against a current that sucked at his boots. Though the creek was usually only four to eight feet across, sometimes it was as deep as his waist, sometimes deeper. Drowned logs and branches posed hazards to his footing, but even so, he found it easier to stay in the water than to scramble up and down on the overgrown banks. The biologist knew salmon should be in the creek. The vegetation along the edges kept the water cool, and the snags in the stream provided cover that would protect young fish. Still he walked for perhaps half an hour without seeing one salmon.

Then, as he was trying to climb around a clutch of branches in the stream he spotted something in the water, its sides a ghostly white. A drowned thing. Using a gaff to pull it out, he saw it was a small coho. He laid in on a little sand bar and went to work.

First he measured it, writing "11" down on the outside of a manila envelope the size of a credit card. Then he needed to determine its sex. It looked like a female, since the tail was badly eroded, as if from hollowing out a place in the gravel to deposit her eggs. Just to make sure he took a knife to the salmon's belly, and, surprised, discovered a sperm sac. He wrote the letter "M" on the envelope next to the fish's length.

The last step in the sampling involved taking scales. Using the tip of his sheath knife, he scraped off three scales from a spot on the coho's side about two-thirds of the way toward the tail. Allori had learned in college that a salmon's life history is revealed in the scale pattern of growth rings. Scales are removed from this particular spot because the fish begins growing its scales there. They show the most complete life history.

Allori drew a piece of blotter paper out of the small envelope and carefully pressed the three scales onto it. He turned the fish over, scraped three more scales from the same location on the other side, and put them next to the others on the blotter paper. This duplication was routine; sometimes scales from one side of the fish were damaged. He sealed the envelope and continued up the creek.

He liked to think about salmon biology. Little things such as their protective coloration interested him. In the ocean, salmon species typically were silvery underneath and blue-black on top. That coloration made it hard for a swimming predator to see the salmon's silvery body against the glare of the sky. Conversely, a flying predator would find it hard to see the salmon's blue-black outline against the dark blue of the ocean.

By the time the fish were in the river and ready to spawn, the colors were changed. Coho and sockeye males, for example, turned a bright shade of red. One common explanation was that red, with it short wavelengths, was a vivid color close underwater but appeared black farther away. So it was ideal camouflage for a fish that needed to signal its presence to a potential mate but didn't want to attract every other fish's attention.

Staying unnoticed by other males was an advantage. Male salmon posed a danger to one another on the spawning beds, where they competed for the females. Biologists had always noticed the distinctive humped back and the hooked jaw that the males of some species developed at spawning time. The Latin name given to the salmon genus, in fact, reflected that observation. "Oncorhyncus" came from the Greek words meaning "hooked nose." The hook and the hump, some biologists speculated, were the result of a kind of arms race. With the hooked jaw, the male gets a bigger bite, enabling him to get his teeth into more of the body of another male. The hump, or in some cases, a bulge, may be part of the defense, in effect protecting vital organs by increasing their distance from the back.

The sexual aspects of spawning were intriguing. What did it mean that salmon spawned only once—effectively putting all their eggs into one basket? It seemed to imply the expectation of a certain stability within the physical environment, at least within the two-to-seven-year lifetime of an individual salmon. Otherwise, the adaptive advantage would accrue to those fish who spawned more than once.

Yet the one-time spawning rule also seemed designed as a hedge against environmental uncertainty. An individual that produced from about two thousand to more than ten thousand eggs, as various species of salmon did, seemed likely to ensure at least some progeny. Under favorable environmental conditions, more offspring might survive. In the wild, fewer than 1 percent of the fertilized eggs would survive to return as adult spawners. The more eggs a salmon started with, the better.

This hedge against uncertainty might also be the reason for the salmon's uncommon genetic makeup. Salmon are tetraploids: they have double the number of chromosomes their diploid ancestors had. The advantage of having a double number, some seventy to one hundred chromosomes, is that the organism has two copies of the genes it uses. A gene that makes an enzyme, for example, may produce one with a structure slightly different from normal. Generally the variations will not be useful, but once in a while one will be. The species will thereby expand its range of survival tricks.

Such elements of salmon biology were all very interesting to the young biologist.

As Allori continued to walk the creek, he came across two more dead salmon, close together. They were a young male and a larger fish, its head missing and body badly decomposed. Perhaps it was a female. Perhaps they spawned together, Allori thought. It was impossible to tell.

Standing on the streambank, collecting his data, he noticed some small black things like snails on the sides of the small male. He recognized them as the larvae of caddis flies, burrowing into the flesh. He stopped a moment to wonder at it. The larvae, growing now on the flesh of the dead salmon, would hatch into flies and perhaps be eaten by a young fish that might arise from the mating of these two dead fish here. Just so, the cycle of life continued in the river.

It was strange to think of, but salmon seemed to be nature's main way of bringing the ocean's productive abundance inland. Few other creatures did this, and Allori found it interesting to speculate on whether the animals of the Pacific forests that depend on the salmon, such as the bears and the eagles, could have ever been so numerous if these ocean-fatted fish had not been present.

Entertaining such random thoughts of abundance, he finished his walk. By the end, he had walked nearly two miles and seen four adult fish, all of them dead. Three were males; one Allori labeled "unknown." The biologist felt bad. Four fish in two miles wasn't terrible, but they were haunted in his mind by the 120 coho of thirty-eight years before. As he trudged his way back to the truck in his waders he consoled himself that one day's spawning survey hardly provided the last word on whether there were any wild coho left in Cullaby Creek, much less whether there were any wild coho on the lower Columbia. Spawning surveys, he knew, were subject to several limitations. More observations were needed to produce a meaningful result, so throughout the spawning season, from late October through February, he would need to continue his surveys. In all he planned to sample each of his creeks about once every two weeks.

But merely repeating surveys was not enough. The sampling of "index" streams was not necessarily broadly representative of the lower Columbia coho runs. Cullaby Creek, for example, had not been routinely sampled in recent years, despite its fish-rearing potential. So Allori had been told to survey more streams. In addition to the three index streams in his area sampled in past years, Allori was expected to walk thirteen more streams routinely, and nineteen others if he had time.

State agency and Fisheries Service officials hoped that such extra effort might give them a better picture of the status of the coho, because everyone had doubts about the validity of the historic data. Experienced biologists knew that streams chosen for spawning surveys were often chosen for their

convenience in sampling. One favorite spot, for instance, was a good spawning area near a bridge, where a biologist could park his truck, get out, and
do the counting job easily. For reasons like that, many biologists suspected
that, if anything, historic surveys overstated the abundance of spawners.

Moreover, the counts themselves still concealed the information that the
Fisheries Service really wanted. Body counts alone couldn't reveal whether
the spawned-out fish were raised in hatcheries or in the wild. That was where
the laborious scraping of the scales and pressing them onto blotter paper
came into use. The scale envelopes were sent to a laboratory in Corvallis
where a specially trained biologist worked.

To read the tiny scales, Lisa Borgerson used a microfiche reader, like the
kind used in libraries. Instead of film, the scale-analysis system employed
thin sheets of plastic. Borgerson made impressions of the scales on the plastic
and then magnified and projected them onto a screen.

The principles behind her analysis were simple enough. As a salmon grows,
its scales also grow, and the growth is expressed in a pattern similar to tree
rings. On the viewing screen, the scale rings, which are called circuli, could
be plainly seen to encircle a starting point. As with tree rings, the spacing of
the rings on the scale indicates the rate of the organism's growth. Tighter rings
indicate slower growth; wider-spaced rings indicate rapid growth.

Although both hatchery and wild fish begin their lives in freshwater,
migrate to the ocean, and return to freshwater to spawn, their growth patterns are markedly different. The key to distinguishing between them was
the variation in the circumstances of their lives, especially in the initial
freshwater phase. Typically, Borgerson knew, a young fish raised in the wild
shows tighter circuli, revealing slower growth, during its first year. Compared to the controlled environment and regular feedings in a hatchery, a
stream is more variable and food is less consistently available. The circuli of
a hatchery-raised fish are generally farther apart in this first, freshwater phase
of life. But when the two different kinds of fish enter the ocean, the wild
salmon often grows more quickly than its hatchery cousin. Ocean entrance
does not appear to be as traumatic for them as it is for hatchery fish, whose
scales may show a narrowing or even an irregular overlapping, indicating that
growth is temporarily stopped.

Borgerson used her knowledge of these and quite a few other characteristic patterns to distinguish between the scales of wild-spawned and hatchery-raised fish. Just the same, she didn't need to rely solely on her own interpretive skill. The department kept a reference collection of scales for all hatchery salmon, so when she encountered a particularly difficult interpretation she could draw on this collection. Most of the time the interpretation was clear, however, and she was confident of it. She had been reading scales for ten years and had examined thousands of them.

After she and other scale readers were done, it would be up to the Fisheries Service to decide how compelling the coho spawning survey and the scale analysis were. A fish's scales could tell if it was spawned in the wild, but the scales might not be conclusive about the fish's genetic history. To be certain, further laboratory work might be necessary to unlock the history sealed in the genes themselves.

Histories inside of histories.

In that winter of 1990–91, those long nights when many Northwesterners awakened to the import of the salmon crisis, many wondered about how the crisis could have happened.

The scales of a fish could lead to thoughts about choices made to produce fish artificially, which could lead to thoughts about why artificial production had been considered necessary in the first place. The Fisheries Service, the Bonneville Power Administration, the industries of the region, the commercial fishermen: They all had histories, often long and sometimes shrouded. Any crisis had roots in the past. It might not be possible to solve the crisis without knowing the histories.

If the salmon crisis of the 1990s was the bitter fruit of some flowering that came before, one might look to the flowering, the climax of an earlier development, for clues. Such a flowering was evident in the 1890s and came to a climax with the great fishing strike of 1896 in Astoria, Oregon. The strike pitted one group of fishermen against another and most of the fishermen against the owners of the canneries, those huge waterfront sheds where millions of salmon were sliced up and packed into tin cans. Like many other strikes this one was bitter and complicated, with conflicting claims of equity and responsibility.

It is possible to consider only such a dark flowering, that moment when everything becomes the most vivid, the most exposed. But to understand it probably takes a further effort. Inevitably, the search leads backward, to the seed.

Two hundred years before the salmon summit was planned, in September 1790, Captain Robert Gray set out from Boston, Massachusetts. His ship, a square-rigged, three-masted, eighty-three-foot-long brig of 212 tons, carried a load of cloth, chisels, and some old muskets, intended for trade with the Indians of the Northwest coast. Little in detail was known about this coast, but it had been visited by Spanish and Portuguese sea captains since the 1500s and, more recently, by the famed British navigator Captain James Cook, who had visited parts of it in 1776 during what would be his final voyage.

Encountering the Indians on the west coast of what became known as Vancouver Island, Cook had bargained for the luxurious warm furs of the sea otter. Though Cook himself was later killed in a dispute with the natives of the Hawaiian Islands, his company continued on its voyage, ultimately selling the otter furs to merchants in China for a handsome profit. Seeing how much money the skins brought them, the crew members had come close to mutiny when the officers refused to return to North America to obtain more pelts. The crew was sworn to secrecy at the end of the voyage in England. But the call of riches was too strong to be silenced. By a decade later the trade of sea otter pelts for tea was well established.

Robert Gray himself had made an earlier voyage in the latter part of the 1780s. In that first trip he had obtained from the Indians more than a thousand otter skins, which had had later sold in China, where he bought tea. The Boston merchants who bankrolled Gray failed to make a profit on the voyage because other merchants were also importing tea from Canton. The selling price dropped in Massachusetts.

Nevertheless, Gray was quickly sent back to the Northwest, bearing letters of introduction for his fur-buying mission from the governor of Massachusetts, John Hancock, and the president of the United States, George Washington. Washington's letter, penned by Thomas Jefferson, his secretary of state, was addressed "To all emperors, kings, sovereign princes, states, and regents," and struck a harmonious note, saying, in part:

> . . . I do request of all the before mentioned . . . where the said Robert Gray shall arrive with his vessel and cargo, that they will be pleased to receive him with kindness and treat him in a becoming manner . . .

After rounding Cape Horn in record time and sailing rapidly northward, by early May 1792 Gray's ship was positioned at the mouth of what was apparently a large river. The river was not on any chart.

On the morning of May 11, Gray entered the river as natives came out alongside the big ship, no doubt wondering what the men on it had in mind. The *Columbia Rediviva* stayed within the river for nine days, the crew repairing and painting the ship and trading with the Indians. For the crew it seems to have been something of an Edenic interlude in their arduous voyage. Not only were the natives "very civill," according to fifth mate John Boit (whose journal's accuracy is considered better than his spelling or grammar), but the salmon, whose Atlantic relatives the New England men knew from their own streams, were "well stocked," he wrote, and of "capitall" quality. The river water, with which they replenished their supplies, was "very good" to drink. He continued:

> During our short stay we collected 150 Otter, 300 Beaver, and twice the Number of other land furs. The river abounds with excellent Salmon, and most other River fish, and the Woods with plenty of Moose and Deer, the skins of which was brought to us in great plenty. . . .

In the opinion of the enterprising Boit, "this river wou'd be a fine place to sett up a *Factory*," by which he meant a trading post. One post here and one north in the Queen Charlotte Islands, he continued, "wou'd engross the whole trade of the NW Coast (with the help of a few small coasting vessells)."

On the day before the American traders left, Captain Gray named the river after his ship. The Americans hadn't stayed very long within the mouth of the Columbia, but their experiences, as witnessed by Boit's observations, set a tone. The mouth of the Columbia would be viewed as the opening to a great, apparently limitless cornucopia of Nature.

The fur trade prospered through the 1790s. Once Thomas Jefferson became the nation's president, knowledge of Gray's fur trading helped motivate him to send his friend and personal secretary, Meriwether Lewis, on a trade mission. He asked Lewis and the frontiersman William Clark to see if they might discover what assets made up the vast Louisiana Purchase territory that he had negotiated in 1803.

"The object of your mission," the president wrote Lewis, "is to explore the Missouri River and such principal stream(s) of it, as by its course and communication with the waters of the Pacific Ocean, may offer the most direct and practicable water communication across the continent."

Lewis and Clark were diligent scouts for the young republic in the first blush of Manifest Destiny. Following the Missouri River as far west as they could and then going overland, they eventually came to the Snake River and to the Columbia. The trek was arduous, and by the time Lewis and Clark had made their way to the place where the Columbia meets the sea, they and their thirty-one companions were thoroughly exhausted.

It was November 1805. The winter rains were beginning to roll in off the Pacific in earnest. Lewis and Clark polled the members of the expedition about where they wanted to stay the winter. They were not happy with the weather, but they needed salt and were weary, so they voted reluctantly to stay near the ocean.

The party quickly built a stockade a few miles in from the ocean and south of the Columbia along a stream. During 106 days of encampment, it rained on all but twelve, and the Corps of Discovery suffered from the cold and the damp and a diet dominated by elk meat. Clark must have been painfully aware of his good fortune only a few months before, when upriver he had enjoyed a feast of fresh salmon. He had come upon a fishing camp where the Indians were busy harvesting the spawning fish. He was invited inside a lodge, and a kind of poached salmon was prepared for him.

As he wrote in his notebook, round stones were placed directly in a cooking fire, and the cook was handed a basket of water "and a large Salmon about half dried. When the Stones were hot he put them into the basket of water with the fish, which was soon sufficiently boiled for use."

Clark ate the fish, describing it as "delicious."

It was during this meal that he made his first substantial observations of the Columbia River fishery, the first by any European-American. The awe of the frontiersman is unmistakable.

"The number of dead Salmon on the Shores and floating in the river is incrediable to say," he noted in his rough-and-ready prose. "At this Season they have only to collect the fish Split them open and dry them on their Scaffolds."

Clark apparently saw beyond the mere physical abundance of the salmon to an awareness of how they shaped the life of the native Northwesterners. In another journal entry, he wrote that an Indian village "lay in the prosperous area of the jumping salmon where life was good and where the red men had time to contemplate nature and God."

If Lewis and Clark appreciated the value of the salmon as a food and as the foundation of a culture, they apparently had little or no interest in what the salmon might represent as a commodity for American trade. They were much more interested in other abundant water animals for which lucrative markets were already established. These included both the otter and the beaver, from whose silky fur men's fashionable top hats were made.

Upon their return east to Washington in 1806, Lewis and Clark published a first account of their journey and suggested establishing a trading post at the mouth of the Columbia River, "for expediting the commerce of furs to China." The account was published in the *New York Post,* where wealthy fur merchant John Jacob Astor may well have seen it. It would have been the extra nudge Astor needed for a plan that he had been considering since probably the early 1790s.

By the early years of the nineteenth century, Astor had become one of the principal fur traders in the world. He thought big. Expanding on Lewis and Clark's published suggestion, Astor envisioned a chain of trading posts strung out across the west. Furs collected in the interior of the continent would be sent to a central depot at the mouth of the Columbia, where they would be shipped to China.

Astor was one of the first Americans to retail the argument known more recently as "what's good for General Motors is good for the country." He wanted Congress to grant his company a monopoly in the western fur trade, and told President Jefferson that one purpose of the company would be to exclude the Canadians from the Louisiana Purchase territory, a goal Jefferson surely shared. Nevertheless, neither Congress nor the president ultimately gave Astor the sort of support he wanted.

Just the same, the businessman couldn't resist the enterprise. In June 1810 he founded the Pacific Fur Company. Since all of his main partners in the company were British subjects, Astor demanded that they swear allegiance to the United States before setting sail for the Northwest coast to establish the China depot. It was an anxious sign from an optimistic man. Astor would be staying in New York, all the while fretting that his competitors, the Northwest Company, were working the same region, and they were British Canadians.

The following March, Astor's gunship, the *Tonquin,* landed just upriver from the mouth of the Columbia. The building of Fort Astoria, the first permanent American settlement west of the Rockies and the intended crown jewel in Astor's empire of furs, began. Establishing the settlement proved brute, hard work. The underbrush was dense and the trees were enormous. Big spruce trees in the area measured fifty feet around and a couple hundred feet tall. None of the men knew about felling trees like these, and it took two months to clear one acre.

During that initial period the Astorians were without shelter, and they ate poorly. It was not long before they had become alienated from their patron. He was interested in pelts collected and sold; his distant employees were more interested in food, shelter, and their safety. When the War of 1812 broke out the following year, and a British warship came to capture Fort Astoria, the occupants had little stomach for a fight. The Astorians were discouraged by the conditions of the settlement there; they weren't getting resupplied with necessities or trade goods.

As it happened, the warship was accompanied by another ship owned by the Northwest Company. Seizing the opportunity, Astor's manager, Duncan McDougall, cut a deal, selling the fort's merchandise and furs for about $80,000. Astor was out his investment of more than $300,000, and his dream on the Pacific had a new name. The British occupants renamed the log settlement Fort George.

After the war, the fort returned to American hands, but later it burned down and the settlement sank into obscurity for a short time, a victim of shifting fortunes in the fur trade.

Although Astor's dream for Astoria never did materialize, the character of settlement at the mouth of the Columbia, begun by Gray and developed by Lewis and Clark, seemed confirmed. This spot seemed less a place to belong to than a convenient point for the collection and transfer of local goods for profit somewhere else. It was an "outpost of progress."

Now, as the business in animal skins declined, the first forays were made into the marketing of salmon meat. The first salted salmon, fifty wooden barrels of it, was packed and sent to Boston in 1830 by a ship's captain who wintered in the Columbia estuary. Shipments of salted salmon continued sporadically from Astoria and from other towns along the Columbia for the next twenty-five years. However, salting, which was the only preservation method available at the time, wasn't really very successful in preserving, much less in promoting, the special qualities of Pacific salmon. Demand for the product was not great.

During this second quarter of the century the salmon runs were probably as little exploited as they had ever been. By the 1830s the number of Indians in the vicinity of the lower Columbia River was drastically reduced. Before the first contact with European-Americans in 1792, the Indian population is thought to have been one of the densest in America north of Mexico, partly the result of the perennially abundant salmon runs. But by 1830 perhaps 90 percent of the Indians of the region had died from outbreaks of malaria. The salmon coursed into the Columbia and their natal streams largely unmolested by humans.

The abundance of the salmon and the favorable location of Astoria was too

brilliant a coincidence to be ignored for long by the growing number of
frontier entrepreneurs. For the period, it was really an ideal location for the
center of commerce in salmon.

To the west, the town faced the largest body of water on the planet, an
ocean with an unimaginable richness of plant and animal life, a seemingly
inexhaustible pasture for the voracious hordes of Pacific salmon. To the east,
the town overlooked a kind of funnel, the last channeling of all the rivers and
streams of a huge land area.

Perched at the mouth of the Columbia, Astoria was at a crowded bottle-
neck in the migratory lives of the salmon. Here each year hundreds of
millions of young fish would make their way out to sea from the vast inland
reaches of the Columbia and the Snake. Just as the millions of juveniles
would go out each year, so nearly every month of the year, hundreds of
thousands of adult salmon would return from the ocean to begin their
spawning journeys to their native streams.

In the area around Astoria some had always been caught. The Indians had
long-term fishing sites on both sides of the lower Columbia and along the
coast at the mouth, facing the sea. Robert Gray, Lewis and Clark, and the first
Astorians had all been nourished by the salmon caught by the Indians. But
the take of salmon by the Indians here and, later, by the salters, was comparatively minor. It was the arrival of the technology of canning that helped
seal the salmon's fate.

Canning was brought to the Columbia in 1866 by George Hume, his
brothers, Robert and William, and Andrew Hapgood, who set up a
cannery on the Washington side of the river upstream from Astoria.
The Humes had come from New England, where the salmon had all but
been exterminated as a result of settlement. In the early 1860s the
Humes and Hapgood tried to make a go of canning on the Sacramento
River in California, but the salmon there were already declining rapidly.
The river was degraded by gold mining activity. The entrepreneurs
saw the Columbia as the next stop, and the best as well, unspoiled and
fecund.

The early canning techniques, which Hapgood had developed, were pretty
primitive. They included painting the cans with a mixture of red lead,

turpentine, and linseed oil. Some of the cans leaked, and the salmon spoiled, but even so the initial pack of four thousand cases sold well.

The canning process itself was simple. Chunks of salmon meat, wrapped in skin and salted, were sealed into the fabricated can and placed into a pressurized oven. The can was cooked under ten pounds pressure for an hour, cooled, and put into cases of forty-eight cans. Three average salmon would usually be enough to fill forty-eight one-pound cans. Sizable profits were possible in the canning business. The Humes paid fifteen cents per fish.

In just a few years canneries boomed and, along with them, Astoria's population. From 1874 to 1876 the town swelled from a few hundred people to nearly two thousand. By 1877 the town contained eleven canneries, and a mere six years later the lower Columbia region teemed with fifty-five canneries. That year, 1883, was the peak of the salmon pack.

The pack increased rapidly from an average 60,000 cases in the period 1867–1870 to nearly eight times that much ten years later, and surged again to nearly 630,000 cases in 1883, valued that year at $3 million. All of the 1883 pack were wild chinook, the Royal chinooks among them.

The salmon canning boom was phenomenal, not just for the speed of growth but for its nature. Some of the fur traders like Astor had cherished a vision of global markets operating from a West Coast port, but it was salmon that put Astoria on the map of international trade. The canning industry there, in the last two decades of the nineteenth century, was probably the earliest example on the West Coast of capitalism on an industrial scale.

The proliferating canneries were fueled by immigrant labor, and into the 1880s the labor was largely transient. In the spring, the workers would arrive by steamer or sailing ship, mainly from San Francisco. Astoria had no roads connecting it to distant parts of Oregon or elsewhere in the Northwest. The cannery workers were almost all Chinese. Individual canneries entered into agreements with Chinese contractors to clean, pack, cook, label, and box the salmon that were delivered to them at a cannery. The contractors in turn had the responsibility for recruiting, hiring, feeding, and paying the laborers needed for the job. This contract system was tailor-made for abuses of the workers.

The fishermen were mainly Scandinavians and Finns, and they were nearly all single men who lived in boarding houses. During the early boom years, Astoria was a man's town and a rough place. One notorious part, "Swill Town," housed most of Astoria's forty saloons, its gambling houses, and the red light district. Much of the city was built on pilings over the mud flats. Conditions would have given a latter day Department of Environmental Quality conniptions. Household wastes and fish processing wastes were both swept directly into the Columbia through cracks in the floors.

Lack of sanitation wasn't the greatest danger to a man's health, however. Far more serious was the practice of shanghaiing, in which men were commonly knocked down in the street and sold away on ships. A man could die easily on his own boat, too. It was not an uncommon sight to see a fishing boat carried out to sea by a change in the tide or swamped by a sudden storm.

The roughness, lawlessness, and danger weeded out the weak, the inept, and the unlucky. For the Scandinavian and Finnish fishermen, solid skills were the key to survival. From previous experiences fishing in the old country or on the East Coast or California the older ones had learned how to set the nets that caught salmon by their gills. A gill netter needed to be strong, to reel in and reel out hundreds of feet of soggy net, and he needed to be savvy, learning how to read the currents, tides, and the weather, to anticipate the movements of the migrating fish. A good man could grow into the work.

But from the old country these gill netters brought something more than their skills. They also carried the attitudes of people with a history of political and economic oppression and a desire to be out from under it. Many of the young Finns, for example, had left their homes rather than be drafted into the Russian army, which dominated Finland. The Finns and the Scandinavians came to Astoria with a consciousness of their class and of the value of their labor. And the Astoria gill netters were ready to fight for what they considered their rights.

As they saw it they had two adversaries.

The first were fishermen who used other kinds of fishing gear, especially traps. The traps were extremely efficient in catching salmon, and they made it difficult for the gill netters to operate near them. Both features were a consequence of the traps' design. The traps were essentially a channel of nets secured to posts that led into the trap proper, a four-posted enclosure of netting. The salmon would swim into the channel and follow it into the enclosure, and since the fish only wanted to go upriver, they would never think to turn around and swim out the way they came. The trap men then needed only to take their boats out to a trap when they deemed it time and collect the trapped salmon.

By law the traps were required to be set far enough apart to allow boats to navigate, but this distance was not enough to allow gill-net fishermen to work their floating nets. Since the salmon naturally hugged the Washington side of the river as they entered from the ocean, and traps were placed in many of the best fishing places along that shore, the gill netters felt themselves very much at a disadvantage.

The second adversary the gill netters recognized was the cannery owners. Disputes over wages and working conditions led to strikes or acts of violence in 1877, 1880, 1883, and 1885. The first disputes were mainly spontaneous affairs, in keeping with a largely transient workforce. But by the second half of the 1880s, an increasing number of gill-net fishermen were able to find other employment in the off-season in logging, millwork, or farming, and thereby became full-time residents of Astoria.

Among all the institutions reflecting the trend toward greater permanence in Astoria, the main institution of the fishermen was the Columbia River Fishermen's Protective Union. Organized in 1886, the union set about to extract concessions from the cannery owners. In two years the price the canneries paid per fish more than doubled, from 55 cents per fish in 1886 to $1.25 per fish in 1888.

From the beginning, the Columbia River Fishermen's Protective Union was plain about its principles. "The greatest good for the greatest number is still an ever-living maxim among our fellow countrymen," a union publication expressed in 1890. The union was equally unequivocal about whom it trusted and didn't trust. "No liquor dealer, gambler, politician, capitalist, lawyer, agent for capitalists, nor persons holding office, whether under national, state, or municipal government shall under any consideration become members," the union's constitution read.

Into this volatile mixture of gill netters and trapmen, of union members and cannery owners, only a spark was needed to set off an explosion.

From the peak of the Columbia River canning pack of almost 630,000 cases in 1883, the pack rapidly declined. The five-year average from 1886–1890 was 385,000 cases; the average for 1891–1895 climbed back to 486,000 cases, but the increase was deceptive. Formerly the entire pack had been chinook, but by the early 1890s more than a quarter was made up of the less desirable coho, chum, sockeye, and even steelhead trout. The machinery of the fishery was running ahead of the fish.

In the spring of 1896, the cannery owners faced a crisis. The nation was in the depths of a depression that had begun three years before. The packers had kept the wholesale price of canned salmon constant, but in 1895 a falloff in sales scared them. They came to believe that they had to lower their prices for the 1896 season. So, after years of competition among themselves, the heads of all but one of Astoria's eleven canneries formed together into the Columbia River Packers' Association. Among the association's first official acts, on April 2, was the setting of prices they would pay fishermen for salmon. Chinook would earn four cents per pound; coho, two and a half cents.

The owners were the steel; only a flint was now needed to make the spark.

"If the cannery men do not pay five cents this season," the union's leader told the *Daily Morning Astorian* newspaper, "the men will not fish."

In the week leading up to the union's monthly meeting, few Astorians would have been uncertain about how the rank and file would vote on the owners' offer. Working class militancy was in the air. A new political movement—Populism—was gaining momentum in the United States. In 1894 the People's Party had elected governors in Kansas and Colorado, and the Populist vote had doubled in California. A thirty-six-year-old Democrat from Nebraska named William Jennings Bryan was rapidly becoming a frontrunner for that party's presidential nomination by promising to crusade for "the masses against the classes." A magnetic speaker, Bryan was capturing the public mood in speeches that did not shy away from a class analysis.

"There are two ideas of government," Bryan said, in one of his stump speeches. "There are those who believe that if you will only legislate to make the well-to-do prosperous, their prosperity will leak through on those below.

"The Democratic idea, however, has been that if you make the masses prosperous, their prosperity will find its way up through every class which rests upon them."

In a mood of rebelliousness, in the midst of a depression, when the union fishermen met on April 9 they voted to strike for five cents per pound for chinook.

The strike made the dispute officially a crisis, but the crisis had really erupted the week before, on the day the packers set their prices. That day as many as forty boats, containing a couple of hundred gill netters, launched a surprise raid on some fish traps on Sand Island, which lay just within the Columbia between Oregon and Washington.

"The gill netters have become tired of being bothered by the traps," the union's leader told the *Astorian*.

The couple of hundred gill netters destroyed most of the traps and cast loose four piledrivers, which set the poles for the traps. A greatly outnumbered group of trapmen from Washington stood off helpless in their boats until the gill netters left the scene.

The response of the trapmen was not long in coming. They appealed to their governor, and on April 10 the Washington National Guard was called out to guard the traps and the fishermen on the Washington side of the river. A steamboat and troops were stationed there, and river patrols began. The next day, some of the trapmen agreed to take four cents a pound for fish delivered to one of the canneries. Other nonunion fishermen along the river quickly took sides. Some not far from Astoria were persuaded by union members not to break the strike; but by mid-month the canneries were able to persuade others in Portland to accept three and a half cents per pound for their catch.

For six weeks, the strike smoldered. The strikers were resolute; the canneries were generally kept from operating. For their part, the packers' association showed no signs of giving in. Then, on May 22, the *Astorian*'s front page flashed a sudden flare-up: "The Fisherman Was Murdered," the headline read.

The first bloodshed incident to the big strike occurred last night near Wallace Island. While the officials of the Fishermen's Union have made every effort to conduct a peaceable strike for what they think is right, the fact remains that the situation is becoming serious. When they begin to feel the pangs of hunger, and when their little ones at homes are subjected to want, men become desperate, and desperate men can not be controlled.

A man named Searcy and his son-in-law were fishing downriver from Astoria when their boat was approached by another containing several men. The men on the arriving boat opened fire and Searcy was killed instantly, shot through the head. He had been fishing for the Hapgood and Company Cannery.

Tensions rapidly escalated. On May 26, the *Astorian* reported that two more fishermen had been beaten and their nets cut adrift. On May 28, fishermen at Rainier, Oregon, were said to have purchased 125 Winchester rifles, "for self defense while fishing." That same week three hundred armed men descended on Cook's cannery to prevent fishing.

The regular monthly meeting of the fishermen's union, on June 7, found the strikers in a defiant mood. Some nine hundred fishermen turned out for the meeting and confirmed their solidarity behind the five-cent demand. On this same day one cannery owner attempted, during an impromptu sidewalk discussion, to persuade a crowd of fishermen to end the strike. Astoria's marshall and constable had to be summoned to escort the owner to safety.

This cannery owner's experience lent additional credence to the perception that the strike was out of control. Two days later the Portland *Morning Oregonian* reported that a regiment of the Oregon National Guard was awaiting orders to board a steamboat in Portland and sail to Astoria. "Every one familiar with the facts knows that the fishermen are already armed to the teeth," the *Oregonian* asserted.

On June 17, the Oregon militia was indeed called out, and 490 militiamen, accompanied by two twelve-pound guns and two Gatling guns, steamed downriver. The presence of the militia soon broke the will of the exhausted and anxious strikers. On June 21, 450 union members showed up for a vote. By a 57-vote majority they called off the strike.

That very night most of the Oregon militia left town. "Many citizens, including a number of ladies and little girls, were at the dock to see them off," the *Astorian* reported.

> Bouquets of flowers were presented to the colonel, and that pop-
> ular officer responded to the gifts of the ladies in most graceful
> language, expressing his appreciation of their courtesy, and stat-
> ing that his command would be ever ready to answer to their call
> of necessity.

With strife banished and chivalry confirmed, the next day everything seemed right with the world. Oregon Fish Commissioner McGuire said that "under the peculiar circumstances it was not his intention to make any strenuous efforts to enforce the closed [fishing] season" that was in effect.

Nor was the unnamed "gentleman" who was in charge of certifying that fishermen had completed their applications for citizenship inclined to do so, saying "this is no time to draw such a line."

"Everybody was happy yesterday," the paper reported the day after,

> . . . and perhaps the happiest people in town were the fishermen.
> Nearly every boat was out, and the returns for the night's work
> were simply immense. A number of canneries were compelled to
> limit their boats to 1,000 pounds each. The boats arriving from
> the north shore were averaging from two to four thousand pounds.
> Two fish were brought in which weighed 143 pounds.

The "high man was Frank Mercurio, with 7,000 pounds," the *Astorian* enthused.

Finally, benediction settled upon the waters.

> It seemed like old times to hear the busy hum of machinery and
> look out over the bay, literally covered with fishing boats.

At the end of it all, to read the *Astorian*, it would seem that Nature had bestowed Her abundance upon a community miraculously restored to liberality and togetherness.

And yet the reader of these newspaper reports one hundred years later might have some lingering questions.

In this restored Eden, was there any evidence left of a Fall?

That modern reader might have found the occasion for some thought in an interview published in the *Oregonian* that summer. Mr. W. A. Wilcox, an agent of the U.S. Fish Commission, was stopping over in Portland on his regular tour of inspection of the region's fisheries. Wilcox, an experienced observer who had made previous tours of the Northwest eight and four years before, offered the paper his assessment of the Columbia's fortunes:

> "The vast volume of fresh water coming down the Columbia will make it almost impossible ever to pollute it sufficiently to drive away the salmon, and it is hardly possible that civilization will ever crowd its banks to an extent that will endanger that [salmon] industry, so I suppose it is safe to say that Columbia-river salmon will always continue to be a choice dish in all parts of the world."

"Of course," Wilcox continued, "the increasing demand for fish and the growing scarcity of the same will call for more aid toward artificial propagation in order to keep up the supply."

But . . ., the retrospective reader might say. But excuse me, Mr. Wilcox. The Columbia River is healthy, you say, and yet you note a growing scarcity of fish, for which you prescribe more "artificial propagation." How is it that, under the circumstances, the need was reached to artificially augment the salmon populations?

Well, Wilcox might have replied, the decline in salmon populations, at least at the mouth of the Columbia, is plain from the cannery statistics, in particular the decline in chinook poundage.

But, the retrospective reader enjoins again, a person with a dispassionate interest in the matter might believe that the cause of the chinook's decline was too much fishing for them. And that artificial propagation was an expedient solution, and did not address the real problem head on.

Ah! Mr. Wilcox would have exclaimed, nodding his head. Such an analysis—that the real problem was overfishing, or overcanning—is not wrong, he might have said.

Yet let met tell you something, he might have continued. To look only at the statistics of fish put into cans almost certainly misses a deeper problem. And that problem, unfortunately, we can do little about.

Turn to the *Astorian* story of June 23, Wilcox might have said—the story about the first big fishing day after the strike? Nowhere in that story does it say what happened to the "extra" fish—perhaps as much as thousands of pounds extra per fisherman—that canneries wouldn't take. It was not reported.

Well, says the reader, what *did* happen to the "extra" salmon the canneries were unable to process in a particular day?

Wilcox would have only smiled, a wan smile. The answer was well known in Astoria. Wilcox surely knew. But few talked about it then.

Years later, a cannery worker from the time left an oral history of his youthful experiences.

"Every other night there would be them fish, beautiful big salmon, all washed and cleaned and ready," Mont Hawthorne remembered. "Then we would just have to go out and shovel them, often by the hundreds, back into the river."

Hawthorne's remembrances are confirmed by others. When the catch was so heavy that the cannery couldn't keep up, the salmon were just wasted.

Another report from the period notes that packers "Brown and George Warren . . . have succeeded much better this season than they expected. Some days they had more salmon than they could take care of, and have thrown 2 or 3 hundred into the river."

Facing this situation, Hawthorne had tried to find some rationale. He may have met Wilcox, though he doesn't give his name in his memoirs.

"A government man did come out to see about building fish hatcheries. He said it was too bad that we was throwing all of the salmon overboard, but he didn't have no authority to stop it.

"I went to talk to him about it. But he was sent out to preserve the salmon by building the hatcheries. At the time he was there we'd often trowed as many as five hundred big salmon overboard every other night. The other canneries was doing the same thing. Some of the fish weighted from forty to fifty pounds apiece."

Hawthorne had a clear appreciation for the endless burden of cause and effect that resulted.

"The town stunk just awful. . . . There wasn't no laws regulating what happened to the fish. The fishermen tried to catch all that they could. The canneries had agreed to take them. Each man tried to live up to his contract.

"Everyone aimed to make all he could."

Ah yes, the retrospective reader may think now. I have heard this before. The Astoria salmon fishery is another example of the "tragedy of the commons." No one has any incentive to preserve a natural resource held in common. Without regulations, each individual recognizes that if he doesn't take the salmon, someone else will. The inevitable result is the destruction of the common resource.

Perhaps, indeed, this is all that this history can reveal, something about the commons and the destructive behavior of groups. Human institutions do have an alarming tendency to suppress our best and most generous instincts, our instincts for life. And yet underneath the behavior of groups and institutions lie the moral impulses of the individual. At this personal foundation, the seed of action, something profound may have been at work in Astoria, out of sight and undiscussed.

For both the fishermen and the cannerymen of Astoria the salmon seems primarily not to have been a living being. It was ultimately and primarily a thing—a thing for human use. There seems to have been no living relationship between man and the other animal. Without such a relationship, the 1890s Astorians seem to have lost a true sense of proportion. Not only were fish wasted. Searcy, the fisherman, and at least twenty other men were killed in disputes over rights to the fish.

Faced with an abundance, most people didn't recognize a need for moderation. They didn't recognize the inevitability of limits. When the abundance was clearly disappearing, their response was not to change behavior. Instead, unequipped to struggle within themselves, they fought each other harder and looked outside themselves for a solution. Hatcheries became popular.

The learning that the opposing sides drew from the strike of 1896 apparently had little to do with the folly of waste. The importance of ownership was the message. The cannery owners saw the power inherent in a unified front among them. The fishermen's union saw that if its members were going to determine the value placed on their labor, they would have to own the means of production. Accordingly, only months after the strike was over, the union organized the Union Fishermen's Cooperative Packing Company. For a time Union Fish was a prosperous enterprise for the fishermen, competing with the private canners.

A century later, no commercial salmon cannery operated in Astoria. The last one had most recently packed tuna, and it too had closed in 1979. In 1990, meanwhile, the city government was busily developing a tourism plan that would portray the history of the bustling cannery years down on the waterfront. What was once the richest salmon fishing site in the Pacific Northwest was a shadow of its former self, erecting memorials to its golden days.

Studies of people with fatal illness reveal a common pattern of response: denial, anger, bargaining, depression, and, finally, acceptance. Back at the salmon summit in January 1991, the participants were still mostly in denial.

For most of the economic interests, the risk of coming up with a plan seemed as great as not coming up with one. The way they saw it, they were trying to solve a complex equation—salmon recovery—that had too many unknowns. The unknowns included the costs to them and the likelihood of success for the salmon.

As 1991 began and discussions continued to drift, Ed Chaney began to pull hard on the oars. The Idaho conservationist was determined that the summit would accomplish something for the petitioned stocks, most of which spawned in Idaho. He wanted to get more water into the upper river to move juvenile fish downstream. He had been arguing the case for years.

In 1978, in a report called *A Question of Balance,* he had written that relations between hydropower and fish needed to be adjusted. "The salmon and steelhead runs of the upper Columbia Basin are at a critical crossroads," he had said then, introducing the "crossroads" idea.

"Unavoidable decisions will be made by design or default within the next

few years. They will either assure the dramatic revitalization or virtual extinction of the upper basin runs."

He envisioned a new era of cooperation among fishery, hydropower, and
irrigation interests. But he argued that "the key to realizing the potential of
the emerging new era of interdependence is assurance that main-stem flow
needs of anadromous salmon and steelhead will be met."

That had not happened, and more than a dozen years later everyone was
in a jam. Chaney was convinced that the solution for the upriver runs was
still better flows.

Why providing water for fish should have been a problem needs some
explaining. After all, the Columbia and Snake river system had been home to
salmon for millennia precisely because the system contained a fabulous
amount of water, widely distributed. The Columbia alone flows 1,200 miles
from its origins in the Canadian Rockies to Astoria. From its drainage basin
of 259,000 square miles, the river pours more water into the Pacific Ocean
than any other in the Western Hemisphere. Its average annual streamflow is
ten times greater than the flow of the Colorado River and twice that of the
legendary Nile.

In scientific terms, the Columbia's annual runoff is 198 million acre-
feet—the equivalent of 198 million acres covered with one foot of water.
That amount was more than enough to put all of Oregon, Washington, and
Idaho under about a foot of water.

One acre-foot is also some 326,000 gallons. The flow coming out the
rivermouth annually, then, was nearly 200 million times those 300,000-plus
gallons. That's more than seven *billion* gallons per hour, which is the aston-
ishing equivalent of 60,000 bathtubs emptying per second. In the abstract,
finding water for salmon should not have been a problem.

The problem was in the concrete. The Columbia and Snake system was
broken up by eighteen major dams and more than five dozen smaller ones.
The river's water was committed to generating hydroelectric power, irrigat-
ing crops, transporting barges, and protecting property from floods. That
wasn't all. Once reservoirs were in place, the Columbia and Snake became
dedicated to providing pleasure boating, sport fishing, and other water rec-

reation where none had been in the past. In short, as historian Donald Worster had put it, the river had died and been reborn as money.

A huge volume of financial activity was indeed bound up in the controlled river, and not just in hydroelectric production. In 1990, for example, the value of exports and imports shipped on the river was more than $9 billion. When water means money, those who have it can be assumed to not give it away easily. That was exactly the problem facing the fish.

For them, the timing as well as the availability of river flows was important. The timing of flows in the regulated river was nearly opposite to the natural flows needed by the salmon. Juvenile salmon relied upon the spring snowmelt and runoff to flush them downriver to the sea, but the Bonneville Power Administration relied upon storing the spring runoff in upriver reservoirs until later in the year. In the summer the agency could use the water to generate electricity for sale to southern California and Arizona, and in the winter the water could be used to produce electricity for heating and lighting the Northwest. As a consequence of the overall regulation of the river, the seaward migration that used to take a matter of days now took weeks, and hundreds of thousands of juvenile smolts died before they reached the ocean.

In 1991, the BPA and its utility customers continued to resist making changes to their annual operating plans to provide what most biologists considered enough water to move Snake River fish downriver. So, in characteristic fashion, Chaney challenged them in a thirty-two-page position paper, which he circulated in January. The new paper was called *Changing Course,* and Chaney was plain about who had to change.

One reason the BPA was reluctant to provide water for fish was that it would reduce revenues from sales of seasonal surplus energy, mostly to California. Salmon advocates argued that Bonneville's problem was marketing, not fish: The agency should find markets for power generated by the water being provided to move fish. But the agency had not, and they were worried about losing revenues.

"For Bonneville, this is no small matter," Chaney wrote. "It has a $400 million per year payment on $4 billion of debt for mothballed and abandoned nuclear power plants."

In December 1990 the BPA announced it owed about $15.3 billion against assets with a total value of $15 billion, Chaney said. "Consequently Bonneville is under enormous financial pressure to squeeze every possible dollar out of the main-stem Columbia and Snake River dams."

Despite its billion-dollar revenues each year, the BPA was also obliged to make annual debt payments to the U.S. Treasury for construction loans on the power system. Although these payments were on the order of a half-billion dollars, virtually every year someone in Congress or the administration clamored for higher payments. The BPA was always nervous about seeming too free with its spending.

And yet, Chaney argued, "fish and hydroelectric energy are not inherently incompatible." If dams were "properly designed," then "fish passage would divert a small fraction, perhaps one percent, of the average annual flow of the Columbia River." One percent, he wanted to suggest, should not break the BPA bank.

Two methods were available to increase the velocity of spring flows in the river system to speed the movement of the juvenile fish. The volume of water coming out of upstream storage reservoirs could be increased. Or the cross-sectional area of the pools behind the dams on the river could be reduced. The principle was that the same amount of water moving through a smaller box would move faster.

Chaney promoted the second method.

"The only feasible way in the short-term is to draw down the four lower Snake River main-stem reservoirs during the spring juvenile migration period, flush the fish through the reservoirs, and spill them past the dams," he wrote.

Over the long term Chaney called for structural changes to the dams to assist the passage of juvenile fish.

Changes in river operations, reservoir levels, and dam construction: Chaney's ideas for moving water down the Snake faster in the spring got the summit participants' attention. In February, Chaney and Idaho Governor Cecil Andrus pushed for the water levels at four Snake River dams to be lowered by seventeen feet. However, a lowering of this magnitude would stop barge traffic and shut down irrigation, and so required much more discussion. All parties agreed to meet as a group one more time, at the Portland Hilton, on March 4.

The meeting place was a ballroom decked out with enough grandiose chandeliers to make anyone feel as if something important should happen there. The added glare of the TV stations' floodlights made men in suits and white shirts look irradiated as they moved to their places at the circle of tables. Bakke and Braun came in looking distinctly like they'd rather be fishing. Bakke put his hat on the table, in full view, as if he was ready to pick it up at any time and go.

Gradually a down-to-business hush fell on the group, and one of the Indians was asked to give a blessing. Levi George, an elder of the Yakama Indian Nation, stood up. The floodlights and tape recorders were turned off by request. George began to sing, in his native tongue, under the chandeliers. The Indians stood up, and most of the white men in the room followed them, some even raising their right hands, palm out, in the traditional gesture of bearing witness.

Whatever George sang about the salmon, most didn't understand. But the chant sounded mournful, and people listened respectfully. For the most part. At the far end of the table, one of the lawyers for the utilities turned to a group of officials with their hands upraised and whispered to them, "Do you know what you're swearing to?"

George's song died out and he began the prayer. He talked softly in English, and people leaned forward to catch fragments of what he said: ". . . the Creator is still going to do his job . . . let's all be happy and accomplish something." He sat down. Somehow it didn't have the buoyancy of the "Star Spangled Banner" and the president throwing out the first ball. But that's the way it was. Everyone sat. The men in suits tried to look optimistic.

Optimism became harder as the day wore on and the negotiations fizzled. At the end, only Jack Robertson of the BPA was thinking positively enough to want to be quoted about it. He told the *Oregonian*'s reporter that "the benefits to fish are substantial" in the plan finally settled on.

Ed Chaney had a different view. "I'm deeply frustrated," he said. After the Idaho plan had come up in February, increasingly the discussions were taken over by the representatives of the four Northwest governors. By the weekend before this final meeting, a "final draft plan" had been put together by these representatives. The process was no longer public, Chaney felt. The best agreement that fish interests could wring from the Corps of Engineers and the Snake River irrigation and shipping interests was not for four drawdowns of seventeen feet, but for a single experimental drawdown of just three feet. Although the BPA promised to increase the amount of water in the system, Chaney just didn't believe it would be enough. He had the numbers to back himself up, if anybody cared.

The *Oregonian* did not report Bill Bakke's reaction. Through the whole meeting Bakke sat looking increasingly like he needed to go out to smoke his pipe. His hat sat on the table in front of him, where only he and Braun knew that it concealed a World War II German hand grenade, real but disarmed. At several moments the gentleman conservationist had to resist a wild temptation to just see what would happen if he threw the potato masher into the no-man's-land inside the circle of tables.

Bakke was beyond words. He thought the whole thing had degenerated into a charade. You couldn't save salmon by consensus among competing interests. Anyone could defeat any measure. All the salmon got were meaningless gestures.

At mid-March the Corps of Engineers seemed to prove Bakke right. The Corps put the one remaining experimental three-foot drawdown on hold for a year, citing the need to develop the plan further and to conduct public hearings.

At this Idaho Governor Andrus erupted, calling the Corps's explanation a "smokescreen."

"It means the end of another generation of smolts, which means we lost another year of salmon," Andrus said. "We're one step closer to extinction."

Mark Hatfield was furious, too, angry enough to have a legislative amendment drafted that would take funds away from the North Pacific Division of the Corps. On the floor of the Senate, on March 21, Hatfield lit into them.

"Over the last five months," he said, "thousands of hours have been expended in this summit process by private citizens, environmental groups, electric utilities, Indian tribes, navigational interests, the four governors, the federal agencies, and others as we've tried to develop an acceptable salmon management plan.

"Imagine how these people feel when the key federal agency—the Corps of Engineers—continues to hide behind a bureaucratic curtain and pretend that it has no responsibility to change the very operations which are killing the fish?

"They feel outraged and so do I."

At the end, he pocketed the amendment defunding the Corps's divisional office, but he expected the agency to pay attention.

The sense of outrage over lack of progress addressing the salmon's problems soon intensified. During the period of the summit, Willa Nehlsen had quietly circulated the final draft of the report on the status of Northwest salmon, soliciting comments and critiques from other professionals. The reviews had come in during the fall and winter, the paper was polished up, and in March 1991 the American Fisheries Society published Nehlsen, Williams, and Lichatowich's "Pacific Salmon at the Crossroads."

Everyone could now see that more than just a handful of salmon and sea-run trout stocks were at risk in the region. The biologists listed 214 naturally spawning native stocks that were depleted. Of the 214, they considered 101 at high risk of extinction, 58 at moderate risk of extinction, and 54 of "special concern." One, the Sacramento winter chinook, was already listed under the ESA.

The stocks at risk were by no means limited to the Columbia and Snake basin. About one-third—76—of the stocks were there. The remaining 138 stocks were spread throughout coastal watersheds, from Washington's Nooksak River, on the Canadian border, down to Malibu Creek, in southern California. Washington's Puget Sound and Olympic Peninsula had their members of the wounded and gasping, as did the streams of the Oregon coast and northern California.

The salmonids in hardly any river system seemed in really good shape. Even so, in a sense, these 214 "Crossroads" stocks were lucky; there might still be hope for them. The authors cited evidence that on the order of 100 stocks in the region had been driven into extinction since the 1850s. The shame of extinction was that it was absolute. The particular traits that made up the Grande Ronde coho, for example, were simply gone, never to be recovered. Such losses throughout the region made it unlikely that salmon could ever be restored in some places where they were extinct, regardless of what measures were taken.

In order to alert readers to the implications of their risk categories, the authors linked the categories to standards developed by the National Marine Fisheries Service for the Endangered Species Act. Nehlsen and her colleagues defined "high risk" generally as stocks whose spawners were declining in numbers from year to year, or whose population overall was fewer than two hundred individuals. The Fisheries Service had indicated that two hundred was the minimum size required to "avoid irretrievable genetic losses." Nehlsen, Williams, and Lichatowich considered such high-risk stocks as candidates for "endangered" status under the ESA. "Moderate risk" stocks were those they considered candidates for "threatened" ESA status. Between the two they had 159 candidates for federal protection.

They minced no words in describing the cause of the crisis. To anyone who had been following the fortunes of the salmon for any time, the list was a familiar litany of woes.

"Habitat loss and damage, and inadequate passage and flows caused by hydropower, agriculture, logging, and other developments" led the list. In some areas of the Northwest livestock grazing posed a problem for salmon and trout as urgent as logging. Cattle tended to eat and trample streamside vegetation, to compact the soil of streambanks, and to defecate in streams. The loss of vegetation raised water temperatures during warm or sunny periods; the loss of vegetation, along with the soil compaction, led to erosion and sedimentation of the stream. Continued grazing pressure frequently led to wider, shallower, and ultimately drier streams. While an individual rancher might not think his herd of cattle was doing a sizable stream any major damage, ranches in Oregon, Idaho, and Washington contained some 4.5 million cattle and calves. The cumulative effects, the "Crossroads" authors understood, could be very bad for salmon. Moreover, "in many cases, the decline of a native [salmon] population is attributable to several detrimental factors," they said. They identified overfishing and the problems caused by hatchery fish as additional threats to native fish. They also recognized that oceanic conditions that reduced the food supplies for salmon could lead to lower survival of adult fish; and they noted that predators such as seals and sea lions constituted a threat.

In manuscript the report ran for thirty pages, giving details on the problems with individual stocks in specific rivers—problems that had been detailed for Nehlsen and the others by dozens of field biologists. But the trio of the AFS endangered species committee had not been content to merely describe the problems. They also proposed a framework for solutions, offering specific suggestions for fishery managers.

In concluding, they called for a new approach to salmon management.

A new paradigm that advances habitat restoration and ecosystem function rather than hatchery production is needed for many of these stocks to survive and prosper into the next century.

Finally, they were adamant that native stocks—wild stocks—were the cornerstone of restoration. They were needed to maintain the natural genetic diversity that would allow stocks to survive major ecological and climatic changes. They were needed to reestablish natural stocks where opportunities occur. They were needed for the genetic viability of hatchery programs.

The "Crossroads" paper, as it immediately became known outside as well as inside the profession, was intended to be a scientific benchmark. It was that, and more. It quickly influenced, even framed public discussion. It had already passed through many hands in taking shape, and sixty fisheries experts had been asked to review it prior to publication. So it came out with high credibility, and everyone took notice quickly—not only biologists and managers but also journalists. It became a topic of numerous news stories in the print and broadcast media.

As the word circulated regionally and nationally, it renewed and spread the call to arms among fish advocates. The magazine *Trout,* a publication of the organization Trout Unlimited, was one that saw fit to republish the essay in its entirety, a first for the magazine. The editor explained that "by devoting such space we honor the urgency of the message. With our broader circulation, we hope to greatly expand its audience and influence. Wild salmonids are in trouble. Their vanishing act will not be stopped until we understand its finality."

The naming of 214 stocks at risk, and the recognition that only a very few were under consideration for protection, immediately begged the question of additional petitions under the Endangered Species Act. Given that whole groups of stocks seemed to be in bad shape, such as coastal wild coho, would there be numerous, or perhaps blanket, petitions?

Andy Kerr of the Oregon Natural Resources Council was thinking that very thing. Even before the publication of the "Crossroads" paper, Kerr was floating the idea. He was not terribly concerned who heard about it. It was like the rumor of a specialized rocket, a V-2 in the fish arsenal. Kerr let it strike terror where it might.

The meaning of the threat of more petitions was made more tangible at the end of March, when the Fisheries Service announced its preliminary ruling on the first of the petitions. It proposed to list the Snake River sockeye salmon as an endangered species.

The decision was not difficult and nearly everyone expected it. The number of sockeye returning annually to spawn in Idaho's Redfish Lake had dwindled from hundreds in the 1950s and '60s to a dozen or two in the mid-1980s, to only one fish in 1989. It was a pathetic situation. The name of the handsome lake, high in Idaho's majestic Sawtooth Mountains, seemed about to become an anachronism. The brilliantly red spawning sockeye were almost no more.

The text of the proposed ruling made it clear that the near extinction of the Redfish Lake sockeye was more than a disaster waiting to happen. Rather it seemed one that had waited too long to be recognized. From the very beginning of European-American settlement, the sockeye of not only Redfish Lake but also the other lakes of the Stanley Basin of Idaho's Salmon River had been mistreated. In 1881, prospectors had pulled 2,600 pounds of sockeye out of Alturas Lake. More recently that lake itself had become worthless for salmon spawning, the Fisheries Service said, as one ranch withdrew all the water from the creek that feeds the lake. In all, sixty-eight agricultural water diversions were counted in the drainage basin that included the lake.

It seemed that few would escape blame, if blame were being passed out. Sockeye needed to pass eight main-stem dams in their migration to and from the sea. The Fisheries Service charged that more than 90 percent of juvenile sockeye would die during this downstream migration. Upstream dam passage often resulted in an additional mortality of about 20 percent of the adults who returned two years later. Everything about the dams seemed to conspire against the sockeye.

Redfish Lake already seemed the destination of a heroic journey for the fish, situated as it was nine hundred miles from the sea and 6,500 feet above sea level. Throughout this immense journey the fish do not feed, so marshaling their energy is crucial to their survival. Yet delays of from one to seven days were common at each dam. Delays of three to four days often killed the fish, the Fisheries Service said.

Fishing compounded the sockeye's problems. Sockeye populations might well have begun their long decline in 1898, when 4.5 million pounds of the species were harvested on the lower Columbia River. Despite population sizes that looked severely depleted as of the 1950s, and a curtailment of commercial fishing for sockeye from 1974 through 1983, commercial fishing had been allowed to resume again in 1984. From 1984 to 1989 the count of sockeye spawners getting past the last upstream dam averaged a mere twenty-six fish.

The fish agencies would not escape criticism for yet another reason. In the 1960s, Idaho's fish agency had deliberately poisoned Pettit and Yellowbelly Lakes with chemicals, killing off the sockeye as they tired to keep unwanted warm-water fish out of the lakes. The agency preferred to stock the lakes with trout. Barriers were put in place to keep sockeye from returning.

Even apparently well-intentioned laws were inadequate to spare the sockeye, the Fisheries Service said. The Fish and Wildlife Coordination Act, which required "equal consideration" for fish in water-resource development, did not require that recommendations of fish agencies be adopted, "particularly when they affect another purpose for which a project may be authorized." The federal Power Act also gave fish agencies the authority to make "recommendations" concerning power projects and their effects on fish, but it too was toothless. The Salmon and Steelhead Conservation Act of 1980 proposed some "very useful" ideas, the Fisheries Service said, but "it was inadequate in providing any additional protection to upper Columbia River salmonids." The gallery of ineffectual laws contained still other not-pretty pictures.

The sockeye listing decision covered some ten closely printed pages of the *Federal Register,* and anybody reading through it could hardly mistake the message. The sockeye were just about down the tubes, and to fulfill its obligations under the endangered-species law, the Fisheries Service would begin requiring changes in the operation of the river to protect the fish. The changes could affect just about every user of the river, from the administrator of the BPA in Portland, to the homeowner turning on her air conditioner in Boise, to the apple grower in Milton-Freewater. Once the Fisheries Service developed a recovery plan for the sockeye the constraints could become hard. Hard indeed.

Back in his Senate office in Washington, D.C., Mark Hatfield read the decision and considered what to do next. He had tried a truly "republican" solution, in the old meaning of that word. He had tried to involve the people in finding their own solution, rather than having government impose it. It seemed to him a worthwhile gamble on the possibilities of cooperation. Others doubted his motives, he knew.

Shortly after the summit concluded, he had read an opinion piece in the *Oregonian,* written by Michael Blumm, a professor of law at Lewis and Clark College and a veteran observer of salmon politics. Blumm had challenged the motives of those espousing local control.

"A basic premise of the salmon summit was that an Endangered Species Act listing would cause the region to lose control over Columbia and Snake River flows," Blumm had written.

"But those flows are now under the control of federal agencies like BPA and the Army Corps of Engineers. The region has no more or less control over those federal agencies than it does over the National Marine Fisheries Service.

"This alleged concern over the loss of regional control masks the real reason for the opposition to a listing: Fear that an agency with some bio-logical expertise would obtain some control over Columbia Basin stream-flows."

Hatfield did not feel that the summit was a mistake. It had gotten people talking to one another, and that was an essential step—one that had never really happened in the forest crisis. And though the results of the summit were not enough, the talk wasn't wasted, he was convinced. Because decisions were to be made with everyone's consent, the summit participants knew they could veto measures they didn't like. This was a problem for reaching con-clusions, but it did encourage people to say what they wanted, knowing they could backtrack later. As a result, each party had a clearer picture of its own interests, of others' interests, and of what might be done to recover the fish.

The region was ahead of where it would be if it had merely waited for the ESA process to run its course. Under that scenario, a recovery plan would not begin to be drafted before the second year, and then the various interests would have staked out their positions. No, Hatfield thought, the summit's efforts were to the good. The Fisheries Service itself could use data gathered by the summit to accelerate its ESA review.

Nevertheless, the summit had not succeeded in developing anything like an adequate recovery plan for the petitioned stocks, the senator recognized. And now the stonewalling of the Corps of Engineers, the whip of the ESA in the hand of the Fisheries Service, and the hanging sword of more petitions, courtesy of the "Crossroads" paper, added up to something bigger yet. No question, the region faced a real crisis.

Hatfield continued to believe in the desirability of a regionally developed solution rather than a mandated recovery plan developed by a government agency. Clearly, though, an institution with a narrow, vested interest in the outcome couldn't oversee the development of such a regional solution. What was needed was an institution that had the authority to affect the status quo. The Northwest Power Planning Council came as close as anything available.

The council members were appointed by the governors; the council and its staff had been developing a salmon restoration program for ten years; they had expertise; they had a mandate. Admittedly, the crisis might not have occurred if they had acted differently during the previous ten years, but they still seemed in the best position to develop a comprehensive, regional salmon strategy. And they should coordinate their efforts with the recovery planning efforts of the Fisheries Service. It seemed to Hatfield like the best chance for success, the best chance to keep local interests addressing the salmon crisis, to keep the crisis out of the courts and outside the Washington Beltway. He pushed the idea in discussions with the Northwest governors and other Northwest members of Congress, and he obtained their agreement.

In May 1991 the council took on the responsibility for solving the salmon crisis, picking up where the summit left off. Everyone knew it would not be easy. The failure of the summit had revealed many things, and the theme of all of them was that the salmon crisis was ultimately not about fish. It was about values. Everyone could agree that the fish were important; that having them in the Northwest was important to some residents' sense of the region. No one would say otherwise. The question was, *how* important?

QUESTIONS OF VALUES

Republicans believed that public life was essentially a matter of the common choosing and willing of a common world. . . . The federalists argued that it was possible—in fact it was preferable—to carry on the most important public tasks without any such willing of a common world. Individuals would pursue their private ends, and the structure of government would balance those pursuits so cleverly that the highest good would emerge without anyone having bothered to will it into existence. It was no accident that this approach to public life was put forward by people who were centrally interested in creating optimal conditions for an expanding commercial and industrial economy.

—DANIEL KEMMIS, *COMMUNITY AND THE POLITICS OF PLACE*, 1990

The whole question of values was on the mind of Glenn Vanselow. Vanselow, an amiable forty-five-year-old, was the spokesman for the economic users of the Columbia and Snake Rivers. As executive director of the Pacific Northwest Waterways Association, he represented utilities, farm groups, barge operators, and river ports throughout the region, from Seattle to Eugene; more than one hundred institutional members in all. He was also the chairman of the Columbia River Alliance for Fish and Commerce, an ad hoc group he organized during the summit to represent the economic interests.

The summit had been for Vanselow a total immersion in how the river's uses affected fish. These problems were something new to him, as he was not a native Northwesterner or a fisherman. But he rather liked the complexity of the problem. Part of him was still the academic, the Ph.D. in geography from the University of Washington who had done his dissertation in the then-new field of psychogeography—mental maps, the images people have of

the areas they live in and how those images influence their actions. The
subject fascinated him.

His own image of the Northwest was nourished by reading such books as
Jane Jacobs's *Cities and the Wealth of Nations*, which made him think hard
about the relationship of cities and rural areas. Jacobs had argued that cities,
not nations, were the primary units of economic life, and economic expansion
depended on close working ties between the resources of rural areas and the
innovative capacity of cities. For Jacobs, the richest economic systems were
like the richest biological systems. They were diverse, and in their diversity
they made efficient use of resources. The system as a whole thrived. Thinking
about such things, Vanselow became convinced that the continued viability
of the Northwest as a region depended upon the continued integration of
rural areas into the whole. In a stint with the Port of Portland in the 1980s,
he worked on economic development planning for small communities along
the Columbia River.

The economic viability of the Port of Portland was clearly linked with the
smaller ports along the river. They put their grain or potatoes or logs on
barges and sent them to Portland; Portland put them on ocean vessels, which
could maneuver that far upriver. From the wheat farmer in eastern Washington to the noodle factory in China the link was Portland, and such links
secured prosperity in several communities.

Still, it was more than the bottom line that interested Vanselow. He
thought of challenges such as diversifying a small port district into a hub of
local commerce as "romantic" work. He used that word when he talked about
it. Keeping rural communities viable, helping them grow so that they could
stay that way, seemed to him not only a sensible but a valuable thing to do.
It seemed like good social policy.

Now, with the endangered salmon, residents of the rural Northwest were
being asked again to consider another value system, one that had been
overlooked. The values in preserving wild creatures and in wildness itself ran
smack up against their own deepest beliefs—that "taming" the West for
humans, making nature productive, were worthy actions.

The apparent virtue of that taming was part of many families' personal
histories and of the community history of towns and small cities throughout

the region over the preceding several generations. It wasn't something people questioned often; it was part of their culture. But it had not always been so, and to see it becoming that way meant looking back at least a generation. The predecessor of Vanselow's Pacific Northwest Waterways Association, the Inland Empire Waterways Association, had been one of the boosters of this view.

The Inland Empire association had published a booklet in 1952 called *Yours Is the River.* Not only was it the booklet's name, "yours is the river" was its expansive message. An anonymous copywriter sought to capture the myth of the newly modernized rural Northwest.

> In a long valley that parallels the Idaho-Oregon border a farmer turns on his electric pump and calls his sleek Herefords to water. He will finish his morning chores in an electrically lighted barn before trudging across the pasture to the irrigation canal that borders his fields. Here he will open up the sluice gates and let cool, rich water flow in controlled abundance to the thirsty roots of his growing crops.
>
> If this farmer is of philosophic bent, he will stop for a moment to gaze across the broad, lush valley with its modern homes and farm buildings, its orchards and fertile croplands, the green pastures and the grazing herds . . . he will pause and look back through the years to this valley as it was when he first came—less than two decades ago.
>
> There was no greenness then, no power lines, no water, no thriving farm communities. Desolation stalked the barren hills, and here in the valley, the rattlesnake, the sage hen, and the jackrabbit vied with each other for survival.
>
> The water came . . . and then the high line . . . and all this was changed. The desert was made to blossom, and productive farmlands replaced the barren wastes.

A real farmer in 1952 would have recognized the artificiality of this account. His own experience had taught him that water and electricity had not arrived as if by magic, but through lots of hard work and cooperation. Even so, the magic in the story was true at a deeper level, and its meaning was widely shared. For people out there, nature in the hinterlands was "barren" and "desolate" until they came along. Now it was productive, and the responsibility of society was to make it more so.

The booklet said this, too.

In 1952 the number of acres of irrigated cropland in the dry areas of eastern Oregon and Washington, and western Idaho, was about 4 million. *Yours Is the River* called for 2 million more. The primary reason for development, the Inland Empire Waterways Association wanted to say, was need, not personal profit. Consider the demand for food:

> In 1975, if people are to eat as well as they eat today, Northwest agriculture will have to produce annually as its share of the national output over a million more cattle and calves, over one-half million more hogs, over 800,000 more sheep and lambs . . .

After 1952, Northwesterners responded to the challenge of population growth by damming more stretches of the Columbia, producing more electricity, channeling more irrigation water, growing more food, and shipping it downriver from new ports through new locks. They thought they had done right. The had made a hard and stingy nature bounteous. They had helped their fellow man and woman.

Vanselow saw himself as the inheritor of this worldview, and saw it as his job to advance it, to update it.

When he worked for the port, he had led the development of the Columbia/Snake Marketing Group. The group had something worthwhile to offer; there was no question of that. The uncertainty revolved around marketing, how to define themselves to the outside world. Under Vanselow's tutelage the rivers became the "development hub of the Pacific Northwest," and the "transportation network to the world."

The marketing group produced a wall-sized map, intending it "to demonstrate the economic unification of the River System and its far-reaching network capabilities."

"The System," Vanselow wrote, "unites a region that is truly whole."

From the very first, Vanselow had recognized that the salmon crisis had the potential to stall the Columbia's engine of commerce. The very day the first salmon petition was filed he had coincidentally been on Capitol Hill, leading a delegation of river users to meet with Mark Hatfield. Hatfield had himself just come from a scientific briefing on the spotted owl, and was visibly upset by the economic implications of owl protection. Protecting the sockeye looked even more serious. The entire Snake and Columbia river system could be held hostage to a fish, he recognized.

Talking with Hatfield, Vanselow was hit hard, too, by the possible consequences, and those consequences kept on hitting him during the salmon summit. The salmon problem was real, and the river users must not deny it. Yet they must not let it overwhelm them. As the chairman of the Columbia River Alliance, Vanselow saw clearly in the spring of 1991 a need for the alliance members to define themselves in the new world of endangered salmon.

Vanselow had no question that the Columbia and Snake should be preserved for what he liked to call "multiple uses" and not be dominated by a single "use," such as salmon. His concern was that the legal machinery of salmon protection had made members scared about the future of their livelihoods. They needed to talk, and they needed to listen. They needed to consider their values in this emerging era.

Vanselow convened a "symposium" titled "Saving the Wild Salmon" for the end of May. The theme, as he expressed it, was "both saving the salmon and saving the river economy." He had arranged it carefully so that there would be a spectrum of friendly viewpoints and a bracing glance at other realities. Rick Braun of Oregon Trout was asked to address the group and respond to questions.

One hundred seventy people came to a hotel in Portland for the event, and settled themselves in to listen to biologists, economists, alliance members, and governors' representatives.

John Carr's speech was not the keynote address, but it might have been. Carr, the executive director of the Direct Service Industries, gave a ten-minute talk that probably surprised most people in the room for its position.

Most in the room knew that the DSI, the consortium of eleven aluminum and chemical companies, accounted for about 30 percent of the Bonneville Power Administration's revenues, payments of some $500 million per year. This meant that the DSI members were in effect paying for about 30 percent of the BPA and Power Planning Council's salmon programs. By the end of the 1980s the DSI salmon contribution had already amounted to $300 million. Carr might have been expected to push some hard-line position that the fish weren't worth so much. But he didn't say that. He was clear that the salmon problem could be solved and that the DSI would play a role.

"We believe that the solution involves a holistic approach to the ecosystem," he said, challenging alliance members with terms that might make them uncomfortable.

"The society that created one of the most advanced, efficient, and reliable energy systems in the world can solve the fish problem without severe economic distress," he said.

"I'm very confident of that."

The keys to the solution were "will" and "know-how," he said. Improved technology could save the wild salmon.

For people who knew Carr, his call for being part of the solution was not a surprise. It was the only prudent position to take, the obvious one to him. Partly he was just trying to keep the wolves from the door.

Andy Kerr had been snapping at the aluminum industry for months. In a position paper developed for the start of the salmon summit, Kerr had written, "As we look to the various sectors of the economy to give a bit so the salmon may survive, we should take special notice of the aluminum industry. That industry consumes approximately twenty percent of all the electricity in the region. It produces less than 10,000 jobs, a mere one-quarter of one-percent of the approximately four million jobs in the Pacific Northwest. Its electricity is provided at a subsidized rate through a socialistic program funded by the ratepayers."

Kerr had his facts about aluminum mostly right. Aluminum smelting consumes huge amounts of electricity, and the region's aluminum producers did consume about 20 percent of the region's hydroelectricity. Also it was true that as wholesale customers of federal hydropower they paid the same average price per kilowatt as large industries served by public utilities in the region. But they paid less than some other private industrial customers. The contractual rate they paid was pegged to the world market price for aluminum.

When the metal's price was in a slump, the aluminum manufacturers on the Columbia got a break on their electricity bill. When the commodity's price went up, they paid more. Since the arrangement was begun in the 1980s, the industry had been paying more than a fixed plan would have dictated. Still, Kerr was concerned about metal market slumps when other ratepayers would subsidize the aluminum companies. To Kerr, this didn't seem altogether the best arrangement for the region.

"We throw away enough aluminum every year in this country to rebuild the entire commercial air fleet four times," Kerr's article continued. "Recycling an aluminum can requires ninety percent less energy than making a virgin one.

"Downsizing and retooling the aluminum industry in the region may be one of the most positive economic and environmental actions that we could take." If the DSI members didn't use so much hydropower, he argued, more water could be available for fish.

Kerr's arguments sounded damaging, and Carr was eager to tell the other side of the story. Most people didn't know that the industry had played a constructive role in the early years of the hydroelectric system, providing a large market for surplus hydropower, thereby justifying the development of publicly owned power facilities. Most people didn't know the various ways aluminum helped salmon, as he saw it.

Showing aluminum as a benefactor to salmon was smart, but then again, Carr was nobody's fool. It wasn't only his beard that made Carr an unconventional sort of executive. His academic training in theoretical math and logic might have seemed strange qualifications for a manager, but they helped him get at the nub of issues. He thought training in philosophy was just the thing for the modern manager.

Under the professional training, Carr felt the tug of personal values. He had grown up around Wenatchee, Washington, where his father was a construction electrician. In the late 1950s and early '60s the elder Carr had helped build the Rocky Reach, Wanapum, and Priest Rapids Dams. Young John had the opportunity to visit some projects as they were being built, to go down to bedrock and see the dams rooted against the flood of the river. People who had never seen it could not know how wild the Columbia was, what a titanic struggle it was to master it.

When he was young, people admired the engineering, the human resourcefulness that reined in the river. The journalist Richard Neuberger captured those feelings in 1938, floridly describing the wild Columbia River and the construction of Bonneville Dam.

> Where the roaring Snake joins it after a rush through the deepest gorge of the hemisphere, the river snarls like an angry monster. Over falls and cascades it booms the mightiest power anthem in North America. Wild and defiant, the river tumbles unharnessed into the Pacific.
>
> The hours of this freedom are numbered.
>
> Down in the thirty-five-hundred-foot canyon of the Columbia a man waves his arm in signal. Another man in a grotesque traveling crane pulls a lever. The crane reaches out like a heron spearing fish. Trolleys whine and cables jerk. A bucket-shaped steel receptacle moves downward, concrete pours from its maw, and one more timbered frame has been filled. Block by block, level over level, the dam rises from the river. The water foams furiously against massive piers that stretch like kneeling sea horses from shore to shore. The river hurls its force against the dam in white-capped fountains of water and spray, but the great barrier stays anchored to the bedrock far below.
>
> The herculean task is practically completed. . . .

There was grandness in the dams and their electricity and in the protection they gave people against flash floods. It was a grandness of building. Carr knew many people who shared this feeling. And he also cared about the fish. He grew up hunting and fishing and remembered well as a child visiting areas around Moses Lake, Washington, before they were irrigated. He hunted coyotes, deer, and jackrabbits there, and over the years he watched the irrigation projects arrive and, as he said, the desert "bloom." He was still an avid elk hunter and a fisherman for steelhead, strictly catch-and-release. If he was asked, he would say without hesitation that the salmon and the elk, among other natural resources, give the Northwest its character. He felt proud to be from the Northwest, and he wanted to protect it.

As a native Northwesterner, and also as a mathematician, logician, and the executive director of an industry tied to a volatile global market, his policy was to try to have it both ways. The fish should be saved—but not at any cost.

As he finished his speech before the alliance members, he declared that the DSI payments for salmon in the 1980s were "heading down the wrong track."

"We hold ourselves responsible in that we wrote a blank check to the fishery agencies," Carr said, "and didn't demand enough accountability for results.

"From now on, we will view our contribution to the regional fish program as an investment, and we will manage it as closely as we would any other investment we make."

This was language the audience members understood, and as Carr sat down he was rewarded with appreciative applause.

A sound investment: That seemed a good principle for action. People settled back, as if they had discovered the philosopher's stone.

Up on the dais, however, one of the other waiting speakers looked distinctly uncomfortable. It might not have been anything Carr said.

It wasn't that Ted Strong was new to discussions about the costs of "saving salmon." His own background was in finance and administration, and he understood the concerns he was hearing from Carr and the other executives.

It was what he was not hearing that made him uncomfortable.

At last he was introduced as the executive director of the Columbia River Inter-Tribal Fish Commission, and Ted Strong rose to speak. He wore a Western jacket and a white shirt; and also a string tie cinched by an amulet. A Yakama Indian, he traveled with the white culture only so far.

"Before the coming of the white man to this land, the Indian people were a ceremonial people," he began. "We were endowed with a feeling that kept us close to all that was created, including the salmon and the waters.

"The salmon were created for a purpose. They were created here to enjoy their life and their existence.

"They were created here to serve mankind.

"Today, with the development of the Columbia River, the salmon do not enjoy their life."

He paused a moment, to let the last concept settle. It seemed natural to him to speak of a salmon "enjoying" its life. He did not know how white people would take such an idea.

He shifted topics from the fish to the people. The "development" of the Columbia had done little for the Indians, Strong reminded his audience.

"Prior to 1890, the tribes in this region harvested five million fish. This year the tribes will harvest thirty thousand fall chinook. When we are asked what will be the impact on tribes of an Endangered Species Act listing we don't have to speculate. We can tell you based on our history.

"That thirty-thousand harvest is about one half of one percent of what we enjoyed."

Strong had a darker speculation of his own.

"Along with that decline in the population of salmon," he said, "Indian people declined from sixty thousand to ten thousand."

Not a sound was heard from the audience in the hotel meeting room as the Indian continued. He sounded sad, but if he was angry he didn't show it in his voice.

"It's not very heartening or encouraging to see the great abundance of billions and billions of dollars being reaped from the Columbia and Snake Rivers. At times we believe it is not 'reaped' but raped. That hurts Indian people.

"Indian people enjoyed the time on this earth when life itself was a value. Today, life *has* a value.

"That is something that is even more frightening to Indian people."

He paused again. That was it, he told himself. The loss of certain values was what he wanted to talk about. What he had been hearing mainly from the others were discussions of costs, losses of money. His face hardened.

" 'Saving the wild salmon'? From what?" Strong resumed, his voice colored with irony.

"From mankind, from our own technology?

"We find it difficult to let go of the materialistic value," he said.

"The value of life is one of the principles we try to keep alive in the tribal perspective. We tribal people try to be cooperative and contributing partners in this tremendous undertaking to keep the Columbia and Snake Rivers from dying.

"And they *will* die, if we continue to weight one side of the equation."

He sensed he was expected to say something forward-looking, to offer hope of a solution, to "save the wild salmon." But he didn't have anything to say that would make the difficulties easier.

He pledged Indian cooperation, but warned that Indians would be slow to choose sides. The main consideration for the tribes of the Yakima,* Warm Springs, Nez Perce, and Umatilla Reservations was the protection and preservation of their hunting and fishing rights, secured by the treaties in the 1850s. The Indians had given up their ancestral lands and many of their freedoms to keep those rights.

Few of the whites knew the accounts of those treaties, how the Yakama leader, Kamiakin, had repeatedly declined to sign the treaty pressed on him by the governor of Washington Territory, Isaac Stevens. How finally Kamiakin was the last to sign, how his lips were covered with blood from biting them in suppressed rage, how he finally signed the paper he was given with an "X." How he said only a few words before departing.

Kamiakin said, "I have been afraid of the white men; their doings are different from ours. Perhaps you have spoken straight, that your children will do what is right. Let them do as they have promised. That is all I have to say."

---

* A January 14, 1994, tribal council resolution proclaimed that the "Yakima" tribe would now be referred to as "Yakama," in accordance with the Yakama treaty of June 9, 1855. The author wishes to respect both the change and historical accuracy, and therefore will use the term "Yakima" when referring to the *tribe's* activity prior to this decision. "Yakima" is also a city in Washington.

The white men's children had not done what their fathers had promised, and though few of those at the meeting knew the history of the treaties, no one in the room needed to be reminded of their consequences, the public disputes and the courtroom battles of the 1960s and '70s. The Indians had struggled to have the federal courts uphold the rights guaranteed to them by the treaties, and they had finally prevailed in a series of landmark decisions. Now they would do everything in their power to preserve those rights. All of this history was behind what Strong said and the false optimism he would not provide.

"We appreciate the opportunity to share a tribal point of view with you," he concluded. "Thank you very much."

He sat down again, to polite applause. He had the same troubled expression on his face as when he began.

Sometimes it seemed to strange, talking to white people; it almost seemed he couldn't go on. They knew so little of the Indians, and seemed to care so little to know.

True, many recognized the Indians were entitled to catch fish for "religious" and "ceremonial" purposes. But they understood little of what that meant. Sitting on the hotel stage, Strong felt that his own strength to speak about the salmon came from these deep traditional beliefs.

Only a few weeks before, he had been part of one of these religious ceremonies at the Satus longhouse on the Yakama Indian Reservation.

The reservation lay in south-central Washington, north of the Columbia River and west of it, too, where the river turned north into the state. To get there, Strong drove east from Portland, through the Columbia Gorge, the chiseled canyon of the Columbia that separated Oregon and Washington. The journey also separated Strong from the wet verdant territory of the Cascade Mountains and propelled him into the drier uplands of the Columbia Plateau.

Past The Dalles, nearing his turnoff for the bridge into Washington, Strong moved through a landscape that looked at the same time gigantic and fragile. The river spread eerily wide here, and the eye traveled warily across its expanse and up by sloping contours to the plateau. It was millions of years ago, Strong had learned, that massive flows of lava had spilled out of the interior of the earth, building up the plateau. Since that time rain and wind had worked the rock, and alongside the river the lava flows now stood weathered into great channeled mounds, like the toes of giants. Above them was a sky broad and empty. The giants were gone. Only the feet remained.

Strong found it hard to drive through this section of the gorge without thinking of the history that had died there. Before the Army Corps of Engineers had built The Dalles Dam and the river had filled up fat and smooth as a harbor seal, Indians had enjoyed one of the great fishing spots on the river. The Indians called the river "Nch'i wana"—Big River—and it shot fast and hard over the falls at Celilo. For countless generations, Indians had fished there with long-handled nets and spears, standing on makeshift wooden platforms over the roaring falls and dipping the nets or spearing the salmon as they leapt up.

The salmon caught at Celilo traditionally fed the local tribes, the Wasco, Wishrams, and Wyams, and the salmon were plentiful enough to be traded with other tribes from as far away as Montana, Nevada, and the Fraser River in Canada. For longer than anyone knew, Celilo Falls had been a thriving gathering point for Indians, a place of abundance. What a time it must have been, when Indians from all over the west would come, bringing buffalo meat and furs and handsome beadwork and sharing their stories and dances for days or weeks at a time.

But Celilo Falls was submerged when the dam backed up the river in 1957. As the falls disappeared Indians stood on the bank and watched. Some wept. No more would the men dare the powerful river in order to capture one of its own. No more would the boys be initiated there in the fishing skills that had passed from father to son, sustaining their people. To Strong, the only sign of the falls that remained was a highway road sign, "Ancient Indian Fishing Grounds," which announced the turnoff for a little roadside park nestled against the new "Lake" Celilo. He passed by and crossed the bridge at Biggs.

The Satus longhouse lay on the plateau, north toward Yakima, Washington. Set out in scrubby, dry lands, the building was a plain one-story affair, constructed of cinder blocks, huddled in a dusty parking lot. On that Sunday morning, a group of teenage boys tended a makeshift barbecue pit in one corner of the lot. On grates made of old mattress springs, they carefully cooked salmon wrapped in aluminum foil. They also cooked the unwrapped, disjointed legs and hindquarters of deer.

They talked a little, but mainly they kept one wary eye on the fire and the other on the kitchen door to the longhouse. Inside the kitchen their mothers and grandmothers moved about quickly, completing the preparations of the other foods. The teenagers were responsible to them to do a good job with the meat.

As the members of the longhouse arrived in their pickup trucks and cars, the dust blew around. If they had not heard the sound as they drove in, as soon as they were outside their vehicles the Indians could not miss the unmistakable, relentless beat—*tum, tum, tum, tum*—and the men's voices, in a high wailing.

Arriving, Strong went quickly inside through the east-facing door to the main hall. There he took his place with the other men, along the north wall. The women were opposite. In between them, at the end of the room on a small raised stage, the drummer-singers stood. The people in the congregation did not look at them, but kept their eyes averted.

The drumming and singing had begun about ten o'clock that morning with two men, but as the morning and the drumming continued other men joined the two until by about one o'clock in the afternoon eight men stood together shoulder to shoulder on the stage. They spoke little or nothing to one another, appearing instead caught up in the songs. When one singer finished leading a song, without cue another one quickly began a new song.

Over the unchanging beating of the drum, the chorus of men sang, in unison mainly. They were songs, but the men were not trying to make "music." The pitches were too high, the volume was too loud; they were not trying to call attention to their artistry. They were up to something else, which they considered more important. The songs were special to the occasion.

From time to time some of the children, dressed up in ceremonial regalia, came out in front of the others and danced, accompanying the songs. The dances were all simple; sidesteps and hops, all the young ones moving together in time with the chanting. They danced around the rectangle in front of their mothers and fathers and the elders, and when they were done, they slipped quietly back into the crowd.

Four and a half hours after he had begun the drumming, Evans Dick, the chief, stopped it, and the male elders fell silent. The invocation was complete. The time had come for the next phase of the ceremony.

The congregation sat on the floor, and woven tule mats were spread between the men and women. The older women, the grannies, brought out the food from the kitchen and gave it to the younger women to serve. They distributed plates, and on each plate, in turn, they placed a mouthful of a particular food: first salmon, next venison, then a series of roots, and finally berries. Each person received a cup, with enough water for two swallows.

Although it was now mid-afternoon, no one in the room touched any of the food or drank the water. After perhaps half an hour everyone had been served, in the correct order. The women then withdrew.

The chief rang a bell, and said *"chiish."* Each of the native people took a sip of water. He rang again and said the salmon's name, *"nusux."* In silence, everyone ate the morsels of salmon.

Again he rang and named, and again, until the morsels carefully arranged around each plate had been consumed. Venison, bitterroot, other wild roots, wild celery, wild carrot, huckleberries, and choke cherries; each was eaten quickly and without comment. At the end, Evans said a few more words of prayer and everyone took a final swallow of water.

The first-foods ceremony was complete, done in accordance with Wáashat tradition passed from generation to generation in the tribe.

The Creator had been thanked for creating the animals and plants that sustained the people.

The animals and plants had been thanked for giving themselves up to be eaten.

Now that the thanks had been given, and the forms of respect observed, the people could feast on these first fresh foods of the spring.

Out came the platters then, filled to overflowing with the same foods that had been consumed as tiny morsels only moments before. Everyone, talking now, hungry after hours of standing and chanting, passed the platters and fell to eating with enthusiasm. It was a feast, with an abundance of food for everyone, and there were happy voices in the room.

It was also a communion.

Few knew all the details of the ritual, but they appreciated that the first-foods ceremony was a community religious rite. Many had helped with the food gathering. Before the fishermen went out, before the women root-gatherers went out, they had had ceremonies to assist them in their tasks; and when they were successful they thanked the animals and plants personally. This was one of their ways.

The Yakama understood the animals and plants as separate beings, endowed with intelligence and will. They referred to the animals as the First People, and they all were familiar with the stories about Coyote, Raven, and Salmon, in which the animals behaved like people. So when the Indians netted salmon out of the river or shot deer in the forest, properly they understood it as a sacrifice of another individual for them.

Out of respect they prayed over the animals. Out of respect they stood during the drumming and singing, keeping time with the songs by beating the rhythm with their right hands, raising the hand in affirmation when the song was over. They also dressed themselves in their best regalia. They were poor people for the most part, but most had brought out something fine for the occasion.

Most of the drummers wore leggings with beadwork; some wore fancy ribbon shirts. Many of the women wore colorful print dresses, topped by tunics cinched by a broad belt. Some wore high-topped moccasins decorated with beadwork. Both men and women wore their hair long, in braids that were often wrapped in the smooth fur of an otter. As Ted Strong looked at his relatives and friends, he smiled.

The leggings of buckskin, the elk-hide drumheads, the deerskin moccasins, the otter-fur wrappings. What did it say about them, after all? Were these "savages," hopelessly backward in a modern world that had gone beyond them?

They believed that hunting and fishing and gathering were essential to their lives, essential because they should take their nourishment from the place in which they lived, from the animals and plants that shared the place with them. Few who were not Indians would understand. The ceremony about salmon and the other foods was an expression of people who were in touch with the terrible mystery of living: the realization that to live, other forms of life must die. It was right to acknowledge this, to try to fathom this.

That was the meaning of the ceremony; that was the reason the songs often sounded like laments; that was the reason the singers made no attempt to make their voices "musical." In the songs they were throwing their selves away, identifying with the salmon, the deer.

For himself, Strong knew as deeply as he was alive that it was important that this tradition should survive. When he looked at the way white people treated the places they occupied, their lack of communal bond to a place and to the other beings of a place, he was deeply concerned. They lived in a place, but they did not respect it.

Respect for the place you lived in and for the natural law was the foundation of what it meant to be Indian. These things were taught through the first-foods ceremony and other rituals. They were good in themselves and could give hope for the future.

He was heartened to know that not only the members of the Satus longhouse but the other Yakama bands, and nearly every tribal group in the Northwest that caught salmon, from Alaska to California, from the coast inland to Idaho, held a ceremony to welcome the first salmon. So important were the ceremonies that tribes which had stopped doing them because the knowledge was lost had begun them again. In the 1970s reservation groups in western Washington, including the Tulalip, the Port Gamble Skokomish, and the Upper Skagit renewed the ceremony. In the late 1980s the Masset Haida on the Queen Charlotte Islands were among those who had also renewed the first-salmon ceremony.

Many of the coast people had a more elaborate and more specific salmon ceremony than the Yakama did, Strong knew. That was right. The form would vary from tribe to tribe, from place to place, although there were common themes.

Traditionally, among the coast Salish peoples when the first salmon run began, no one was allowed to fish until the first catch had been ceremonially welcomed. Children, or sometimes elders, bathed and painted themselves and were sprinkled with bird down, then went to the beach to receive the fish from the fishermen. The fish was carried on outstretched arms up the bank to the fire pit, where it was placed on a bed of ferns and butchered so that its spine was left intact. The flesh was skewered and roasted over coals.

A leader prayed that the salmon would look kindly on the people and return in great numbers. The whole community then shared in the cooked fish, eating all of it. When they were done, they carefully collected the bones and entrails in a basket or mat and ceremoniously returned them to the river or the sea. In that way the salmon would come to life again and lead their companions to the Indian fishing sites.

Indians had lived along the Columbia for at least ten thousand years, Strong had read, and their inhabitation was perhaps four times as long along certain parts of the Northwest coast. He had read the studies that said that prior to the arrival of the whites, fifty thousand Indians from the Columbia River tribes had harvested an average of 18 million pounds of salmon and steelhead. And yet they seemed not to have jeopardized the runs. It seemed to Strong a sure thing that ceremony was a factor.

So now as he sat on the dais in the Portland hotel, looking out at the audience, he had to wonder about who these white people were. What were *their* ceremonies? What did they really want?

Out in that audience, looking up at the panelists, another of the speakers sat listening, puzzling it all out. He smiled placidly, but his eyes blinked rapidly behind his wire-rim glasses. Angus Duncan was ripping through the ideas that mattered to him.

You could think the big thoughts about the endangered-species problem, he told himself. The behavior of one species was endangering many of its companions on the planet. Certainly it was symptomatic of the last quarter of the twentieth century. It was unprecedented in scope and magnitude as an environmental problem. From any big perspective it was frightening and required immediate action.

But that was the problem with the problem.

It might be planetary in scope; it might be profoundly moral at root. It *was* frightening. But any lasting solution was going to have to be based on understandings and agreements forged among the people within the region in which a particular species was in trouble.

Take the salmon, for instance: Nongovernmental groups could only do so much. Their job was to bring the crisis to the attention of the government, to use whatever tools were at their disposal. Petitions were fine. But the salmon summit? It was naive to think that a solution was going to come through a mediated process among adversaries. It wasn't only that too much was at stake. The parties just didn't have the skills. They didn't know the language that would let them forge the solution.

Listening to them now, they sounded as if they came from different planets.

For better or for worse, in the United States the government was supposed to shape solutions. That was what all these people at this conference were looking for: a framework in which to find solutions.

Duncan took it as axiomatic that if you wanted to contribute to solutions, the best role to have was as a decision-maker in government. As he sat there in the audience triangulating the various speeches, looking for a path through the clashing values, Angus Duncan felt secure he had something to contribute, and he quietly relished the fact that he had the position in which to do it. He was one of Oregon's two members on the Power Planning Council.

Duncan always thought of himself as a leader. He was raised the eldest son of a Democratic politician, Robert Duncan, and grew up hearing politics at the kitchen table. While in high school he gave campaign speeches during his father's political campaigns. He liked talking to people, and what his father did intrigued him.

Bob Duncan was one of those independent politicians Oregonians seem to love, a liberal on most human rights and social issues, a conservative on fiscal and environmental affairs. He had been an amateur boxer, a good one, then a lawyer, a speaker of the Oregon House, and finally a U.S. congressman for five terms.

He had run for the Senate and been beaten by Mark Hatfield in Hatfield's first campaign. Duncan had supported the Johnson administration's Vietnam policies.

The Vietnam War proved to be a crucial test of the politician's son, too. Angus had signed on, then freshly graduated from Harvard, to be an advisor to the South Vietnamese government. Why he had signed up to go to Vietnam was another story, one that had to do with reading too much Hemingway in his teenage years and having come away from it hell-bent to find out what war was about. Getting out of Harvard in 1967 he knew that he might be drafted anyway, so he had signed up in order to have the experience at least somewhat on his terms. Among the other things he hadn't counted on was the living arrangements he would encounter on the job.

Since he had studied the Vietnamese language for a year, and was quick with it, arriving in Vietnam he was assigned to quarters with a local commander, a Major Vang. When the fresh-scrubbed Duncan introduced himself, the major wasted little time expressing his expectations about their shared living arrangements. As the major, he would take the bed near the back of the room.

"You," Major Vang said, "take the B-40 bed."

"B-40?" The Harvard grad hadn't heard of that.

The major smiled, in a nice way. Soon after, he told Duncan that B-40 was the name of a Viet Cong hand-held rocket. When the shelling came through the wall, the man in the front bed was more likely to take the hit.

That was the way his Vietnam tour started. Two years later, Duncan had come through his experience with no lasting damage and with one big personal advantage. He knew something about being under fire. He knew what a real conflict looked like. It helped put things in perspective elsewhere when he was taking heat.

After Vietnam, he went to Washington, D.C., to work on the McGovern campaign. From it he learned a little more about the collision of idealism and electoral politics, not much of which he was happy to find out. Afterward, tired of D.C., he bummed around the Caribbean. He spent time on sailboats and worked his way to a favorite beach in Belize. But politics drew him back.

One of his political acquaintances was Neil Goldschmidt, a bright, charming, hard-driving guy who happened to have both political ambitions and the skills to realize them. In 1973 he was voted the mayor of Portland, Oregon. At age thirty-two Goldschmidt was the youngest mayor in the United States, and was widely considered a rising political star. Goldschmidt named Duncan, age twenty-nine, his administrative assistant for policy in 1975. Working with Goldschmidt, Duncan learned a lot more about the practice of politics, and he saw that he liked influence. In that area after the OPEC oil embargo, he became interested in energy policy. It suited him as a topic; it was big enough to be a challenge, and new enough so that a person could make a mark.

His first chance to influence the Northwest's own energy policy happened in a unplanned way. In 1977 Goldschmidt had learned that utilities and the BPA were meeting behind closed doors in Seattle, hatching an arrangement that would have kept the public out of regional energy planning. The Young Turks didn't like that at all, so Goldschmidt and Duncan threatened to fly up to Seattle and confront the plotters. Goldschmidt issued an ultimatum.

"Either you let us in and discuss the city of Portland's concerns," he said, "or I do a news conference."

Invited behind the door, Duncan proposed the idea of a planning group, a council, that would be broadly representative of the public in regional energy decision-making. With that was born the idea of the Northwest Power Planning Council.

Duncan represented the city in the drafting of the Northwest Power Act, which ultimately gave many people who had been on the outside of regional energy planning a seat inside the room. It went way beyond what Duncan had been pushing for; the link between fish restoration and energy planning was the revolution within the revolution. Those who hadn't lived through it found it hard to believe that before 1977 the fish managers from the agencies and the tribes would go with hat in hand over to the Corps of Engineers and beg for changes in river operations that would help the fish. The Corps and the BPA held all the cards. With the signing of the Northwest Power Act, the rules changed.

By the time that had happened, Duncan had already moved on. In 1979 he had left Portland, restless to try other doors. He followed Goldschmidt to Jimmy Carter's Department of Transportation. Goldschmidt was secretary of transportation; Duncan became director of energy policy. He learned more about linking politics and energy planning from that experience, too, and with Carter out of office, Duncan took what he had learned and tried to make a new start in the private sector. He became an executive with two wind-energy companies, and moved to California. But wind was slow catching on. He was trying to sell a new, untried, and more expensive form of energy during a period of energy surplus and political indifference. His timing was off. With a certain amount of relief, he moved back to Oregon.

Through the 1980s he never lost touch with the Power Planning Council. For a time that was particularly easy. In 1986 his father was appointed to the council by the outgoing Republican governor, and was retained by the incoming Democratic one, who just happened to be Neil Goldschmidt. In 1987 the elder Duncan was elected the council's chairman. Father and son talked often about council policies and politics, which continued to fascinate Angus, who was now working for an Oregon utility company. The elder Duncan retired from the council in 1988. Goldschmidt filled this vacancy, but in 1990 the governor had another council vacancy to fill, and Angus approached his friend for the job. "Who's more suited for this than I am?" he asked. Goldschmidt gave him a seat at the table he had helped to create.

The two members from each state tended to divide the council's portfolio of energy and fishery responsibilities. Initially Duncan thought he would specialize in energy, since that was his background, and Ted Hallock would concentrate on fish. Of course, Duncan was interested in environmental issues, but to him that meant the big things such as the greenhouse effect and global warming. Biology and management of fish just couldn't be enough of a challenge.

But fish was where the political action was going to be, he saw, and when the salmon summit came up, he went to newly elected Governor Barbara Roberts and asked to be the state's new representative to the meetings. His experiences there told him that finding a regional solution was going to take a framework that the council was in the best position to provide. It also made him recognize clearly, for the first time, something that he was hearing again at the alliance symposium. To really solve the endangered-salmon problem, you had to be sensitive to people's values.

Sure, you could legislate all the solutions you wanted. But particularly in political circumstances such as those around endangered species—where time was running out and people felt threatened and you needed cooperation—you wouldn't get cooperation if you disregarded the values of various groups and just ran roughshod over them.

For the Indians, that meant acknowledging the importance of their traditional ways, and their determination to preserve them. For some of the businesses, such as the farmers, that meant recognizing that they had made investments and commitments based on a reasonable expectation of what the rules would be, and now the council would be changing those rules. For the conservationists, it meant trying to respond to their concerns for a viable future. The challenge was to try to make all of them see that they were partners in a solution, rather than victims of one another.

That's why, as he listened that day and thought about the remarks he would make, ad lib, he was particularly offended by what Washington's Republican senator, Slade Gorton, and Oregon's Senator Packwood had said in their keynote comments. Both had fingered the Endangered Species Act as the enemy and the good people of the Columbia River Alliance as its victims. The ESA needed to be changed, they said.

"For those of you who feel as I do about these issues," Gorton had said, "it is not enough to nod in agreement and grumble about the excesses of the Endangered Species Act. You must share your views with your neighbors, you must talk with your local newspaper, television station, and radio station. You must let your local, state, and national political representatives know how you feel.

"You must let those people know what the specific impacts of endangered species listings will be, and express to them how you weigh the trade-offs between human progress and the preservation of the state of nature."

Duncan thought this "trade-off" between "progress" and "preservation" was not only baloney, it was bad politics. When he was introduced to speak and made his way to the lectern, he was reminding himself not to let Gorton and Packwood become the focus of his talk. What he himself had to say was more important.

Standing at the lectern he wasn't what anyone would call imposing. Slight of build, with a neatly trimmed blond beard and conservatively tailored suit, Duncan was a bit tweedy perhaps, but unexceptional. Nevertheless, there was something about the expression, the bearing, that inspired interest. He smiled confidentially. He looked relaxed. As he began to speak, he projected a sense of intelligence and reasonableness.

"With the exception of several comments heard today," he began, "we have generally avoided inflammatory statements and predictions of doom.

"There has been no surge of salmon 'recipes' on bumper stickers, no barge parades, no people sticking pins in Bill Bakke dolls. We've avoided splitting along the natural fault lines of this problem: upstream interests, downstream interests; tribal fishermen, nontribal. We have not ignored or papered over the differences, but we have negotiated.

"Contrary to Senator Gorton, we have contemplated costs and benefits, and have found measures—not *without* costs, but with manageable costs that the public is willing to pay."

That was about the best construction he could think of putting on the summit. There were challenges enough ahead, and he wanted them to focus on the council's prospects. He had a short list of what the council must accomplish.

"One. Keep the decision-making within the region.

"Two. Achieve a rough equity among users.

"Three. Manage costs.

"Four. Resolve uncertainties for users.

"Five. Avoid breakdown of political dialogue."

He didn't see how anyone could object to these. He didn't think he could have gone any softer. So he thought it fair to go a bit on the offensive in this Republican gathering. He challenged Gorton again.

"It's a political red herring—a false issue—to pit the Endangered Species Act against the people," he continued.

"The ESA, handled responsibly, is not about stopping projects. The most it's about is slowing—barely—the accelerated rate of species disappearance due to human intervention.

"It's an important warning about the stresses we place on the environment."

It was time the audience should hear a little broader perspective than most politicians were giving them.

"The true issue is a profoundly conservative one," he continued.

"The lesson we have to learn is to live within our means, to live on the interest that our natural resource capital throws off, without consuming that capital—whether water, land, airshed, energy—on which all living species, including ourselves, ultimately depend.

"This 'living within our means' is the true meaning of the elusive concept of 'balance' that we hear so much about."

At this definition little glimmers of insight passed across faces out in the audience. "Living within our means" sounded awfully familiar and sensible.

At the end of Duncan's talk, measured applause accompanied him from the lectern. Duncan knew that translating applause into support was not going to be easy. The council had to figure out what credible actions, on what timetable, would be sufficient for the salmon. But it also had to figure how much time and what sorts of adjustments needed to be made so that these members of the "Alliance for Fish and Commerce" would be part of the solution. There were no set formulas, and Duncan liked that. It gave him room in which to work his reasonableness and persuasiveness. He thought he knew the chances.

Whatever comfort Duncan, Ted Strong, and other nonalliance participants took from the salmon conference, at its close alliance leader Glenn Vanselow was considering the session a definite success. His members had some shared information and perspective from which to take strength during the assaults that were now sure to come.

The next salvo was not long in arriving. A month later, at the end of June, Rollie Schmitten announced that the National Marine Fisheries Service proposed listing the petitioned Snake River chinook as a threatened species under the Endangered Species Act. At the same time, the Fisheries Service declined to list the lower Columbia River coho.

Although most people familiar with the issue expected listings, the reaction in the region was immediate, and much of it was negative. Nobody really liked the "threatened" listings. The Columbia River Alliance members now needed to look their anxieties in the eye. The environmentalists were satisfied that listings were proposed, but it seemed to them that the Fisheries

Service had adopted a weak posture. The fall chinook ruling seemed to them especially wishy-washy. In 1990 the Fisheries Service estimated that only seventy-eight adults had survived to the Snake River to spawn. Given a new rule of thumb that at least two hundred fish were necessary for populations to maintain their genetic viability, it seemed that the fall chinook should easily have qualified for "endangered" status. The agency's own biological review team had concluded that the fall chinook "face a substantial risk of extinction."

It wasn't only the fall chinook that environmentalists were chagrined about. The agency had decided to lump together the spring and summer chinook stocks under one "threatened" listing, arguing that the two runs could not be distinguished. Both environmentalists and industrial interests speculated openly that the decision to list chinook as threatened rather than endangered was self-serving. The Fisheries Service's traditional constituency was commercial fishermen, and a "threatened" listing under the ESA gave the agency flexibility in allowing continued, limited fishing on those stocks. With an "endangered" listing, any "directed" fishing on them would be off limits.

The chinook listings were less than desired, but they were listings nonetheless. The ruling that really upset Bill Bakke was the failure to list coho at all.

Before the turn of the century the annual run of coho in the Columbia was 500,000 fish or more, all of them wild spawners. But now the lower Columbia wild coho, like the Snake River coho a few years before, were pronounced extinct. Schmitten issued a kind of institutional apology.

"What we found was we have done a very good job of hatchery homogenization," Schmitten said. "We have bred out wild stocks. The hatcheries did what we asked them to do, but we weren't smart enough to see what they were doing to the wild stocks."

It wasn't quite the argument that Bakke would have made, though it was on the right track. From his point of view, it wasn't just that hatcheries had overwhelmed wild stocks. Fisheries managers had decided to turn to hatchery production because they wanted to have fish available for fishermen. And they had sacrificed the wild stocks willingly in the mixed-stock fishery that resulted.

Bakke had publicly argued the folly of the managers right to their faces at the meeting of the Oregon chapter of the American Fisheries Society, just that winter.

"There is no policy for the conservation of native salmon stocks or the genetic resources they represent," he had said in an invited talk. "Today's salmon managers are commodity brokers consumed by the authority to allocate access of special interests to the resource.

"Let's stop the charade that everything is OK, which is what we've been hearing for years from the Oregon Department of Fish and Wildlife."

But, for all that, Bakke was angriest about the coho decision not because the Fisheries Service said the coho were effectively extinct. The coho status review had left open the possibility that some wild coho still spawned in the tributaries of the lower river, after all. Scale analysis done by Washington and Oregon—lab work done by Lisa Borgerson and her colleagues, following on the field surveys by Chris Allori and many others—had suggested as much.

To Bakke, it looked like the agency was dodging the political fallout of a listing. It looked like the Fisheries Service was trying to prevent a discussion of the loss of habitat, of the misuse of hatcheries, and the abuses of harvest— all problems associated with fisheries agency management. It even looked like maybe the agency had dropped the lower river coho so it could just keep the public's attention focused on the faults of the hydropower system. The upriver chinook were best for making that case.

He was determined not to let the coho drop. Either wild fish remained, or they didn't; the ESA didn't let the agency just write them off on a presumption. Bakke and Braun began looking into the merits of a formal appeal, and of measures short of that.

Nevertheless, as Bakke rightly perceived, the listing decisions allowed virtually all of the public attention, and that of the council in particular, to be focused on the problems of the dams.

Before considering the contentious dams, the Power Planning Council warmed up to its new salmon-recovery planning by prescribing some non-controversial actions that could quickly benefit the salmon. They identified some $18 million worth of projects, calling on Bonneville Power Administration ratepayers to provide half that amount, federal taxpayers $6 million, and the Northwest states the remaining $3 million. Of thirty projects, the big-ticket item was $6 million for purchase and installation of screens to keep juvenile salmon from being swept into irrigation canals and ditches. Over the years, untold millions of fish throughout the region had been killed in this way.

Overall, the first projects were small compared to those the council would be prescribing when it tackled the dams. Prescriptions, however, would come only after the members had heard from the public. During the summer they began inviting proposals from the region on the key problems of salmon survival through the dams, harvest by the commercial, sport, and Indian fisheries, and "production." During the early fall they received more than one thousand pages of proposals from various interest groups, including the utilities, the fish agencies and tribes, and the conservationists.

Much of the concern expressed by the fish interests focused on providing additional water to move juvenile salmon downriver faster. For most fish advocates, the dammed-up, harnessed river continued to be the fish's worst enemy.

No advanced theoretical training in fisheries was needed to realize that salmon would probably do best in a river like the free-flowing one the species had evolved in over millions of years. Nor did it take some specialized insight to predict that the dams, which turned the river into a series of slow-moving pools, would cause problems for the migrating fish. Fisheries scientists only explained what common sense already suggested: The fish had evolved to migrate to the sea as juveniles during the spring and early summer, when the snow melted off the mountains, sending a surge of water down the creeks into the streams and into the main stem of the river.

Before the construction of the dams and the reservoir system, juvenile salmon took about twenty-two days to migrate from the Salmon River in Idaho to the lower Columbia River. With the main-stem dams in place, that same journey could take over fifty days. The more-than-double duration of the migration put the fish at serious risk. Increases in migration time meant that the physical changes that enabled the fish to survive in salt water could be delayed beyond acceptable limits. The biological "window of opportunity" could close.

The more that biologists learned about them, the more the fish's preparations for salt water appeared subtle and intricate. While still in their streams, juvenile salmon began undergoing profound changes in their anatomy and physiology. Not only did their colors change, the shape of their fins and teeth changed. The thyroid hormones became active, causing them to be less territorial, less aggressive, and less resistant to the increased flows ready to whisk them away. Other hormonal changes altered the functions of their kidneys and gills, enabling them to regulate their blood chemistry in salt water.

While genetic factors and the stage of growth appeared to predispose a juvenile to migrate, environmental factors such as longer day-length, streamflow changes, and increased water temperatures also served as migratory cues. Once migration began, the little fish tended to be swept along passively in the current, for active swimming wasted precious energy. That was an additional difficulty for the juveniles in a dammed, slow-moving river: They might have to expend energy just to make headway.

The slack-water ponds between the dams harbored other dangers. Predatory fish such as the Northern squawfish preyed more easily on the smolts when the flow was slower, when the water was clearer, as it was in a slower flow, and when the fish might be stressed from the effects of warmer, slow-moving water.

All of these dangers of migration were in addition to the physical impediments of the dams themselves. A tiny fish could be chewed up in turbines or even sometimes hurt in passage through the powerhouse bypass system. It could also die from the equivalent of the scuba diver's dreaded "bends" when spilled over the dam and dropped into a foaming plunge-pool perhaps forty feet below. The air they breathed in the pool had a higher concentration of nitrogen than normal, as a result of the extra air trapped in the falling water.

Research done in the 1970s seemed to confirm that the faster the fish went downriver, the better they survived. If slower travel rates and higher mortality was the problem, higher flows during migration seemed to be the solution. As a result, the fisheries managers of the agencies and tribes began in the Power Planning Council's very first year to call for water to be dedicated to flushing the salmon downriver in the spring. To enhance the flows in the Snake River they requested an additional volume of water amounting to more than 1.6 million acre-feet.

In 1982, the council responded by developing a "water budget" to provide some additional flows. But the planning agency refused to accept the advice of the fish agencies and tribes on the volume of water the fish needed. The council reduced the recommended volume in the Snake River by one-fourth, to 1.2 million acre-feet. In the following years, the flow levels desired by the agencies and tribes were rarely achieved.

Observers criticized this failure variously. Michael Blumm, the salmon-law professor, called it the major failing of the council that the planning body and its staff put itself above the fisheries specialists, as a kind of "super fish and wildlife agency." Others complained that the council's ruling was po-litically motivated; that the regional agency was too accommodating to the BPA, which held the purse strings for its programs, and to the utilities and industries that funded the BPA.

During the fall of 1991, as the council was reconsidering fish passage needs, fish advocates again urged the group to adopt the flows proposed by agency biologists. The Columbia Basin Fish and Wildlife Authority, the representative of the region's fish managers, chose not to focus on overall volumes. Instead the authority called for flows of 140,000 cubic feet per second to be made available in the lower Snake and mid-Columbia Rivers during the spring migration period, from April 1 to June 15. It also called for 300,000 cubic feet per second to be provided by water managers in the lower Columbia.

The fish managers reminded the council that the flows might be achieved in more than one way. Flushing water out of upstream storage reservoirs was one method. Drawing down the water level in the reservoirs between the dams might accomplish the same results. Adequate water velocity was the issue, not just the volume of water displaced. The Fish and Wildlife Au-thority left it up to the water managers to find the best way to produce the velocities the fish needed.

Dan Rohlf of the Northwest Environmental Defense Center was among the endorsers of the Fish and Wildlife Authority's proposal. In his letter to the council, Rohlf reminded the members that "the Northwest Power Act requires that measures to improve fish migration and survival be based on 'sound objectives.' Unfortunately," said Rohlf, "recent discussions on mainstem passage have had little to do with biology.

"Politics cannot save a single smolt," he continued. "Fish simply need humans to operate the rivers in the Columbia Basin so that they behave more like rivers."

For their part, the utilities called for flows only a bit more than half the rate prescribed by the fish experts: 85,000 cubic feet per second upriver rather than 140,000; and 160,000 downriver rather than 300,000.

In his letter to the council, utility executive Al Wright said that the utilities' recommendations were "based upon the best scientific information obtainable coupled with a balancing of measures based on cost effectiveness."

It seemed that everyone wanted to claim the "best scientific information." The science that the Pacific Northwest Utilities Conference Committee preferred related fish travel time to flows in one of the Columbia pools. The model showed that increased flows always cause reduced travel times, but above a certain velocity the reductions taper off, becoming less "cost effective."

Ed Chaney preferred the science of the fish agencies, and he developed his own "travel-time objectives" from the Fish and Wildlife Authority's proposal. It should take the fish sixteen days to travel from the Washington-Idaho border to below Bonneville Dam, Chaney calculated. "Target 16" he called it. In his straightforward won't-get-it-if-you-don't-ask way, he submitted language that the council could just incorporate directly as its own:

> Given the imperiled status of Snake River salmon, the council has determined that emergency action is required. Therefore, it establishes a deadline of March 1, 1994, for operational and regulatory entities to achieve Target 16 travel time objectives.

Reading through all the thousand pages of assertions and counterassertions, Angus Duncan was as puzzled as anyone would be. It would have been easier if the council could have blindly followed the recommendations of any one biological "expert." Unfortunately, the matter was not so simple. True, the Power Act required the council to give "due weight to the recommendations, expertise, and legal rights and responsibilities" of the fish agencies and tribes. But, as Duncan understood it, the law didn't say *capitulate* to the agencies and tribes. Responsibility for its program still rested with the council. There didn't seem to be any way around the council looking into these complex technical issues for itself.

When council staff went back to the original studies that supported the Authority's proposal, they found uncertainty. Most of the support for the relationship between increased flows and survival depended upon only one primary source, a 1981 report prepared for the National Marine Fisheries Service by Carl Sims and Frank Ossiander. That paper summarized a number of years of data collected by Fisheries Service researchers in the 1970s. On closer examination significant errors were found in the report.

One small but revealing error involved 1977 and 1978. Although the fish being counted in the studies actually passed a different number of dams and reservoirs—six dams in 1977 but only five dams in 1978—the report used the same total, six dams, for the "per project" survival estimates. Those estimates were thereby skewed. A bigger problem with the Sims and Ossiander report was that conditions under which data were collected changed drastically during the years of the studies. The number of dams and turbines in operation increased significantly—a negative factor for the fish; while, on the other hand, the Corps of Engineers took steps to improve bypass conditions at the dams—a positive factor. The Fisheries Service data may have also been affected by ever-increasing numbers of predators in the main-stem reservoirs and by the increasing percentage of hatchery fish among the juvenile migrants. Hatchery fish survive migration often at lower rates than wild fish.

Such developments presumably affected the calculations of fish survival through the dams, and yet bore little relation to flow. As a result, considerable doubt was cast on whether the relationships describing travel time and survival were exact.

Not only were the methods and conclusions of the principal background study apparently flawed, council staff calculated that if the Fish and Wildlife Authority's flow proposal was met, not enough water would remain in the system to refill the storage reservoirs. Moreover, even if the region's reservoirs were emptied to try to provide the flows, the Authority's targets might still not be met.

The uncertainties over the science made it difficult for council members to know what to do. Should they do nothing until more conclusive studies were conducted? To Duncan that wasn't tenable, either. Action was necessary.

During September, the council staff sifted through and reconciled the various proposals with their own views and made recommendations to the council. During October the council held public hearings and consulted with dozens of citizen groups, agencies, and utilities. In November the council met in Helena, Montana, and the members came up with the outlines of a plan that they could endorse. They called for an additional 3 million acre-feet of water during the smolt migration in the spring to increase flows to 85,000 cubic feet per second in the Snake and 200,000 cubic feet per second in the Columbia. These levels were near what the utilities argued were biologically defensible, but only about two-thirds what the fish biologists specified.

That the position of the utilities on a biological issue appeared to have swayed the council more than those of biologists had something to do with the uncertainties of the science. But the council had also long felt the political influence of the utility industry. Ted Hallock himself said so.

Hallock, Duncan's Oregon partner on the council, had a reputation for independence and outspokenness. At seventy-three, he was a decorated combat veteran of World War II, a former jazz drummer, and a public relations executive. As an Oregon state senator for twenty years, he had guided much progressive environmental legislation, including the state's nationally recognized land-use planning law. After Hallock was elected council chairman in October 1991, he irritated the utilities by telling a newspaper reporter that, from the start, the council had been "totally dictated to by the power industry." Hallock promised a "golden era" free from domination by the industry.

At the December meeting, the council was supposed to complete its program amendments on fish passage. The members had heard from hundreds of people and had worked through two preliminary versions of the amendments they wanted to make. They were ready to conduct a final review and vote. Angus Duncan prepared himself for a showdown on flows.

He knew it would be difficult to obtain increased flows for fish migration if the discussion revolved around costs to the utilities. It seemed to him the way the council talked about costs was fundamentally skewed against the fish. The burden of proof was placed on the fish to justify their getting more water, and more water was consistently seen by the utilities as a cost. In the salmon crisis, however, options were being eliminated—living beings were falling toward extinction. In such a case the burden of proof logically should be placed upon those who wanted to eliminate options. So the hydropower interests should be required to explain why they could *not* provide water for fish. The burden of proof should be on them.

Pure logic would dictate such a process, but Duncan didn't expect the council members to suddenly all become philosopher kings. Nonetheless, he hoped that by presenting a clear argument he might change some attitudes and, perhaps, some votes.

At the meeting at council headquarters, the members went one-by-one through the language of some 170 amendments to their draft plan. Many amendments sparked little discussion and needed only the experienced hand of Hallock to steer members to vote and move on. Others were guaranteed to be the scene of pitched battles.

Duncan sat at the far left of Hallock, the chairman, along the curved conference table. John Brenden of Montana sat at the far right. It probably wasn't deliberate, but the placements seemed appropriate. Duncan and Brenden couldn't have been more opposite.

Brenden was a real estate investor and an operator of a wheat ranch in the remote northeastern part of his state—Big Sky country. He didn't much care to rein himself in. He said what was on his mind, and not much of it sounded like it came out of Harvard in the 1960s. He had chaired the Montana Republican Party and cochaired Stan Stephens's campaign for governor in 1988. He took his seat on the council as a plum for getting Stephens elected.

The showdown between Brenden and Duncan came as the council considered three alternative approaches to providing flows in the mid-Columbia. The alternatives described the amounts of water to be provided for fish migration, based on a fifty-year period that was modeled on the previous fifty years' experience in the Northwest. The model forecast thirty wet years and twenty dry ones, eight of those catastrophically dry.

The alternatives were known in shorthand by the number of millions of acre-feet of flow from storage reservoirs that they provided: "100–80," "90–80," and "90–70." The important difference between the options was that they gave more (100–80) or less (90–70) water to the fish in certain dry years. Duncan favored the 100–80 option and he attempted to convince skeptical council members from Washington and Montana that the utilities could afford his option, and the fish could not afford to be without it. The other options provided less water.

"They take it from the driest of those years," he emphasized. "It is clearly a trade-off of dollars saved for the power system for water not provided to the fish, when they need it.

"This is about as clear a trade-off of water for fish for cost to the power system as we're likely to be presented today," he said again.

Brenden wasn't going to have any of it, and he requested permission to speak.

"Mr. Chairman, I would hope that my colleagues would vote this down. Because here we go again; we're trying to create nirvana for fish, so that they don't have to suffer any pain. And I don't know any segment of society or anything else that has nirvana year after year after year.

"Myself," Brenden continued, "I think 90–80 is too high and I'm going to talk to my governor about 90–70. There are times when fish and wildlife are going to have to suffer just like humans.

"I'll go back to one illustration. I'd like to be protected from drought every year as a farmer. But that isn't possible. So I don't think we can create nirvana for fish or any other fauna or person either."

If Brenden had been a steer, Duncan looked like he would have made hamburger out of him. Brenden was impossible, the Oregon Democrat reminded himself all over again. The Ronald Reaganism of "here we go again," or the deliberately contemptuous way he pronounced "nur-vanna," or the preachy "there are times when fish and wildlife are going to have to *suffer*"!

Duncan seethed. *Get off it, Brenden, why do you think we're here? What do you think they've been doing?*

He seethed, but he kept the comments to himself. There would be other battles.

No one else felt the need to say anything after Brenden, and Hallock called the roll. The four council members from Idaho and Oregon voted for Duncan's proposal. The four from Washington and Montana voted against it. It failed in the tie. Without much further discussion, Idaho abandoned Oregon to vote for the 90–80 plan, which would save the utilities some money. So much for the clear trade-off, Duncan thought. He had hoped for better.

And yet, when the day's battles were over, he and Hallock and the Idaho members had won some partial victories for the salmon. Despite the defeat on the flows during the twelve dry years, the measures the council adopted for the worst eight years represented a significant improvement over current operations. Council staff had analyzed those lowest years and estimated that salmon survival would increase under the new plan by nearly 20 percent. Overall, the council's plan was always better for the fish than was the status quo.

Among the partial victories involved a new position by the council on drawdowns. Although Ed Chaney, Cecil Andrus, and many others had wanted the drawdowns to begin the previous spring, the council as a whole still wanted to go slowly. Recognizing that drawdowns would take preparation, they called for plans to be conducted by the relevant agencies and submitted to them by 1993. Unless the drawdowns were found to be "economically or structurally infeasible, biologically imprudent, or inconsistent with the Northwest Power Act," the council further said that drawdowns should begin in 1995. It might not be fast enough for the fish, Duncan worried, but it seemed to him the political reality. In the meantime, the four main-stem Snake River reservoirs should be operated during the spring migration at the minimum level needed for hydropower, barging, and irrigation. In addition, Idaho should also provide enough water to raise the flows in the lower Snake River to 85,000 cubic feet per second.

While the simmering controversies over the uses of the Columbia and Snake Rivers were coming to a boil that fall of 1991, the controversies over managing federal forest lands were boiling over. Beginning in 1987, the success of legal efforts to protect the northern spotted owl and its old-growth-forest habitats had at first worried, then infuriated members of the Northwest timber industry. Members of Congress had subsequently felt the heat. Northwest congressional members knew they needed to get the boiling pot off the stove, but the old-growth-forest crisis seemed politically too hot to handle. It was a witches' brew of environmental passions, economic fears, and management confusion.

For the timber industry, the owl represented the end of business-as-usual. For environmentalists, it represented the end of a forest that had persisted for millennia. For both, these outcomes were unthinkable. Meanwhile, the Reagan and Bush administrations seemed either in disarray on the issue, if one were feeling charitable, or in simple, bold-faced defiance of environmental laws.

Back in 1981, the Fish and Wildlife Service had undertaken the first review of the status of the spotted owl and concluded that, though it was "extremely vulnerable" to logging of old forests, the small bird was not a candidate for the endangered-species list. In 1987, the ESA petition brought by environmentalists prompted the agency to again review the owl's status. Once more, the wildlife agency announced a listing was not warranted. This decision was appealed by conservation groups in 1988, prompting yet another review, which finally resulted in a proposed "threatened" listing in 1989. The agency then convened a team to review the proposal, which delayed the listing one more time.

Because of uncertainty surrounding the management of habitat to sustain spotted-owl populations, the Forest Service recommended formation of an Interagency Scientific Committee to develop a "scientifically credible conservation strategy" for the owl. When the heads of the Bureau of Land Management, the National Park Service, and the Fish and Wildlife Service agreed, a seventeen-member team of biologists began work. They were led by Jack Ward Thomas, the chief research wildlife biologist with the Forest Service's Pacific Northwest Research Station. A recipient of the Aldo Leopold Award, the profession's highest honor, Thomas was regarded as one of the preeminent wildlife biologists of his generation. He was also respected for his political savvy.

As it happened, professional and political ability didn't help Thomas's efforts avoid controversy. His committee's report, released in April 1990, recommended establishing "habitat conservation areas" for the spotted owl. These areas were designed to ensure the distribution of the owl within its natural range, provide blocks of habitat big enough to maintain about twenty pairs of owls each, and space the blocks so as to allow dispersal of owls from one area to another. The result dictated that no more logging should be permitted on some 5.2 million acres of owl habitat in the federal "owl forests" of the Northwest. In Oregon the timber harvest would drop to 1.7 billion board feet per year, a little more than half the amount proposed in official forest plans. Even so, the Interagency Scientific Committee predicted that the protections would still result in a decline in spotted owl numbers.

The projected decrease in harvests on federal forests angered the timber industry, and in late 1990, Cy Jamison, the director of the Bureau of Land Management, responded with his own plan, calling for a timber cut in western Oregon about 69 percent higher than the Thomas plan. Environmentalists were furious, and several organizations prepared to bring suit to force the BLM and the Forest Service to implement credible owl-protection measures.

By the spring of 1991 many in Congress saw clearly that the Bush administration was not about to solve the owl and forest problems. Out of frustration, four influential Democratic congressmen decided to seek some expert advice. Congressmen Kika de la Garza of Texas, Gerry Studds of Massachusetts, Harold Volkmer of Missouri, and Walter Jones of North Carolina chaired committees and subcommittees of the House of Representatives that had jurisdiction over forest issues. They asked a quartet of scientists for help.

John Gordon was the dean of the Yale University of Forestry and Environmental Studies and a specialist in forest management. While at Oregon State University's College of Forestry, he had been intimately involved in the development of old-growth forest studies, and in 1984 he had served on a scientific panel of the Society of American Foresters which urged the creation of old-growth-forest reserves. That report was ignored by the Reagan administration.

Jerry Franklin was the Forest Service's chief plant ecologist. At Oregon State University in the 1970s and '80s, Franklin had led the efforts that discovered the ecological values of old-growth forests. He was a gifted scientist with a knack for communicating new ideas.

K. Norman Johnson, another forestry specialist at Oregon State University, had developed FORPLAN, the computer model that the Forest Service used in the 1980s throughout the national forests for resource management planning. Politically alert, he had been an adviser to Governor Neil Goldschmidt on forestry issues.

The fourth member of the panel was Jack Ward Thomas.

It was unquestionably a knowledgeable quartet, arguably the best-qualified scientists in the country to lead the study. Congress called them the Scientific Panel on Late-Successional Forest Ecosystems—"late-successional" referring to the concept that a forest matures through a succession of stages. Late-successional was a more scientific label than "old-growth." Scientific niceties aside, the group soon became known by a simpler name, one that put a mischievous light on their political role. They became known as the Gang of Four.

Their charge was broad. In the seventeen "owl forests" of western Oregon, Washington, and northern California they were to identify old-growth forests and "mature" forest areas—those approaching the old-growth baseline of about two hundred years. They were to decide which of these areas warranted inclusion in a regional reserve. They were to develop alternatives for protection of old-growth ecosystems and species, including "but not limited to" the northern spotted owl. They were to map the protection alternatives on the region's national forests and show the effects of these alternatives on timber harvests.

They were being asked to embrace the basic questions that no one else had dared touch: *What would protection look like, and what would it cost?* The questions themselves, let alone the complexities of providing the answers, would have convinced most people rash enough to consider them to go slowly. But with characteristic enthusiasm, Jerry Franklin told the four congressmen that an analysis could be done in about two weeks. The scientific panel was given about four weeks for the job.

As rumors of the intended congressionally sponsored analysis circulated, an aide to Mark Hatfield began thinking around the edges of the House Democrats' plan. Mike Salsgiver had heard from Andy Kerr that a solution to the forest crisis that did not take the salmon into account would not satisfy environmentalists. "Fix the salmon along with the owl," was how Kerr had put it.

Salsgiver was not about to ask Kerr for advice, but he understood Kerr's point. For advice, he turned to another environmentalist for whom he had respect, someone with whom he had had successful dealings before. He talked with Bob Doppelt, the executive director of the Oregon Rivers Council, based in Eugene. "What might a solution that involved both the owl and the salmon look like?" Salsgiver said.

"It's funny you should ask," said Doppelt. "We've been thinking about that very question."

The Rivers Council was different from other environmental groups addressing the problems of salmon. Its orientation was not primarily toward fish, like Bakke's Oregon Trout, nor primarily toward public lands, like Kerr's Oregon Natural Resources Council. Its focus on the rivers themselves linked fish and lands. Doing creative things just outside the expected frame reflected Doppelt's personal style.

He had years of experience as a professional river guide, and there was something sturdy and reassuring about him. He was the sort of fellow you could depend on to negotiate the rough spots in a river. But the river guiding was a sidelight. His academic training, including advanced degrees, was in psychological counseling. He had worked for four years as a counselor with delinquent kids and dysfunctional families—training, he joked, that was good preparation for politics. With this background, it wasn't surprising that he sometimes talked about his environmental work in therapeutic terms, calling the Rivers Council a "catalyst for change." As denial and stalemate increasingly seemed to dominate the dealings of others on the forest and salmon, Doppelt looked for ways to affect the "health," as he put it, of river ecosystems.

The autumn before, in October 1990, Doppelt had asked his staff to convene a national group of scientists to help the Rivers Council develop a new strategy for ensuring the health of river environments. The workshop was to be held at a Forest Service old-growth research forest in Oregon's Cascade Mountains. Among the fifteen scientists invited were Gordon Reeves and Jim Sedell.

The two of them were primed for the event by their own recent studies. Reeves had concluded the review of habitat rehabilitation projects on Forest Service and BLM rivers that he had begun in 1987, and he had come away certain of a few things. Rehabilitation projects could improve the quality of degraded rivers for fish, under favorable conditions. But habitat rehabilitation, no matter how good, was a poor substitute for habitat protection. The proverbial ounce of prevention was again worth pounds of cure, Reeves had found. But it wasn't only that preventing degradation was almost always less costly than repairing it. The dark truth he had found was that some habitat damage and loss simply could not be undone.

While Reeves had been evaluating the effects of remedial efforts, Sedell, with his penchant for historical comparisons, had been looking into management-caused changes in certain river environments over the previous fifty years. He had discovered a unique set of data collected just after World War II that described the extent of large and deep pools in salmon-bearing rivers on federal forests in the Northwest. Such pools are needed by salmon for rearing and for refuge from the extremes of summer heat and winter cold.

With help from Fred Everest, Sedell had gone back out and reexamined the same streams. He found that about 60 percent of the large pools had disappeared, victims primarily of nearby logging and grazing practices that had filled the pools with silt and sand. The best pools he found were in wilderness areas, off limits to the timber and livestock industries.

So when Doppelt asked them for advice about salmon and forests, they knew they had something to offer. If good fish habitat was the goal, both men were seeing from their research a radical, though probably unsurprising truth. No human disturbance was best.

Doppelt hoped that the scientists he asked to the meeting would be able to offer the Rivers Council something authoritative and perhaps something new. But he didn't expect what happened. In the quiet enclave of the Andrews research forest, amid towering Douglas-fir and clear creeks, the fifteen researchers spent three days, on their own time, conducting an internal seminar. They considered the best of what they knew about river health. What Doppelt heard there overturned his previous assumptions.

Most environmental protection strategies began with the assumption that the worst conditions needed to be addressed first. Attack the most polluted spots, the most degraded conditions before they got any worse, that was the conventional wisdom. What the river scientists told Doppelt was that, first of all, that approach was often very costly. More important, it usually did not buy much of lasting value. But worst of all, they said, focusing energy on the most degraded areas often allowed attention to be diverted from areas that were temporarily better off. Over time, the result was that all areas became degraded equally.

The experience of these biologists, from all over the country, gave Doppelt a national perspective on the seriousness of the river crisis. Many of the statistics he heard were frightening. More than 70 percent of all streamside vegetation in the United States was gone, they estimated, removed to permit people to establish ranches, farms, roads, and cities. At least one third of all North American fish were at some risk of extinction. In some places, the continuous deterioration of a river system had led to wholesale extinctions of river species.

On the Illinois River in that state, Doppelt was told, two-thirds of the fish species had disappeared since 1850. The commercial harvest of fish on the Illinois had declined to almost nothing during the 1980s, although earlier in this century the Illinois had been second only to the Columbia River in commercial catch. Declines of fish populations on the Illinois, the Missouri, the Colorado, and the Columbia itself seemed clear testimony to the general deterioration of river systems.

Rather than the old, ineffective approach of trying to restore the worst, the strategy that should be followed instead, said the scientists, was to identify and protect the best areas first. Put resources into *securing* the best areas, making sure they stayed that way. That, in itself, would be a huge task. Done right, it might fulfill at least some of the century-old vision of establishing salmon parks or sanctuaries. After securing the best, efforts could turn to restoring the next-best areas and then linking them together. That was what restoration should be.

Doppelt, attuned to seismic tremors in the professional world around him, picked up a clear, new signal from these scientists. *Forget about first fixing things. Think about first protecting them.* The message instinctively appealed to him.

It appealed to David Bayles, too, the Rivers Council's staff director on public lands issues. In the follow-up to the meeting, Bayles turned to members of the Oregon chapter of the American Fisheries Society, including Dan Bottom and Chris Frissell, asking them to help the Rivers Council define what a protection-first approach would look like in Oregon. Where were the remaining healthy areas?

During the spring of 1991, this group of fish biologists developed a preliminary map showing the location of salmonid habitats that were still in comparatively good condition west of the Cascades. When they were done, the biologists outlined seventy areas that they felt should be protected as refuges for the fish.

So when Mike Salsgiver asked him in May, Doppelt could say, yes, he might have something interesting to show him, and he invited him to have a look. Salsgiver studied the map, asked Doppelt and Bayles some questions, and left the Rivers Council men with the distinct impression that they were taking a direction that Mark Hatfield would not oppose. Nothing was committed, of course.

Meanwhile, Doppelt had been in touch with Norm Johnson, of the Gang of Four, who also came to see the new map. Johnson noticed an important feature of the map, that a significant percentage of the salmon refuge areas were already included in the Thomas plan's owl set-asides. But, equally significantly, about 40 percent of the salmon refuge acreage was new— acreage beyond that which would be needed for the owl alone.

Johnson immediately recognized that if the Gang of Four were to deliver on their charge to deal comprehensively with "old-growth ecosystems, species, and processes," they were going to need some professionals with expertise in salmonids. Doppelt referred Johnson to Sedell, whom the forester did not know at the time. Johnson called Sedell and asked what he thought of the Rivers Council's approach, of identifying refuges. For reasons that Johnson did not fully appreciate, Sedell thought the approach was sound. Johnson asked him if he would advise the Gang of Four, and Sedell suggested Reeves should help as well.

Reeves was flattered, and his first instinct was to jump at the chance to be involved in advising Congress. However, his first *thought* was to hold back. Was this going to be another political exercise? Would this just be another study that some higher-ups wanted, until they saw what it said—and then the recommendations would sit on a shelf, collecting dust? To his mind, the whole old-growth crisis had been a frustrating mess, and with the Bush administration in office, the prospects still didn't seem good for resolution. He didn't like much of the Forest Service timber politics he had been involved in so far. The Elk River dispute had only become the more unsavory the longer it had gone on.

Although Reeves had advised Siskiyou Forest officials against logging the North Fork, they hadn't agreed, and they had presented a fisheries model that, they claimed, supported their reasoning. When Reeves learned about this, he was outraged. The model was adapted, without his knowledge, from work he had done.

The model predicted the cumulative effects of alternative land management practices on fish habitat. As used by Siskiyou officials, the model purported to show that there would be no effect on the fish habitat from the proposed timber sales. That was a misuse, Reeves let them know. One alternative would be more or less likely to have a greater or lesser impact on fisheries compared to another; but the *cumulative* impacts model could not be interpreted to say that there would be no impacts.

Reeves complained to the Siskiyou Forest about the use of his model. Memos were exchanged, meetings held. Through 1990 the issue festered. The forest officials modified but refused to withdraw the proposed Elk Fork and Wolkrab timber sales, so in September the Oregon Rivers Council and others filed a court injunction to stop them. Finally, after other court actions went against them, and members of Oregon's congressional delegation were brought into the issue, in January 1991, forest officials quietly dropped the proposed sales.

It took some doing for Sedell to convince Reeves that the Gang of Four was going to be something different. Reeves knew that Gordon, Franklin, Thomas, and Johnson were top-notch scientists, and he felt pretty sure they were agile enough not to set a trap for themselves politically. But he still had doubts when he and Sedell went up to Portland to discuss with the other four how the two of them could be involved.

The congressmen had not specifically told the Gang of Four to consider salmon. But Norm Johnson was sure it would be fine.

"After all, Congressman Volkmer told me," said Johnson, " 'Now don't have us be surprised by some damn fish.' "

Volkmer was probably only half joking, Johnson thought. No one in Congress needed to be reminded of the uproar over the snail darter, the little fish that nearly stopped construction of the giant Tellico Dam in the 1970s.

Over breakfast, Reeves and Sedell outlined the extent of salmon problems associated with the owl forests, and by the time the plates were cleared away, all had made up their minds that the fish scientists needed to be closely involved in the process, as equal scientific partners. It was Gordon who stated the rationale.

"Gentlemen," he said, "fish are going to sell this effort.

"Few people know what an old-growth ecosystem is. Few care about the spotted owl. But you tell Joe Blow on the street that he's losing his fish, and Congress will pay attention."

If fish were to be central to the effort, Reeves felt he now was hearing an offer he couldn't refuse.

In June the Gang of Four "Plus Two" were joined in Portland by nearly one hundred field biologists and other resource specialists. They came from twenty-three Northwest units of the Forest Service and BLM, gathering in a large hall next to the Memorial Coliseum.

At the outset Jerry Franklin laid down the ground rules.

"This process is only credible as a *scientific* process," he told the group. "If there is political interference, or the appearance of political interference, we lose credibility."

Franklin had wanted to exclude agency officials from the process entirely, but too many knew information that would be important. So he warned them.

"We cannot have any sense that people are intimidated. I expect you, on your honor, to keep what dialogue goes on here, here."

For the time being, all talk of timber supplies, timber sales, "allowable sale quantities," and all the customary business of the Forest Service was off limits.

They went to work. To the outside world they pulled down the blinds. No one who was not invited was allowed into the room with the workers. As the species-protection maps were developed none left the hall without approval or without being signed out. People stayed on task, often ten or twelve hours a day.

Reeves was caught up in the possibilities. He was putting in at least ten hours a day, and on some weekends he didn't get a chance to go home to Corvallis and spend time with his wife and two sons. But he told his wife, a lawyer who specialized in environmental policy, that his involvement with the study was the highlight of his career. Partly it was the uplift of planning forest management without timber targets. The Gang of Four participants seemed liked "masters of the universe," he told her over the phone, laughing.

"I mean, the people on the ground, the ones who know the most about their forests, are being asked, 'OK, if you were God, what would you do?' "

It was enormously liberating; that was part of it. But it was more. He had never dreamed he'd have a real chance to influence national policy about the things he cared deeply about, the forest and the fish. This seemed the chance of a lifetime.

The scientists framed their report as a wide range of alternatives for managing the late-successional forests. They planned to present Congress with fourteen major alternatives in all, and options under those alternatives, a veritable alphabet-and-number-soup of options. Some of the alternatives would require substantial changes to current practices; all would require reduction in logging below levels outlined in the official forest plans.

The federal "owl forests" comprised some 24 million acres, of which 14 million acres was considered potentially appropriate for timber production. The forest plans considered 10 million acres of that suitable for harvest. The Gang of Four's alternative 11, meanwhile, reduced that acreage to about 6 million acres, some 40 percent less.

At the end of July, the long days of staring at maps and glaring at computer screens came to a close for Reeves, Sedell, the other four, and their hundred associates. The report was sent off to the four congressmen who had requested it.

After initial briefings, the report began to circulate in Washington, D.C. Top Forest Service officials there and in Portland were not pleased with the report, and not pleased with the fish element. Two internal reviews were begun, ostensibly to learn whether other Forest Service fish biologists agreed with Reeves and Sedell. But Reeves wondered whether the real motive was to discredit them. From his reading of them, Reeves saw that the local forest plans themselves admitted they degraded fish habitat and populations. It shouldn't have been a big mystery back in D.C. So when officials inside the agency started getting on him, asking him where he got *that* information, he'd raise his eyebrows and say to himself, *Hell, it's in the Umpqua Forest Plan . . . it's in the Siskiyou Forest Plan. Don't they read the plans?* It reminded him of David Bella's discussion of the systematic distortion of information—how people on the ground say one thing and administrators never get it.

As the summer of 1991 turned into early fall, Reeves heard tantalizing bits and pieces about the two internal reviews. They sounded supportive, but sometimes drafts said one thing, final documents another. He stopped worrying about it. He was sure that his and Sedell's conclusions would be vindicated. If they weren't now, they would be later. Just the same, he called Doppelt and urged him to make sure that when hearings were held on the Gang of Four report, fish would get their day.

He got his, too, in October. He had never been invited to a congressional hearing in Washington before, but on October 8 he found himself sitting in front of a row of congressmen in a Capitol Hill hearing room. He looked around at the important men in their expensive suits, and the aides scurrying about whispering messages, and wondered exactly what the congressmen would think to ask him.

The whole idea of national government was strange. It was good that people from Texas and North Carolina and Massachusetts cared about the forests of the Northwest. But to have the fate of those forests in their hands? What did they know about getting up in the middle of the night, putting on a face mask, and plunging into a river so cold that the fillings in your teeth ached—all so that you could see a three-inch salmon lurking behind a dark boulder, holding herself strongly in the cold current, doing the things required by that place, that time, that life? That world seemed all so far away, so tuned to its own laws. It seemed impossible its fate should be set by the laws of this other world in Washington, D.C.

Reeves felt out of his element, and he was glad he was not scheduled to give a prepared statement. He was content to listen to the other four.

One by one, Gordon, Franklin, Thomas, and Johnson presented highlights of the report, which covered some sixty notebook pages and a dozen pages of explanatory maps. The highlight of the hearing for Reeves was when John Gordon read the congressmen the panel's conclusions.

"The current forest plans do not provide a high level of assurance—that is, low risk—for maintaining habitat for old-growth-dependent species," Gordon said.

Changes were needed. Gordon told them they would not be easy.

"We think there is no free lunch," he said.

None of the fourteen management alternatives the panel offered provided both abundant timber harvest *and* high levels of habitat protection for species associated with late-successional forests.

Gordon looked up at the congressmen, to see if they were following this.

He had only one more thing to say.

"We think we have provided a sound basis for decisions," he said. "Science, at least as exemplified by us and those who helped us, has done what it can within the time allotted.

"We think it's now up to others to carry the process forward."

The hearing went on for three more hours, but that was the take-home message: No free lunch. That was what the newspapers reported the next day.

If Congress wanted intact old-growth ecosystems it would have to settle for lower timber harvests and fewer timber jobs. That was reality; the nation's lawmakers could no longer feign ignorance.

Reeves thought the hearing had gone well. The report itself marked the beginning of a new vision for Northwest forests, and at least some in Congress seemed to understand its meaning. It seemed impossible now to go back to the old blinders of "jobs versus owls." With the fish in the picture, no one could fail to see clearly that the discussion wasn't just about protecting owls, but preserving ecosystems. Whatever came politically of the report, it was no longer possible to pretend that the owls were the problem.

Laying the foundation for a forest ecosystem approach had been talked about for years, but people in government agencies said it couldn't be done because of the complexity and scope of the issue. Now the Gang of Four had done it. He was still amazed by what they had been able to do in four weeks. When the institutional constraints were removed, it was wonderful what could be accomplished.

And yet, for all the political sophistication of installing ecosystems as the cornerstone of a solution, the greater sophistication was in not prescribing a particular solution. They had not said there was one "correct" management plan. The fourteen management alternatives they arrayed were all possible. The choice depended on what Congress's preferences were: timber . . . owls . . . whole ecosystems. An unintended effect of having fourteen alternatives was that alternatives seven and eight would seem middle-of-the-road. The adoption of any of alternatives eight to fourteen, the Gang all knew, would be a radical departure from the past.

In the five watershed and fish alternatives, which began with alternative seven, Sedell and Reeves had outlined measures that would go way beyond what was provided by official Forest Service plans. They had been blunt about the need for such provisions.

"On numerous federal lands, many watersheds and riparian zones and much of the fish habitat have been degraded," they wrote in the report.

To maintain and restore fish habitat, they recommended a variety of improvements. Logging should be prohibited from streamside zones; the more important the stream, the wider the no-logging buffer zones. Noting that tens of thousands of miles of logging roads snaked through the owl forests, they called for either improving or removing hazardous roads. Such roads led to landslides, catastrophic mudflows, and other problems for fish. Roadless areas should be left unroaded, they added.

Finally, they recommended extending the amount of time between timbers harvests—the "rotation" period—to 180 years in certain "key watersheds." Here was the realization of the strategy first expressed to the Rivers Council the year before.

During the preparation of the report, Forest Service and BLM fish biologists had identified 137 key watersheds. These were defined as areas of six square miles or larger that contained high-quality water and habitat for potentially threatened stocks of salmonids. These watersheds made up the best of what was left. They contained the habitat of ninety of the at-risk stocks identified in the "Crossroads" paper.

In sum, Reeves and Sedell were unequivocal about how to help save those salmon.

"Changes in management of federal forests can directly affect the habitat and recovery of those stocks," they wrote.

The science might well have been top-notch, but Congress naturally wanted to know the price tag for doing what the scientists recommended. What would a holistic solution cost, one that gave what the scientists labeled "at least a medium-high probability" of retaining enough old-growth forest to ensure viable populations of owls, salmon, and other dependent species?

When Northwest congressmen saw the figures for the first time, many of them blanched. Under the report's management option that allowed for most logging but that also included the key watersheds, timber harvest in the owl region would be no more than an estimated 1.5 billion board feet per year. This compared to the average 1980–89 harvest level of 4.5 billion board feet.

Timber jobs would decline, perhaps by thirty thousand from levels of the go-go 1980s.

Never mind that the employment effects of protection would be only a fraction of the employment effects caused by mill modernization in the early 1980s. Never mind that the logging levels of the early 1980s could not be sustained. In the fall of 1991, such strong medicine was hard for many in Congress and the Bush administration to swallow.

How far apart congressional fish advocates and Bush officials were was revealed by an exchange between Jim Jontz and John Beuter. Congressman Jontz from Indiana was the principal sponsor of the Ancient Forest Protection Act, while Beuter was deputy assistant secretary of agriculture. This exchange occurred at a second Gang of Four hearing, two weeks after the first one.

Before he turned to Beuter, Jontz had queried the chief of the Forest Service about his views of the watershed and fish protection options. Chief Dale Robertson had tagged two of the watershed suggestions as "drastic." One was a cornerstone of the watershed concept—not putting roads into the 1 million currently roadless acres. The other was placing timber harvests on a 180-year rotation in the key watersheds.

The chief had asked, "Is it worth it?"

In returning to the discussion with Robertson's boss, John Beuter, Jontz was taking on a knowledgeable adversary, a former forestry professor in Oregon, the author of a report in 1976 that predicted the increased pressure to cut trees on public lands. Like Robertson, Beuter cast doubt on the benefits in salmon protection, given the costs.

"How much additional protection, vis-a-vis the other problems that fish are having, are we buying?" said Beuter, in response to an opening question from Jontz.

That was about where Jontz wanted him, and he replied, "The question as you put it, Mr. Secretary, is the cost, and we have to make some trade-offs. I have another chart I'd like to pull out, if I could show you this for a minute."

Jontz displayed a chart with a big round circle. At the top was a thin slice, showing 2 percent of the total.

The circle, he said, represented the total average production of timber on state, public, and private forests, in Region 6—Oregon and Washington—for 1980–89. The annual average total harvest was 14.5 billion board feet.

Protecting watersheds for fish, according to the Gang of Four, would cost 290 million additional board feet, he said—2 percent of that annual total.

"Now," Jontz continued, "has someone in your agency done any economic studies of what the costs of *not* protecting fish are, just in attorney's fees for you when you have to go to court . . . Have you done any studies of the economic impact of not protecting fish?"

Beuter now could see the lure. He told Jontz, "I'm not sure what kind of a conversation we're having. You're asking if I've advocated one or another of their alternatives. I haven't talked about them at all. If we want to protect fish, to the extent shown, we certainly want to consider those options."

Jontz was not going to let him get away so easily.

"Is that too high a price to pay, 290 million board feet," he continued, "for maintaining the viability of fish populations and all the attendant benefits . . ."

"Those are the questions we have to ask the people who live in the region who are going to be affected by it," Beuter snapped back.

The hook was set. Jontz let out some line.

"Well, it seems to me that the law, with regard to maintaining viable populations of species, doesn't say 'balance.' It doesn't say 'maybe.' It says 'do it.' It's a requirement. Your own scientists came forward and recommended to us what they consider to be reasonable prospects for maintaining viable populations," Jontz continued. "And I want to know on what grounds you dismissed those recommendations."

"On the grounds," said Beuter, struggling, "of the multiple-use charter of the national forests, in which we are required to have a balance."

Jontz tightened up and cited the law, the National Forest Management Act.

"NMFA says, 'maintain viable populations,' period. It doesn't say that you balance that. It says that's a prerequisite."

"Well, that's the easy thing," snapped Beuter. "Let's just walk away. If we leave, that will maintain the viable balance."

The two men scowled at each other. This tug-of-war seemed not likely to be resolved that day.

It looked unlikely to be resolved that month, or that year. When Congress adjourned for the Christmas holidays of 1991, the solution for the ecosystems of the Northwest, and the wild animals and the people who occupied them, was still somewhere off in the distance.

As Christmas approached, Andy Kerr was becoming impatient. It was like those seasonal newspaper stories about helping the neediest. Everybody wanted to feel good about their sympathy for the salmon. But who was really doing enough?

The Power Planning Council had completed the second phase of its salmon strategy, and measures such as the proposed drawdowns sounded good. But the council had little authority to make anyone follow its directives. The National Marine Fisheries Service and the state fish agencies were jawboning one another about taking "proactive" steps to help troubled salmon populations. But how those steps were helping wild fish was hard to see. Now the big national conservation groups were starting to get involved. The Wilderness Society had set up salmon offices in Seattle and Portland and announced a new research program. Talk was fine, but nothing significant, as far as Kerr could tell, was being done for the fish at risk.

At least 200 of the 214 stocks of wild salmon identified in the "Crossroads" paper were still in danger of becoming extinct—if some weren't extinct already. And yet the environmental community, the one bunch you should be able to count on, seemed to have gone soft.

No petitions had been filed for salmon under the Endangered Species Act for over a year, when Kerr and Bakke and Reeves and the others had gotten together on the three chinook and the coho. At the rate of four petitions per year, the two hundred other stocks would take fifty years to petition for. They sure as hell didn't have that sort of time. Kerr hated the idea of sitting around waiting for somebody else, so he called a meeting of salmon conservationists for February 1992, in Portland. The agenda was to discuss the next petitions under the ESA.

In a letter to the others Kerr made it plain that the question for him was not about petitioning itself. He was not opposed to the development of regional solutions to restore salmon, but he doubted that the economic interests were involved in discussions because they wanted to save the fish.

They just wanted to avoid the constraints of listings under the ESA. He remembered his experiences with timber executives, who for years engaged environmentalists in "dialogue" while they kept their mills running flat-out. The fish couldn't afford much more of this sort of dialogue and cooperation. It was cooption, not cooperation. He was convinced that more petitions were necessary.

As he thought it would, his assertiveness got people's attention. On the day of the meeting forty conservationists assembled from Washington, Idaho, California, and Oregon, and crowded into a too-small conference room up-stairs from the Oregon Natural Resources Council's offices. All the leaders from the major groups were there—Bakke, Chaney, Doppelt, Bayles, Lori Bodi from the American Rivers Council, and many others. They sat in folding chairs in a circle along the walls until the chairs ran out, and then they sat on the floor or leaned against a table in the back. The latecomers and the restless ones stood in the hallway outside with their hands cupped around their ears to hear.

A person who had dropped in from another country would have been hard pressed to see a common denominator among the group of conservationists. They ranged from their twenties to sixty years of age or older, though the largest component was men in their late thirties and early forties. Many of the men wore beards and jeans, but many were clean-shaven and wore sports jackets. There were also quite a few women, and they were not at all retiring amid the men. Perhaps the one thing all of them looked was worried.

To set the stage for a group strategy session, Kerr had invited Dan Rohlf and Vic Sher, the spotted-owl lawyer from the Sierra Club Legal Defense Fund. Rohlf and Sher were to give their views on the legal pros and cons of peti-tioning under the ESA. Rohlf had continued to bird-dog the treatment of the salmon petitions by the Fisheries Service, and he had concerns that the service seemed to be trying to make it harder to petition successfully. The agency, he said, had misconstrued its obligation under the law to judge petitions on the basis of the best scientific information available. It had misconstrued the ob-ligation by establishing, *de facto*, a new definition of species.

The law, Rohlf reminded the others, granted protection not only to what everyone usually thinks of as species and what biologists call the taxonomic species, but also to subspecies and "distinct population segments." The Fisheries Service had decided it must define what the legal term "distinct population segment" meant in biological terms, in order to decide whether petitioned salmon stocks qualified for listing.

"They didn't need to do this," he said. "For the bald eagle, the Fish and Wildlife Service decided that 'distinct population' simply meant geographically distinct." Back in 1978, when the Fisheries Service itself had first considered listing Snake River salmon runs, an agency lawyer had concluded that a "distinct population segment" was merely one that had "esthetic, ecological, educational, historical, recreational, or scientific value." A decade later, when the agency ruled on the Sacramento winter chinook, he told the other conservationists, it had still not thought a new definition was needed. But the Northwest Region of the Fisheries Service had felt it needed to go ahead with the definition.

So, to qualify now, Rohlf explained, a stock needed to be classified as an "evolutionarily significant unit—an 'ESU.' "

Around the room eyes rolled back in their heads when he said the phrase.

The lawyer gave his listeners a sympathetic grin.

"Yes, I'm glad you asked that. What *is* an 'ESU'?"

To be an ESU, Rohlf explained, a population needed to meet two criteria. First, it must be reproductively isolated. That was fair enough in terms of salmon biology. Actual stocks were understood not to interbreed with one another, at least for the most part. Second, it must be an " 'important component in the evolutionary legacy of the species,' " Rohlf said, quoting.

To determine whether it was, the Fisheries Service said certain questions should be asked: Is the population genetically distinct from other populations of the same species? Does it occupy unique habitat? Is it uniquely adapted to its environment?

The Fisheries Service conceded that the methods to address these questions would not always provide clear-cut answers. So the net result, Rohlf underlined, was that the agency could apparently reject a petition with a subjective interpretation of whether a stock was evolutionarily "significant." As the lower Columbia coho decision seemed to show, the burden of proof was placed on petitioners to prove that the population in question was an ESU, instead of putting the burden of proof on the Fisheries Service to prove that a population was *not* an ESU.

This did not seem like a great improvement in science or policy to Rohlf. But the ESU ruling did something else, he said. By focusing so much attention on the biological identity of the species, it effectively kept the discussion away from the importance of conserving ecosystems.

"Look," said Rohlf, "Congress said, right in the opening section of the ESA, that one purpose of the law is to 'provide a means whereby the ecosystems upon which endangered species depend may be conserved.' "

Battles against the ESU definition and for ecosystem conservation were not going to be easy, and not easy to win, Rohlf concluded. He urged the other conservationists to at least petition for stocks for which the biological information was good. The strategy for conserving ecosystems was harder to see.

While Rohlf leaned toward the theoretical, Vic Sher leaned toward the jugular. Sher was a trial lawyer, and he thrived on righteous combat. He had been the environmentalists' chief advocate through years of spotted-owl lawsuits, and his success there meant that the salmon conservationists looked up to him. Environmentalists tended to like their lawyers anyway. Everyone was equal before the law, which was one reason politicians and managers hated lawsuits. A single effective lawyer working for an organization outnumbered and outspent could work seeming miracles.

Sher told the salmon leaders that he liked the Endangered Species Act, but he wasn't married to it. It was a tool. To his mind, the ESA should be thought of as part of a broader strategy to make the responsible governmental parties act responsibly. He had seen how other environmental laws could be used in court to serve their purposes, and he urged the others in the room to recognize the value of the National Forest Management Act, the Clean Water Act, the National Environmental Policy Act, as well as the ESA, for achieving their objectives.

"We can kick them where it hurts most to change agency behavior," he told them. He raised a few smiles, and a few heads nodded.

Different laws could accomplish different things, but Sher left no one uncertain about his fundamental bias. Species were not going to be protected by cooperative regional plans and nonbinding agreements. The salmon conservationists should not be afraid to use the range of laws at their disposal.

Using the law was Kerr's bias, too, and as the afternoon discussions began, he showed a few maps prepared by Chris Frissell, the Oregon AFS biologist. Frissell had gathered together the information from the "Crossroads" paper and from other scientific sources and had drawn some preliminary region-wide maps. They were extremely helpful; they showed geographically the status of the salmon.

The coho map was particularly stark. It showed that pretty much all the way from the central California coast through the southwest Washington coast, coho stocks were either threatened or endangered, according to the best information. At least one reason was not hard to find. Coho required protected habitat off the main channels of streams, but land settlement, logging, and farming practices had eliminated or degraded many of those off-channel areas.

"We don't need to argue that each coho stock qualifies as a distinct population segment under the Endangered Species Act," Kerr told the others. "The whole coho species looks to me like it's in trouble.

"Why not petition for the taxonomic species?"

Why indeed not? Kerr restated what he had urged them all to consider in his invitation letter. He didn't see any reason the salmon conservation community couldn't begin petitioning right then for all ten species and principal races of Pacific Northwest salmon. Winter chinook, spring and summer chinook, coho, chum, sea-run cutthroat trout, winter steelhead, summer steelhead, fall chinook, pink, and sockeye: All of them had multiple stocks identified by Nehlsen, Lichatowich, and Williams as being at some risk of extinction.

Kerr asked them to think about attracting national interest to the salmon.

"We need to nationalize this issue, the same way we have with the ancient forests," he said.

"If the public thinks the problem is just with the Redfish Lake sockeye salmon, or the Snake River fall chinook, they won't see what the big deal is.

"The big deal is that it's not just this or that stock. It's nearly all of the coastal coho, for instance. The wild salmon are going down the toilet."

It would be nice to believe that lots of people would worry about the salmon, that Congress would take tough actions, that the agencies would do what was necessary, without an obvious crisis. But Kerr had given up such fantasies. The way to get attention, he firmly believed, was to make the crisis in the political world equal to the crisis in the natural world.

"If we start petitioning now, we could be done petitioning for all of them by the end of 1993," Kerr said. He raised his eyebrows and smiled, in challenge.

What about money, some wanted to know. ESA petitions took staff time, which was always limited; and petitions took attorney fees, never cheap. How much could they afford to do in the next year? How much could they afford politically? Petitions that covered broad regions would be sure to provoke anxiety among lots of people, and the local political fallout could be intense. The ESA was up for reauthorization in Congress in 1992. It was also a national campaign year. Did they want to give Mark Hatfield and other Republican senators an excuse to change the law? Did they want to give Bob Packwood ammunition to fire on a candidate who would support the ESA?

Broad petitioning seemed very risky.

And what about advice they were getting from others?

The "Crossroads" authors—Nehlsen, Williams, and Lichatowich—and a geneticist colleague, Anne Kapuscinkski had faxed Kerr an urgent memo the day before. Many of the conservationists had seen the letter, and because the scientists were well known to them and well respected, the forty leaders in the conference room brooded about their views. They tried to factor them in to their own assessments of how to proceed.

The four scientists were adamant.

"We do not support a strategy that relies primarily on Endangered Species Act petitions to recover salmon and steelhead populations," they had typed, in boldface. The problem, they said, was one of emphasis: part, or whole?

"A strategy that relies primarily on the ESA focuses on species, not on the broader target of ecosystems. We think that a strategy that relies *primarily* on ESA listing will fail because it focuses energy in the wrong place.

"While effort is given to protecting one species at a time (among the infinite variety of species critical to ecosystem function), the ecosystem is falling apart. More and more species keep entering the endangered species pipeline, requiring more and more effort to save them.

"Focusing on species sets us up for a task that is humanly impossible, simply because ecosystems are so complex."

Instead, the four scientists urged the conservationists to give their attention to "conserving the integrity of ecosystems." They should use the ESA only as a last resort, or "when a species is in such straits and of such priority that there is no other choice."

It was quite a warning. *Do not petition first,* their scientific advisors were telling them. Then what should they do?

Even before they received the scientists' letter, Bob Doppelt and David Bayles were troubled by Kerr's proposal. To them, too, the question wasn't to petition or not to petition. They were not opposed to petitions for endangered species. But now they argued to the group their concern that conservationists were about to spend financial, political, and legal capital without having a clear sense of biological priorities, much less of political consequences.

They might not be able to predict the political consequences, but the consequences would certainly be easier to defend if their arguments were strongly based on the best science. Which species and stocks should be petitioned for first? Which were most vulnerable? The responsible and also safer approach, Doppelt and Bayles argued, would be to complete the scientific homework first.

The Rivers Council proposed to begin a consultation with Nehlsen, Williams, Lichatowich, and other scientists that should provide answers about these priorities. They proposed to have a ranking scheme ready by late summer 1992.

Wait for better information, or petition now? That's what it boiled down to. For two hours the debate volleyed, then spaghettied around the room, getting more tangled, nothing really seeming to become resolved. By the end, a consensus seemed to emerge that the Rivers Council should go ahead with its ranking scheme, and other groups would try to wait. Many had misgivings about the cost to fish of waiting.

As they said good-bye that chilly winter evening in 1992, Andy Kerr felt only more impatient. Bob Doppelt and David Bayles felt like they had the momentum for moving conservationists in a sensible new direction.

HOPE AND DREAD

As he plotted the next steps for the Rivers Council, that winter of 1992, Bob Doppelt kept thinking about the fate of the Redfish Lake sockeye.

Not one adult sockeye had returned to the lake in 1990. In the summer of 1991 three adult males and one female had been trapped returning to the lake. These fish had been spawned, and about two thousand fertilized eggs were being carefully raised up in two laboratories, one in Idaho, the other in Seattle. Meanwhile, in the spring of 1991, fish biologists had captured hundreds of smolts as they were migrating out of Redfish Lake. These, too, were being raised in a laboratory and would later be spawned.

The rebuilding program for the sockeye was costing more than a million dollars a year, and it was only part of the management, administrative, and legal costs involved with keeping the species going.

Doppelt didn't argue with the money being spent. But it was like the nation's health-care system. Rather than investing in maintaining good health, Americans spent extraordinary sums on terminal illnesses. And just as with crisis medicine, technological novelties were part of the endangered sockeye strategy, too. Researchers were prepared to freeze—"cryopreserve"— the sperm of returning adult males, if no adult females were available in a given year. Doppelt looked at the nationwide results of the emergency-room heroics with endangered animals, and he felt there just had to be a better way to sustain species.

The General Accounting Office reported that from 1974 through mid-1991, the federal government had placed 650 species on the endangered species list. Of those, the Fish and Wildlife Service and the National Marine Fisheries Service had determined the critical habitat needs for only 105. And on the crucial task of establishing recovery plans for the listed species, the Fisheries Service seemed lost in space. Of the twenty-four recovery plans for which it was responsible, the agency had approved just seven.

The longer-term prospects did not look any better. Beyond the 650 listed species, in 1991 the Fish and Wildlife Service recognized 600 other species as worthy of listing proposals. But where was it all ending up? Only 16 of the original 650 listed species had recovered well enough to be removed from the list. No fish species has ever recovered enough to be removed.

The GAO report was only one internal government review of the short-comings of Endangered Species Act administration. The inspector general of the Department of the Interior slammed the Fish and Wildlife Service in a 1990 review, questioning whether its ESA program could ever succeed under the program's structure and funding.

In the 1980s, thirty-four known species of plants and animals had become extinct in the United States because of inadequate ESA protections, the inspector general said, and the situation was only going to become more demanding. Apart from the six hundred additional species the Wildlife Service recognized as worthy of proposals, the inspector general noted an additional three thousand "probable" candidates. The problem with administration of the act was money. To carry out the law properly would require some $4.5 billion, according to the inspector general. But Congress had appropriated about $39 million in 1991 for endangered-species administration. For comparison, that sum was less than the $42 million Congress had appropriated that year for repair of the Woodrow Wilson Bridge, which spanned the Potomac in the Washington, D.C., area.

As disheartening as the news was from Washington, the news from the Northwest wasn't much different. The GAO had been asked by Senators Packwood and Gorton to look into the costs of past actions to assist Columbia River salmon and what benefits those expenditures had bought. From 1981 to 1991, the GAO found, federal and regional entities had spent $1.3 billion on helping salmon. The single largest expenditure, $537 million, was for hatcheries. Costs for protective screens and bypass systems at the dams were another $455 million, and research alone cost $262 million.

What had these expenditures accomplished? The GAO noted a "continuing decline of salmon runs," such that in 1990 only 1.1 million adult salmon returned to the Columbia River Basin. Of them, only 300,000 were believed to be either wild or naturally spawning fish.

Some things were clear to Doppelt, reflecting on all this. Petitioning grabbed public attention, but ESA listings didn't guarantee recovery of a depleted species. Worse, getting a species listed didn't even assure development of the required recovery plan. So putting much faith in the effectiveness of the ESA was not wise, if restoration of a species was the goal.

If you were concerned about salmon specifically, California provided additional discouragement; the listed Sacramento winter chinook seemed grim proof of the limitations of the ESA. The Fisheries Service was spending much of its time weakly battling with powerful irrigation interests for control of the water the fish needed to survive. While the people fought, the chinook were slipping into oblivion. Only 190 had returned in 1991. So much for salmon protection and recovery.

If your concerns were broader, if you really wanted—as Willa Nehlsen and her colleagues had advised—to protect the functioning of the ecosystem, then petitioning for fish species one by one under the ESA seemed an even less adequate approach. Attention narrowly focused on coho, for example, would be unlikely to help salamanders or owls or the old-growth Douglas-fir forest upon which all depended. The Gang of Four analysis had set the framework for solutions based on a comprehensive, watershed approach. Doppelt felt it was time to try to defuse the ticking time bomb of the salmon and forest crises, time to try to get ahead of crises by taking steps to protect and restore watersheds.

It was time to start showing how to do it.

Charley Dewberry was a former Forest Service fish technologist who had worked with Gordon Reeves, Jim Sedell, and Fred Everest. Dewberry had assisted on research projects in the Siuslaw, a timber-rich national forest of the central Oregon coast, since the 1970s. In the winter of 1991–92 Dewberry began working for the Oregon Rivers Council to develop a project that would demonstrate how stream restoration could be done. Their efforts would focus on Knowles Creek.

The creek is an eleven-mile-long tributary of the Siuslaw River, within that national forest's Mapleton Ranger District. Mapleton is a small logging town on the bank of the Siuslaw, about fifteen miles upriver from the mouth at Florence. The modern river is broad there, straight, and shorn of big trees. The district itself is infamous among conservationists as the site of severe landslides that had blocked Knowles Creek and other streams, precipitating a series of bitter legal actions against the Forest Service for allowing the road-building that had precipitated the landslides.

The in-stream version of landslides are known as "debris torrents": masses of soil, rocks, logs, and water that move down tributaries as a unit. Observing a debris torrent on Knowles Creek in 1980 had had a strange, contrary effect on Dewberry. It had started him rethinking everything he thought he knew about them.

At that time the conventional wisdom still held that debris torrents were bad—just more junk in the river. They seemed to choke off the stream, and the evidence of the apparent choking was that you could walk in tennis shoes on the lower creek and never get the bottom of your shoes wet. The flow there was about one quart per minute. The miserably few juvenile salmon that survived had managed to find cracks and pockets in the bedrock, to which the stream had been stripped by repetitive debris torrents.

But the upper few miles of Knowles Creek were in old-growth forest, and Dewberry knew that evidence of a natural debris torrent could be found at every stream junction. This piqued his interest. Old trees would have been much more common before logging began. He began to delve into some of the history of the Siuslaw and its tributaries.

He read journals of the Hudson's Bay Company from the 1820s describing huge log jams across the coastal rivers, including the Siuslaw:

> Jeaudoin and his companion went in Course of the afternoon some
> distance up the North Branch of this River Siuslaw but finding
> the Navigation much impeded by fallen trees they returned at
> dusk conceiving the Obstacles insurmountable.

He also read through the available fishery reports and estimated that in the 1890s, before logging of the Siuslaw's watersheds began in earnest, the annual run of coho salmon had numbered about 220,000 fish. In the 1980s that was more than the total annual number of coho spawners for the entire Oregon coast. Perhaps debris torrents and salmon abundance were linked.

As Dewberry's own observations, and studies elsewhere by Sedell, Reeves, and others, gradually showed, logs and rocks falling into a stream *naturally* were not a problem for salmon. Rather, they were vital. Debris jams caught sediment behind them and set up pools above and below them. The sediments and gravel distributed over time, providing the needed materials for salmon spawning. The pools created habitat for coho, steelhead, and cutthroat. The logs in the stream created side-channel areas that protected fish during flash floods after winter and spring storms. Finally, the log jams kept the stream from forming one straightened channel and cutting its way down to bedrock.

However, from the 1950s to the 1970s the policy on Knowles Creek, as elsewhere in the Northwest, was to remove log and debris jams from rivers, as presumed barriers to migrating fish. But once removals were stopped on Knowles Creek, starting in 1978, Dewberry noted that for ten years afterward, half of the juvenile salmon in the creek were found to live in pools above debris torrents. The problem was that perhaps three hundred years of debris torrents had all occurred over about a thirty-year period, as the result of road-building and logging. As Reeves had also seen on the North Fork of the Smith River and in other streams, all the materials for this creek system for decades, if not for centuries, had apparently already come down. The solution for Knowles Creek, Dewberry told Doppelt, was to reestablish the structure the stream needed.

Over the long term, restoration would not be complete until mature conifers were present throughout the entire floodplain of the stream. Once they were back, the old trees could become part of the large wood that fell into the stream naturally, enhancing the structure and function of the stream ecosystem. Standing and live trees, meanwhile, could contribute to the shade and habitat needed by riverine species such as insect and beavers, which played key supporting roles in the lives of fishes.

To start this redevelopment process, the Rivers Council should build up the stream channel. It sounded simple, but it would take engineering and heavy construction skills. Dewberry learned about some pioneering watershed-improvement work being done in California's Redwood National Park. For the Knowles Creek project, Dewberry and other staff members also went about gaining the assistance and cooperation of the Forest Service, the state forestry and fish agencies, and the landowner of the surrounding forest lands. Together they planned to put more than one hundred large logs and boulders into the creek in the summer of 1992.

Downstream, the logs would be cabled into place and glued with powerful epoxies to the streambed or to adjacent boulders. Upstream, most of the logs would be left uncabled, so they could move and reestablish themselves in a natural manner. Dewberry's guiding philosophy was that the people cooperating on the project would set up the log jams, but that nature would build the habitat for salmon. He held to a radical concept: Let nature work.

It was radical because it would take time and test society's commitment.

But, the way he saw it, if forestry and fishery practices had removed nature's work of hundreds of years, why should people think the results of restoration would be seen overnight? Restoration would take decades to be visible and centuries to complete. But at the end there would be a truly restored eco-system, able to provide people and many other species, including salmon, with all the benefits of nature's design.

That was the vision. The problem for Doppelt and the Rivers Council was that the plans of human organizations usually did not encompass decades, much less centuries. But Doppelt felt that if conservationists were serious, they'd have to lead the way on tasks that might not show a payoff for a very long time. Part of the success of long-term restoration ventures was going to depend, he knew, on building working alliances not only inside but also outside the conservation community. Doppelt and David Bayles had begun making connections the previous fall, around the Gang of Four report.

In November 1991, they had persuaded some forty other groups to join with the Rivers Council in a letter to members of Congress. The letter urged that watershed-protection policies outlined by the Gang of Four be included in any upcoming ancient-forest legislation. The Independent Troll Fisher-men of Oregon and the Oregon Salmon Commission, both of them repre-senting commercial fishermen, were among the signatories. So were sport fishing groups, including Trout Unlimited and Northwest Steelheaders, and mainstream national conservation organizations such as the National Audu-bon Society and the Wilderness Society. Many of these individual groups had had little to do with one another before, and many would have felt uncom-fortable with other policies of the same groups. But Doppelt and Bayles had found an issue that crossed old lines.

Forming links between conservationists and commercial fishermen was essential to political success, Doppelt and Bayles believed. They felt keenly that conservation initiatives had borne too long the stigma of economic costs: "jobs *or* the environment." For too long, activities that could harm fisheries—dam-building, road-building, logging, cattle grazing along streambanks, irrigated farming—were narrowly evaluated from the standpoint of their economic benefits. But the jobs and other benefits associated with dams and logging and the other activities carried heavy costs, not only to the environment but also to fisheries workers who depended upon the aquatic environment—not to mention to the society as a whole. Everyone depended upon the integrity of water resources.

The common practice within the economic system of "socializing and hiding the costs while privatizing the gains," as Doppelt thought of it, had to be exposed for the scam it was. The issue to him was not "jobs versus the environment." It was "jobs versus jobs." In his view, long-term, sustainable fisheries jobs were hostage to short-term jobs that degraded natural resources.

Doppelt and Bayles found a ready interest among fishermen in calling attention to the vulnerability and the value of their jobs, and in January 1992 the Rivers Council issued a report linking salmon habitat protection to big economic benefits. Twenty other fishing and conservation groups signed on to the announcement of this report.

Prepared by private economists from data collected by government agencies, the report provided a new perspective. In the Northwest, commercial and recreational salmon and trout fishing produced over $1 billion in personal income per year and employed an estimated sixty thousand people, the report said. The commercial salmon fishery contributed an average $234 million annually during the 1980s, while the recreational fishery added another $930 million to the region of northern California, Idaho, Oregon, and Washington.

The $1-billion-plus personal income probably surprised many by its magnitude, but the amount summed three different kinds of economic impacts of the salmon fishery: "direct" impacts in the form of jobs for fishermen and fish processors; "indirect" impacts generated by the purchases of goods and services by those fishermen; and "induced" impacts, created by employees of each "indirect" industry spending money derived from the fisheries. As big as a billion dollars surely seemed, the report wanted to assert that the potential of a restored fishery would be substantially greater.

But any economic benefits to fisheries carried a simple message, Bayles and Doppelt told the reporters who picked up the story. The salmon jobs depend on the habitat, they said. If the public wanted to retain the economic benefits of fishing, then protection and restoration of habitat upon which the fisheries depended was essential. Since most of the remaining good-quality habitat was on public land, the Rivers Council and its allies called for protection of remaining productive watersheds in Bureau of Land Management and Forest Service lands. Specifically, they called for the immediate protection of the 137 key watersheds identified by the Gang of Four.

In the spring of 1992, the Rivers Council seemed on a roll. Its plan to develop a priority list for petitioning, its Knowles Creek restoration demonstration, its forging of new political alliances all looked like constructive actions that could help bring solutions to the salmon crisis, at least on public lands. Doppelt was too smart to assume this process was more than just begun; but he had to believe that once the public was widely aware of the economic benefits of the salmon fishery and the degree to which those benefits depended on public lands, support for changes in the way those lands were managed would grow. Perhaps the region could get beyond the endangered-species-of-the-month club. To him that seemed like good science and intelligent public policy.

M eanwhile, on the Columbia River, the solution that everyone seemed to love or hate was being put to a test. The Army Corps of Engineers had been preparing for a test drawdown in March 1992 ever since declining to conduct one following the salmon summit.

In their environmental impact statement on the test, the Corps confirmed what Cecil Andrus and the fish advocates had been saying: lowering the water in the reservoirs behind the dams could accomplish what taking water out of Idaho's storage reservoirs could not. There was simply not enough water available in all the reservoirs to achieve the 140,000-cubic-feet-per-second current that the state and tribal fisheries biologists called for. But drawing down the reservoirs behind the four lower Snake dams could provide that velocity. At least theoretically.

The practical questions, however, were not trivial. Drawdowns of forty to fifty feet would be required to attain the recommended velocity. Fifty feet was ten times the normal range in which the reservoirs were operated. Below the normal five-foot range, barge traffic stopped.

For the test, the Corps proposed to lower the reservoir not the full fifty feet, but thirty-six feet, citing too many unknowns to go further. The engineers were particularly concerned about the power turbines. How great a loss in efficiency would result from the lowering of the "head"—the distance the water drops before going through the turbines? Would changes in water flow cause mechanical problems to the turbines? Would, for instance, the bearings in the turbine get too hot?

Many other questions loomed. Would heavy flows—of 100,000 cubic feet per second—damage the spillway on the downstream side of the dam? How badly would embankments along the reservoirs slump as the water level went down? Would highways and railroad tracks along the river be damaged by the slumping?

While the Corps worried about its facilities and the effects of the drawdowns on the physical environment, users of the lower Snake worried about the effects on their businesses. As the representative of many of these users, Glenn Vanselow had opposed the test drawdown from the start.

When the idea was first floated at the salmon summit, Vanselow said it was OK for the Corps to proceed with a feasibility study, but that an official environmental impact statement was going too far. In his view, supporting an EIS seemed to endorse the test before the positive and negative biological effects were known. He wanted to know beforehand whether the test was going to make any difference for the wild salmon.

The drawdown was a precedent he didn't like. Too much was at stake, as far as he was concerned, for too little known benefit. The National Marine Fisheries Service had declined to have the test address biological questions, because the agency worried that the dams weren't set up to protect the fish during a drawdown. So the test had been scheduled for March, before the start of the spring migration of juveniles.

Vanselow and members of his Pacific Northwest Waterways Association had prevailed on members of the Northwest congressional delegation to limit the drawdown test. Instead of all four of the lower Snake dams and pools as originally planned, the test would be conducted at only two, Lower Granite and Little Goose. Instead of a six-week test period, the test had been shortened to begin and end in March. And the Corps had been appropriated $8 million to dredge the Snake River channel at some thirty sites in an effort to protect ports, marinas, and other facilities from the expected effects of low-ering reservoirs to minimum operating pool. However, there was no certain protection below that level.

Not only the physical facilities at the ports—the levees, docks, and pil-ings—but also the businesses that the ports served, such as agriculture and wood products, would certainly be affected. With the river drawn down, people wanting to ship would have to use rail or truck. Vanselow had been on the phone constantly, trying to get some estimates from barge operators, grain cooperatives, and ports about what all this would cost.

In mid-March, halfway through the test, he drove out to the lower Snake region to see for himself what consequences the test was having. As he drove along he thought again about the testimony he would give to Congress the next week, and what was at stake.

Four hours outside of Portland, and just outside of Irrigon, Oregon, was a spot Vanselow had always liked, where the roadside gave the first clear illustration of what irrigation had done for this arid plateau country. All around, the natural vegetation was dominated by bunchgrasses and sage-brush. But right next to these dry, brown, dusty places were stretches where the landscape was carpeted green with wheat and alfalfa. When he looked, somewhere amid the green he would see the elevated water pipes and rotat-ing sprinkler heads of the movable irrigation systems, snaking across the land on rubber tires.

Back along the river Vanselow found himself admiring again a vista of buttes sloping down to the river's edge on either side. One after another they receded into the distance in shadows of brown and black, the broad flat river shining a dark mirror between them. It had once been a lonesome spot, Vanselow figured, but now a small port crouched up against the big water. The Walla Walla Grain Growers had a facility there, and a small harbor protected a few brightly colored sailboats from the winds that exploded through the gorge. A sign identified the little haven as Port Kelley. No town was anywhere visible, just the grand vista of buttes.

Crossing into Washington, Vanselow soon was driving through the roll-ing hills of the Palouse, where trees were few and nearly every hillside was farmed. The slopes seemed almost painted, so regular were the bands of crops from one to the next. In the early spring the new growth looked like fuzz on a peach.

People who lived in Portland or Seattle, or really anyplace west of the Cascades, where it was sometimes too wet for comfort, were prone to forget how comparatively dry much of the eastern parts of their states were, and how that could change everything about a person's views concerning water. Where water was less plentiful, it was hard not to be possessive about it. Western water law had in fact enshrined the idea that water was property— private property. Vanselow saw that all the complex social arrangements around water rights were being challenged by people lobbying for fish.

Although he was hired by the Pacific Northwest Waterways Association to work on a variety of federal public policy issues, ever since the salmon summit most of his time had been consumed by salmon. He had been forced to ask the organization's members for extra money to hire another staff person to work on the other issues on their agenda—trade, transportation, and energy.

Vanselow usually thought of his work as an enjoyable challenge. Some-times he proposed a position on a policy issue and then brought members around to it. Other times he acted more as a facilitator, educating members to the demand of federal or state laws or regulations and helping them find common ground. But the salmon issue was a different sort of challenge. It wouldn't stay put. From the beginning he had encountered resistance; some members asked him why they needed to be involved in "saving the salmon." With the drawdown the resistance was growing more acute.

He saw that when he arrived at the port of Clarkston, Washington, late in the afternoon. Rick Davis, the port director of operations, took him on a quick tour. Down along the port's riverfront the Snake had receded, leaving an oily mudflat. As the water was withdrawn, the banks had begun to slip away at some places and cave in at others. Davis showed Vanselow a dock that had two weeks before been at water level. Now it looked like it was on stilts and leaning dangerously toward a nosedive into the mud.

Of greater concern to Davis were cracks he had discovered in the concrete footing under the port's giant crane, which was used for moving materials between the shore and the river. Would the crane pitch itself into the mud?

Davis was plainly worried about it; and he was also nervous about what bank slumping might do to the concrete pipe that ran from the city's sewage treatment plant.

"I'm really starting to sweat," he told Vanselow. "I don't know what the effects of the drawdowns are going to be. I don't know what the effects of the refill afterward are going to be.

"This is a disaster for us."

Minutes away, just across the state line, at the neighboring port of Lewiston, Idaho, port manager Ron McMurray had decided that he had done enough sweating. He was determined to make some other people sweat instead.

McMurray was the push behind a recent boom at the port of Lewiston—the "gateway to the world for Idaho and the inland Northwest," as the port's promotional brochure put it. McMurray had built up the port in the previous five years, touting it as the "most inland seaport on the U.S. West Coast"—situated four hundred sixty-five miles from the Pacific Ocean. It was indeed a marvel of modern engineering, courtesy of the Corps of Engineers, that a waterway went as far as Lewiston at all. But now the drawdown was making the port's slogan, "Catch the Current in Lewiston," an embarrassment.

McMurray had gone on the offensive. He was a born politician—quick, cunning, full of strong opinions. As he welcomed Vanselow into his office, he joked about Governor Andrus's attack on him in the newspaper earlier in the week. Andrus had said that McMurray, a native of Idaho, was politically motivated; he aspired to being lieutenant governor in a new Republican administration, Andrus said.

"Can you believe him?" McMurray said to Vanselow. " 'Everyone in Lewiston would be for drawdowns if it weren't for McMurray'!

"I didn't know I was that powerful," he said, winking.

The drawdown was taking its toll on the port, he told Vanselow. Physically, the port was in much better shape than neighboring Clarkston. But McMurray was worried about the "psychological" effects.

A wood products company was spending twice as much to move its milk-carton stock by rail rather than by barge, he told Vanselow. Farmers couldn't afford to pay higher prices for moving their wheat, they told Mc-

Murray, and he had been getting inquiries from farmers in Montana asking about the "stability" of the port. Insurance companies said they wouldn't compensate the port and its customers for losses occasioned by the drawdown test.

"They call it an 'act of God,' " McMurray snorted. That was choice. The Corps of Engineers was God.

There was no question in his mind: The Corps should compensate the victims of the drawdown. The agency had done it deliberately. It wasn't as if these troubles hadn't been predicted.

The port commissioners had voted back in January to obtain a court injunction against the Corps to stop the test, but McMurray had been talked out of it. Now a McMurray-led coalition opposed to the drawdown was gaining new members hourly. The money was flowing in, and more than $100,000 had been raised quickly. Sentiment against salmon wasn't limited to Lewiston, he told Vanselow. A lot of Idaho farmers were furious at state legislators who had proposed a law trying to claim water rights on behalf of fish.

In the long run, McMurray thought that the opponents of "turning the river back to the fish" would win. He was not terribly worried about the Power Planning Council. Its member were creatures of their governors. By the time drawdowns were supposed to begin, in 1995, the Democratic governors in Oregon and Idaho, Roberts and Andrus, would be out of office. Booth Gardner in Washington would be out in 1992, and a Republican was likely to follow him. Republicans were a pretty good bet in Montana. So the council would change. You just need to keep the pressure on them, he told Vanselow.

Vanselow handed McMurray a draft of his proposed testimony to the House Energy and Water Development Subcommittee. He outlined its highpoints: $10 million to repair property damage resulting from the drawdown, $3 million to complete emergency dredging of Snake and Columbia river facilities.

He would explain to Congress that whenever the reservoirs are drawn below minimum operating pool, navigation completely stops, irrigation pumps on some pools go dry, marinas are dry, and power production drops. The costs could be substantial, he would say. Farmers would lose a potential $300 million for crops. Lost power generation could cost up to $116 million.

Fine, fine, said McMurray. But tell them what the real problem is. The Endangered Species Act. It needs to be changed.

"You need to push that, push that, push that," he said, stabbing the air with his finger.

Vanselow nodded sympathetically and rose to go; he wanted to take some photographs of the port to use in his testimony.

McMurray joined Vanselow to the door, stopping in the hallway alongside photographs of the port taken at different times over the years. The theme of the photo arrangement was "progress."

"A river system you can't use is like a plane you can't fly," McMurray said.

"We want to maintain an atmosphere in which the free market can flourish."

Back in his car Vanselow drove down to the waterfront, and pulled in where he could view the confluence of the Snake and Clearwater Rivers. He got out of the car and walked to the edge of the levee. The Snake was way down and the mudflats were ugly. He clucked his tongue, raised his camera to his eye, and took a picture.

Later that day, Angus Duncan arrived in Lewiston, came down to the waterfront, and took that same look at the confluence of the Snake and the Clearwater. The mudflats looked ugly, the Snake was way down, but Duncan noticed that, where the Clearwater entered the Snake, a current was clearly visible. He felt good about that. A real, moving current was, from his point of view, what the drawdown was all about.

Duncan had flown out with Idaho and Washington members of the council to see for themselves what was happening. He listened to McMurray's concerns. McMurray was quite the whirlwind, quite the representative: He crackled with belligerence and unbridled energy. Duncan was sympathetic, up to a point. He knew the arguments about the costs, to the port, to the farmers, to the barge operators. The council had already agreed, in principle, to help local parties directly affected by the council program. Some help seemed likely in this case.

But he also knew that others had evaluated those costs and taken different perspectives on them. A trio of professors of agricultural economics at the main agricultural universities in the region—the University of Idaho, Oregon State University, and Washington State—had analyzed the effect of lower Snake River drawdowns on barge transportation. They concluded that the effects on grain farmers might not be large, because farmers would adjust to scheduled drawdowns by shipping grain beforehand. Anyway, only about 5 percent of total annual shipments out of the Port of Portland came from lower Snake River ports during the drawdown period.

The professors believed that fully compensating those who suffered losses from the drawdown might inhibit long-run economic adjustments. One barge company, for example, controlled about 80 percent of barge capacity in the lower Snake area. At the same time rail transport had sunk into disuse; eastern Washington alone had over one thousand miles of abandoned rail. If increased demand for rail transport were to result from the drawdowns, the long-term effect might be to make the rates charged by the barge company more competitive. So it might not be good public policy to jump too quickly into compensating affected parties.

Even without these fine points, Duncan was feeling a bit short about complaints from the lower Snake ports. The fact that Lewiston and Clarkston had grain transshipment depots was the result, after all, of a national subsidy. As he said privately, nowhere did the Bible say "There shall be slackwater navigation to Lewiston, Idaho." This was an act of government. The development of navigation features on the Columbia and Snake system as a whole had cost taxpayers on the order of a half-billion dollars over the years.

Such a subsidy was OK, in Duncan's view; it was good for people. But some of the river had to be given back to the fish if they were going to survive. A lot of people were going to have to bear some costs. But those costs were associated with benefits they had enjoyed for many years.

Where people had made investments based on reasonable expectations of government policies, they were entitled to transition time and assistance. But they weren't entitled to drive fish runs to extinction in the name of current income, Duncan believed. When ports on the lower Snake complained that the river didn't have enough water to make some available for fish, the complaint rang a bit hollow. Agricultural irrigation in the upper Snake, in southeastern Idaho, consumed about 7 million acre-feet of water. Storage and manipulation of water there led to dramatic water reductions in the lower Snake in the spring. The reductions were on the order of 20 to 30 percent of the natural flows. So severe were the withdrawals that some sections of the middle Snake dried up in the summer. So, to the extent that agriculture was affected by the drawdowns, farming interests were only giving back some portion of what they had borrowed from the fish.

The Lewiston squabbles had yet a darker side, as far as Duncan was concerned. The earlier threat to file a court injunction was part of a subversive outlook. If people started bringing suits over parts of the council's recovery plan they didn't like, it would unravel. Duncan was truly anxious about that. For himself, he was convinced that the political center he had tried to craft must hold, or anarchy would be loosed upon the salmon's world.

If not anarchy itself, at least a certain species of confusion seemed to have gotten loose in America generally, during 1992. It was, after all, an American national election year.

Political journalists like to refer to an election campaign as "the silly season," and to an impartial observer it would have seemed that some kind of brain fever had indeed spread among politicians during the campaign. The fever was noticeable whenever the topic of the Endangered Species Act came up.

"I voted for the Endangered Species Act when I was in Congress, but I was thinking of saving tigers and elephants and rhinoceroses and those kinds of animals. I wasn't thinking of the mess we were going to get into with it." So said America's top wildlife official, the secretary of the interior. Manuel Lujan, Jr., made the elephant and rhinoceros remark during a campaign appearance with President George Bush and Senator Bob Packwood in Oregon.

Lujan's next-in-command, Cy Jamison, director of the Bureau of Land Management, went further in a campaign visit to the state. "No matter how you look at it, the root cause to our problems is the Endangered Species Act," he told reporters.

Candidates up for reelection sounded the most alarmed of all. To some, the northern spotted owl seemed to have become Public Enemy Number One.

"The main issue in this campaign," candidate Packwood asserted in an appearance in May, "is who is going to be tough enough to amend the Endangered Species Act to make sure people count as much as birds."

In August, a newspaper reporter quoted Senator Packwood paring his argument down even further, to a fine point. "I think there's nothing wrong with saying people count as much as bugs," he said.

President Bush himself, in a campaign swing through Oregon, echoed the senator's sense of hierarchy. "It is time to make people more important than owls," Bush told a lumber company audience.

But the president was eager to do more than talk.

"The law is broken, and it must be fixed," he told the rally. "I will not sign an extension of the Endangered Species Act unless it gives greater consideration to jobs, to families, and to communities."

Republicans were not the only ones prone to this particular fever over the ESA.

"We're going to want to cut every tree in the area to feed our children," said independent candidate Ross Perot. "Nobody will think about the spotted owl if they're starving, except maybe to eat him."

What was one to make of this outpouring?

Well! American politicians say the darndest things! But they don't really mean them.

Something like this is the usual explanation for such talk. But the truth was probably otherwise. All the candidates were quite serious. By election time the land-use struggles associated with the spotted owl had made the bird a ready target for the slings and arrows of those whose fortunes were outraged—and for those who wished to side with them.

That the forest crisis was attributable to the Bush administration's handling of federal forest-protection laws was not a perspective Republican candidates shared themselves or wished to share with the electorate. But that federal agencies were in defiance of certain laws, not only the ESA, was a fact.

For a year, new timber sales in the west-side forests had been under an injunction ordered by U.S. District Court Judge William Dwyer. Earlier,

Congress had required the Forest Service to revise its owl-management plan by September 30, 1990. But on May 23, 1991, Dwyer ordered the halt to the sales, explaining his decision with a blunt critique of federal misman-agement.

"The Forest Service did not even attempt to comply with the congres-sional requirement," Dwyer said. "The secretaries of agriculture and interior decided to drop the effort. The public was not told of this decision to ignore what the law required.

"More is involved here," Dwyer continued, "than a simple failure by an agency to comply with its governing statute. The most recent violation of the National Forest Management Act exemplifies a deliberate and systematic refusal by the Forest Service and the Fish and Wildlife Service to comply with the laws protecting wildlife."

Such disregard of the law was not the doing of the scientists, rangers, and other field personnel, Dwyer said. "It reflects the decisions made by higher authorities in the executive branch of government."

Compliance with environmental laws didn't improve much in early 1992. In March the Forest Service released its owl-management plan, as required by Dwyer, but it ignored new information about the rate of decline of the bird. It also ignored other new information about thirty-two additional species newly identified as dependent on old-growth ecosystems. In July Dwyer told the Forest Service its plan was inadequate, and he ordered the agency to prepare a broadened environmental impact statement to explain how they would protect old-growth-dependent species. Dwyer gave the agency until August 1993 to comply.

These rulings notwithstanding, the Bush administration and its support-ers persisted in blaming the ESA—even though the National Forest Man-agement Act was the basis for Dwyer's rulings. The situation in 1992 was odd. The vanguard of the environmental movement, for its own reasons, was also dissatisfied with the ESA and its applications, and wanted changed to endangered-species policies. But private economic interests and their polit-ical allies were pressing a much more radical agenda. They wanted to weaken or even kill the law itself.

"Loggers are an endangered species too" became a favorite timber industry slogan. From the environmentalists' perspective, underneath the superficial, incorrect biology of the slogan the statement was true enough—though not in the way the loggers intended. The timber industry wanted to keep doing what they had always done, and loggers saw themselves and their way of life in danger from environmental constraints. The environmentalists argued that the timber workers' jobs had been put at risk by the policies of the Bush and Reagan administrations and by forces intrinsic to the industry—automation, historic overcutting of the forests, the export of raw logs to other countries, the abuse and collapse of forest ecosystems. To the environmentalists, the irony was that if the timber industry got what it wanted—the opportunity to cut the remaining federal old-growth forests—it would have to face the same problems of job loss once those trees were gone. And the forests would be in even poorer shape. To attacks on the ESA, environmentalists steadfastly replied that the law was not the problem.

It seemed to make little difference to its opponents that the ESA did contain provisions for "taking people into account." Under the act, only the decision to list a species had to be based solely on biological information. Once a species was listed, economic considerations can be brought to bear on the measures taken to save it, including the amount of habitat needed for the species' recovery. Indeed, the General Accounting Office reported in 1992 that fewer than 1 percent of development activities scrutinized under the law were prohibited due to concerns over their effects on protected species.

Where affected parties believed that their proposed projects were still being unduly restricted by the law, they could apply to the federal government for a special exemption from its provisions. If the exemption request was accepted by the secretary of the interior, a cabinet-level committee was assembled to decide the case. (Since this committee effectively plays god with the listed species, it has been dubbed the "God Squad.") Requests to convene the God Squad were rare, and only one exemption—to allow construction of the Tellico Dam regardless of the snail darter—had ever been granted. Yet the mechanism was available.

The clamor to change the ESA continued in 1992 despite these provisions, and environmentalists fretted. Killing the messenger of bad news would not change the message that species were tottering on the brink of extinction. A little extra negligent push would surely put the owl and the salmon over the edge. They might just inadvertently get knocked over anyway in the prolonged pushing and pulling among the parties. Nevertheless, the disgruntlement over logging declines linked to owl protection became part of a broader private-property-rights backlash, which styled itself the "Wise Use" movement. In Oregon, its main voice was the Oregon Lands Coalition.

Formed in 1989, the Lands Coalition claimed fifty-one member organizations in 1992, including timber, farming, ranching, and mining groups. Battling the ESA became a focus of the coalition's activity. In 1991 it was instrumental in persuading the Bush administration to convene the God Squad to consider exempting certain timber sales in western Oregon. The sales, on 4,600 acres of Bureau of Land Management forest, were rejected by the U.S. Fish and Wildlife Service because they would jeopardize spotted owls. When hearings began in January 1992, the coalition was an official intervenor on behalf of the BLM, and was represented at no charge by the Mountain States Legal Foundation. The foundation had been started by James Watt, the prodevelopment head of Ronald Reagan's Department of the Interior.

In March, as the Northwest awaited a ruling from the God Squad, the debate over endangered species had become so inescapable a topic of public discussion that it was ripe for a television talk show. In Portland's case that fixture of modern American political life was the locally produced *Town Hall*—a name probably intended to evoke images of the old town meeting where everyone had a chance to be heard. Many participants were indeed invited. In practice, though, the show was more like a debate with a stopwatch. The idea seemed to be that speed stripped people's ideas down to their emotional core.

For the installment titled "Who's Endangered Next?" Andy Kerr and Valerie Johnson had been particularly invited, since they were widely recognized as the main spokespersons of their opposing camps. Surely, the producers sensed, they would crystallize and dramatize the debate.

Kerr was riding a wave of notoriety that seemed to generate its own froth whenever he appeared in public. He had become a public character, a favorite of the news media. Reporters had great fun with his appearance, comparing his receding hairline to a clear-cut in a forest, and noting his facial resemblance, with his beard and hooked nose, to a spotted owl. To which Kerr would reply with mock umbrage, "That really ruffles my feathers."

His quotability made him good material, but it also ran the risk of graduating him from environmental point man to scapegoat, and just maybe to martyr. One timber industry bumper sticker read, "Kiss My Ax, Andy." A year before, at a public meeting, one logger threatened to kill him if he didn't leave. An *Oregonian* story called him the industry's "most hated man in Oregon." *The Lake County Examiner*, a small southern Oregon newspaper, went further, labeling him "Oregon's version of the Anti-Christ."

To all of which Kerr responded in deadpan. To the irate logger he said, "It's fun to want to blame me and kill me, but the change is coming anyway." About Oregon's congressmen he was fond of saying, "To expect the Oregon congressional delegation to deal with the ancient-forest issue would be like expecting the Mississippi delegation to solve segregation in 1959." He had a certain Oregon vernacular sense of the truth—thumbs in the suspenders, head cocked to the side, a smile emerging at the sound of foolishness.

Valerie Johnson was supposed to shake up Kerr and his friends. As chair of the Oregon Lands Coalition, she had gained a reputation as a clever spokeswoman. The daughter and granddaughter of southern Oregon mill owners, Johnson, nicely dressed and well spoken, brandished the flag of family and community values while decrying environmentalists as the real "special interests," self-serving and socially destructive in their actions.

When the *Town Hall* show began she was the first to speak, and she wasted no time launching into the coalition's critique of the Endangered Species Act.

"The original intent of the ESA," Johnson asserted, "was to raise the conscious level of our society to not deliberately and willfully push species to extinction.

"But unfortunately those who would use the ESA as a means to lock up all of our resources and eliminate human uses and human benefits have pushed it to such a radical end that it's no longer workable."

She did not seem impressed by arguments that the salmon might represent part of a billion-dollar industry in the region, and that preserving that economic activity and those communities dependent on it meant preserving the genetic diversity of the fish—through the ESA, if necessary. There was entirely too much talk about the needs of other species, she countered.

"Human beings are also animals who need food, clothing, and shelter, and so 'balance' is the key word here. Balance is the word we should be repeating over and over and over."

While the moderator, Jack Faust, asked if anyone disagreed with the concept of "balance," Johnson slipped in her next point.

"Let's talk about how we access resources which are the source of every new dollar in the economy and the source of every commodity that we human beings need. The environment is not separate from us. We are an integrated world. We are an integrated ecosystem globally. And *their* rhetoric about how we have to be concerned strictly with the ecology of this and somehow make people aliens is absurd. We can't continue this approach."

Faust turned to Andy Kerr. "Valerie Johnson says you are denying people access to the benefits of their environment. How do you respond to that?"

"Short term versus long term," said Kerr, not to be outdone for brevity.

"What do you mean?"

"If the timber industry had been here a hundred years earlier, or the National Cancer Institute a hundred years later, we wouldn't have knowledge of the Pacific yew—a 'weed species,' so called, that grows in the old-growth forests," said Kerr. "So it is self-interest on all sides; just that environmentalists take a longer-term point of view.

"These people are sincerely frustrated," Kerr continued, "but the timber industry isn't up against an owl, it's up against an ocean. The rich are getting richer and others are being left behind, and rather than talking about equity, justice, and fairness for us as a species, they're taking it out on the poor owl or the poor salmon.

"*Their* problem," Kerr said, "is overcutting. Their problem is log exports. Their problem is the economy is changing like it is for auto workers."

Johnson would have none of that argument, that loggers were anachronisms, the whalers of the 1990s.

"Their agenda," she shot back at Kerr and the other environmentalists, "is social and economic control.

"They want to limit the resources to a minimum number of people. They will claim that their values—that the worship of the earth and the natural environment—deserves a ranking above the consideration of the majority of people."

Again, Faust asked Kerr for a response, and again Kerr tried to sound temperate.

"Environmentalists are interested in human self-interest. I want to be around, and I want generations to come to be around, and the way we're behaving, with holes in the ozone layer, the greenhouse effect, and with species die-offs at massive rates, we're not going to be. Environmentalists don't want to go back to the Stone Age. We're trying to prevent us from going *forward* to another one."

So the back-and-forth went, with many other guests chiming in, until the end when Johnson was invited to make a final comment. She emphasized her main theme.

"We'll have balance when we recognize that there are more natural laws at work here than just the environment. The other natural law is the economy. We've got to balance both those natural laws."

Faust nodded to Kerr for reply.

Kerr had heard the "balance" argument before, so many times that during one of his evening baths, when he dreamed up and tried out his one-liners, he had thought of the Bible.

"Isaiah 5:8," Kerr said now to the studio audience and to the television camera.

" 'Woe unto those who join house to house and field to field with no place to dwell alone in the midst of the earth.'

"The balance we must strike," he said, "is not between the parts of this generation but with the generations to come. And we're not leaving them any legacy."

He looked toward the monitor, flashed his trademark ironic smile, and delivered his favorite aphorism.

"Environmentalists may be hell to live with," he said, "but we make great ancestors."

To a sputtering of applause for Kerr, Faust wrapped up the show. There wasn't much agreement between the camps, he said, so government would likely have to step in and solve the problem.

Outside the studio, Kerr felt tired. He had scored some points, but he hated having to waste energy on the "Wise Use" movement.

Gifford Pinchot had started this business that conservation was "wise use." But "wise" did not seem part of the "Wise Use" agenda to Kerr. "Use"—old-fashioned, unregulated—did. What was new about the self-styled "movement" was its use of public-relations techniques.

What was it that Johnson had said about the economy? That it's a "natural" law? It didn't make any sense as a statement. "Natural" did make sense as a word to appropriate. "Natural" was good. Forward-looking Americans liked "natural."

Appropriation and twisting of terms seemed to be the "Wise Use" game. It was more of the same old topsy-turvy name-game world of public relations, the same world where a multinational manufacturer of weapons systems and nuclear reactors styles itself as bringing "good things to life," and a giant timber-cutting firm becomes a "tree-growing" one. Kerr was sick of it. It made him dizzy. In a world where words flopped around, people lost the ability to think clearly. No wonder that government was called in to resolve problems. They said what words would mean.

Mark Hatfield was himself thinking over what "endangered species" should mean that spring of election year. He was not facing election at this time, so he had a bit more leisure to reflect on such questions, and he was troubled about the Endangered Species Act. He had introduced the legislation in 1972, although it failed that year because Congress couldn't decide whether to include protections for plant life. Hatfield cosponsored the bill that passed (and which included plants) in 1973. So he felt a kinship to the ESA.

But he felt strongly that the law was being misused by what he considered extremists, people like Andy Kerr. He had a definition for the extremists. To him, they were people who proved their commitment to the environment by being dedicated to no utilization of resources.

The endangered-species law was up for reauthorization in 1992, and Hatfield was convinced that it had to be "fine-tuned." But given the election year and the unwillingness of legislators standing for election to grapple with a controversial law, he knew it would not be reauthorized that year. He would battle to keep the act funded through the appropriations process, and he was prepared to see funding for an additional year if it meant getting a consensus on the new law that was moderate and reasonable, from his point of view.

What seemed moderate to him was a reconsideration of the way the law defined "species." He was not at all sure that considering subspecies and population segments was a good idea. Protecting every chinook run, protecting every variety of owl, those things weren't part of his original expectation for the law, and they had to be looked at anew.

Personally, he was offended. When Congress had said, during the early debates over the law, that wildlife is of "incalculable value," he assumed everybody thought human life was, too. Now he thought that perhaps Congress would have to go back and spell out that "*human* life and wildlife *are* of incalculable value."

He thought of the costs. The financial costs of saving the listed salmon alone were in the billions. The Army Corps of Engineers predicted that modifications to the dams to allow annual drawdowns of the Snake River reservoirs would cost upward of a billion dollars and take years to accomplish.

But the financial costs were only part of Hatfield's calculus. He thought of himself as someone who worried about the human costs. He worried about the ripple effect of job loss and homelessness and community instability. Mark Hatfield worried, and the thought kept coming back. The Endangered Species Act had to be better balanced.

B*alance.*

The word was maddening. It had the ability to conceal or confuse more than it did to clarify. Not only Valerie Johnson and Andy Kerr spoke of balance and meant different things. The Republican president and the Democratic vice-presidential candidate, who had titled his book *Earth in the Balance*, demonstrated the same split when they spoke about the environment, the economy, and "balance." If nothing else, the frequent use of the word did reveal that it had become the touchstone of a society that, for all its differences, apparently shared a common perception that "balance" was a quality lacking in its world, and a quality desired.

In September the Northwest Power Planning Council completed its own attempt at striking a balance, its much-discussed salmon strategy. The negotiations had been precarious all along, and on the day the members were scheduled to vote on the final program, agreements almost came unglued. The Montana representatives wanted some provisions that the Oregon and Idaho members couldn't live with. A deal was finally worked out that reconciled almost everyone. When the vote came on adopting the program, seven voted for it. Only John Brenden of Montana voted against it.

The culmination of two years of public tinkering, the region's vehicle to carry salmon into the future had a partly aluminum engine and ran on a mixture of water and good will. How far it would go was anybody's guess.

The council put the best shine on it that it could. Always savvy in its own public relations, the council issued its report in two models, a one-hundred-page formal report, bristling with directives to those who needed to implement the program, and a stripped-down summary with stylish drawings, intended for the general public. It was crucial to have the public on board.

"We can rebuild salmon populations in the Columbia Basin if we act quickly, carefully, and cooperatively," the council's report summarized. "And we can accomplish this goal without eliminating other uses of the river, or jeopardizing our efficient and economical supply of electricity."

The council established as its goal a doubling of Columbia Basin adult salmon populations. The council had proposed the same goal before, but this time it added that the doubling should not diminish the biological diversity of the salmon that remained in the basin. For the council, it was hard to overestimate the significance of this addition. It was nothing short of revolutionary. It was substantially the result of the efforts of Willa Nehlsen.

As Nehlsen had been obliged to turn her attention away from identifying endangered stocks, she had focused her attention on conserving the genetic diversity of the basin's salmon. As coordinator of the council's salmon and steelhead research, she had convened the most knowledgeable fisheries geneticists from around the country to see if they could synthesize their work and make it understandable to the council. Early on, this committee had agreed that in order to achieve sustainable salmonid production it was essential to "maintain genetic resources of salmon and steelhead . . . with no avoidable and irreversible losses of genetic diversity." That concept was finally embraced by the council as part of its fundamental goal.

The council's fish supporters, Ted Hallock and Angus Duncan in particular, were pleased with the clarification of the goal. In the past the regional planning group had just wanted to double the runs without distinguishing between hatchery and wild fish. Now they recognized that the only real guarantee of fish over the long term was preserving the genetic material left in the region, material that resided primarily in wild fish. The historic indifference to wild fish was being recognized and asked to be corrected. Wild-fish advocates, Bill Bakke among them, were encouraged by the change.

The rest of the plan described the measures needed, both immediate and longer-term, to reach the goals. There were more than one hundred new measures, directed at what insiders had come to call the "four h's"—harvest, hatcheries, habitat, and hydropower. Among the notable measures were interim targets for rebuilding the Snake River salmon listed under the Endangered Species Act. The targets were runs of fifty thousand spring chinook, twenty thousand summer chinook and one thousand fall chinook. The plan also called for increased flows in the Snake River during spring migration to reduce the travel time of juvenile salmon. Drawdowns of Snake River reservoirs were still scheduled to begin in 1995 unless "infeasible," "imprudent," or "inconsistent with the Northwest Power Act."

On hatcheries, the council hedged its bets. The members wanted an audit of hatchery practices throughout the region, citing the need to improve the practices so that hatchery-bred fish were better able to survive in the wild and did not harm naturally spawning fish. At the same time the council also called for evaluation of a different sort of hatchery production in which hatchery fish would be bred to supplement diminished wild populations. These fish would be genetically compatible, presumably, with the wild stocks and would be released into streams early in their lives, to adapt naturally. The Indian tribes were particularly keen on supplementation, and most politicians were sensitive to their desires. However, the effectiveness of such supplementation was unclear, and the council prescribed close monitoring of efforts.

The council also directed more attention to watersheds. They said that salmon rebuilding actions should "take a watershedwide approach to habitat and production improvements." How exactly such a watershed approach should operate was not detailed, only that it should be "cooperative" and "involve local landowners and governments." Still, the council seemed almost daring in advancing the idea of managing the region's natural resources on a watershed basis.

With so many parties affected by the plan, no one at the council was surprised that hardly anyone greeted it with open arms. The environmentalists most concerned about the listed Snake River salmon were discouraged that the council did not support greater flows for the Snake River juveniles. Dan Rohlf, for one, was depressed. The council had again ignored the flow recommendations made by the region's fisheries agencies and tribes for over a decade. To him, it just looked as if the council finally found the issue too difficult and too controversial to deal with. All he could hope was that the consultations required by the ESA between the Fisheries Service and the hydropower operating agencies would result in better flows.

Angus Duncan knew that the actions the council prescribed for 1992 through 1994 weren't by themselves going to recover the listed upriver runs, but he was inclined to see the new strategy as a good beginning. The council's call for an 85,000-cubic-feet-per-second flow in the Snake River during the spring migration would cost the hydroelectric utilities revenues of up to about $70 million per year. In the worst case the total costs could be over $200 million per year.

Duncan thought he had done about as well as he could with the plan. He continued to worry about the package as a whole, not the individual pieces. He worried most that various players—the fish advocates, utilities, port districts, farmers, whoever—would decide, like the Port of Lewiston had, that they did not like what the council plan did for or to their interests, and they'd ignore, challenge, or resist the strategy. The federal and state agencies might follow suit. Once the Corps of Engineers or the BPA began backing away from parts of the council's plan that their constituents criticized, then fishermen and their management agencies would head for the exits just as fast. When that started, Duncan worried that the region would be basically with the fish where it was with the owls and the timber industry. Only the salmon crisis would be much, much bigger.

Stalemate on the salmon would be a disaster, he felt. The river users would suffer, the region would suffer, and after a little while, the fish would just disappear. Duncan believed his job was to help avoid such a collapse of public cooperation. The council's statutory authority to compel other agencies was limited, so the plan was really only as good as the cooperation it received. Duncan was determined to be as effective a politician as he knew how.

Still, he wanted to be clear that the old ways of balancing interests were out of joint with the times. He took all the opportunities he could to promote the council's program, and in a speech at the National Governors Conference in October 1992, he tried, once and for all, to explain what was wrong with the old hobby-horse of "balance" that the private economic interests perpetually wanted to ride.

" 'Balance' is a word that sounds pretty good, but here it's profoundly wrong," Duncan told the governors.

"It relies on a notion of natural resources as a pie that can be sliced into ever-thinner pieces to accommodate new people and their always growing demands. With each redivision—a little more water to power, a little more to irrigation—what remains to support other species diminishes."

True balance, he wanted to say, was obtained not by preserving the old shares in a shrinking pie, but by telling some people with plates that they'd already had seconds. Others were still waiting to be served.

The old-style balancing act, he continued, "reached its inevitable, predictable end in the Columbia Basin when those runs whose share had declined below a threshold value began to fail.

"Unless we restore to them a share that will sustain them, as a species, over generations, they will not recover. And where biology can give us no precision as to the amount of that share, the benefit of the doubt at the margin must go to the fish, the burden of proof to other users.

"Our failure to establish and respect these thresholds condemns us to a string of heroic but futile and frustrating rescue attempts. Natural systems don't survive on smaller and smaller shares, in the name of 'balance.' At some point they shut down."

That was what Duncan had learned from biology, that the realpolitik of "balance" was at odds with the real biological principles of thresholds.

The way his mind worked, he had tried to apply the same insight to the social inequities caused by the salmon decline.

The prevailing social solution of taking a little from everyone seemed unimaginative and unhelpful. The creative task was in keeping people from slipping beneath essential economic thresholds. So Duncan turned his attention to commercial salmon fishermen. They were the ones vulnerable to additional restrictions, for two reasons. Unlike farmers or utility executives their jobs *obviously* involved catching and killing fish, some of which were of endangered or threatened populations. And on the scale of electrical utilities, farmers, port districts, and aluminum companies, fishermen were politically weak. Because fisherman caught fish, reducing their harvest should make some sort of difference, and the council had had few qualms about calling for harvest reductions.

Even though the council itself did not manage fish harvests, the agencies that did have the responsibility took their suggestions into account in developing the 1992 season. The season that resulted was overall the most restricted one ever for most Northwest salmon fishermen, and they were not happy.

Oregon and Washington's two main groups of commercial salmon fishermen were the trollers, who fished the ocean with lines, and the net fishermen, who worked the Columbia River. In both states, Indian and non-Indian fishermen had separate fishing locations and seasons. On the river, for instance, non-Indians fished the first 140 miles to Bonneville Dam; Indians fished the next 130 miles to McNary Dam, at Umatilla, Oregon. By the summer, all of them, trollers and netters, felt the pinch of harvests designed to protect listed and other weak salmon stocks.

Offshore trollers were on their way to their second-worst season on record.

Oregon trollers' catch was limited to about 300,000 fish, down 80 percent from a 1970–80 average of 1.5 million salmon. Along with the decline in numbers came a precipitous loss in income, down some 88 percent over the same period. But even the plight of the trollers paled by comparison with that of the lower Columbia River gill-netters. Since the gill-netters were the first in line in the river, getting salmon past them was important, and their harvests must be restricted. While the Oregon trollers might expect their catch to be only half that of the year before, the gill-netters were looking at more like a quarter, or less. Duncan tried to soften the blow of the restrictions by building some compensation into the council's program.

He figured that the utilities would find it less expensive to increase adult spawners by paying fishermen not to catch the fish than by releasing water at the dams. He was right. One utility study found that the cost of reducing by half the commercial gill-net harvest on chinook would be about $4.7 million per year, about one-tenth to one-fiftieth what the utilities were expecting to pay yearly for increased river flows. Paying the fishermen not to fish seemed comparatively cheap. Duncan floated the idea of fish license lease-backs.

Duncan thought he had found a nice interim arrangement. It seemed to help the fish, the utilities, and the lower river fishermen; and the utilities would pay. The deal seemed like a model for the kind of cooperation he was trying to foster. The test would be whether all the parties bought it.

When gill-netter Jim Hogan became involved in discussions about the deal in the spring, he supposed that the arrangement would take his finances into account well enough. But like other fishing industry leaders, he was still wary of it. The way he saw it, it didn't seem to take his life into account.

Hogan looked like he was born to be a fisherman. Tall, strongly built, with a salt-and-pepper beard and weathered face, the forty-eight-year-old had the bearing of a man who preferred to work outside and often worked by himself. He was reticent and soft-spoken, and didn't talk much unless he had something to say. He smiled easily, and thought, in general, he had much to smile about.

Although he looked like he was born to gill-netting, he had come to it by choice. He had grown up near Portland, in Oregon City, where the falls of the Willamette River generated hydropower for factories, and he had gone to work in the Crown Zellerbach paper mill near there, working a machine eight hours a day. More often than not he worked the graveyard shift, and he had grown to dislike the repetitive work in the windowless, noisy room.

He had his first taste of the gill-netter's trade when he took up with a young woman who was the daughter of a Finn fisherman. He had gone out on the river with her relatives back then in 1972, and he was hooked. Hogan couldn't believe people could work in such a beautiful environment and get paid for it. He had moved to the river, to Clatskanie, married the fisherman's daughter, and in 1979 made the break from mill work for good. There were good fishing years and bad fishing years—more of them bad than good recently—but "the worst day fishing is better than the best day working." He had to smile at that saying. There was truth enough about it in his own life.

Clatskanie was a small town about midway between Portland and Astoria along that stretch of the Columbia where the river meanders through small islands and backwater sloughs. The town's name came from the Indian word *tlats-kani*, meaning a trail alongside a stream. Hogan's daily commute to work took less than ten minutes from the main intersection in Clatskanie, the one with the stoplight.

Driving north toward the river, it was only a couple of minutes before the downtown shops, the motel, and the houses on a little ridge were behind him, and he turned his pickup across the railroad tracks alongside the mill where they made the cedar fencing. He was out then on the narrow road through the diked bottom lands, lush and green, laid out flat and open as a hand and veined with the backwater sloughs of the Columbia.

Turning across one bridge, he passed a blueberry farm, the bushes blue and green in the late spring or flushed a deep red when the coolness of fall was upon them. Turning again and crossing another wooden bridge, he passed a field of cottonwood, the new, hybrid "super" cottonwoods, which are cut for pulp in less than a decade. The cottonwood farm was laid out in rows, succinct, a kind of techno-triumph over the thickets of blackberries and morning glory that would have occupied the place before.

The truck kept on, more turns, more crossings, the road accommodating the twists of the waterways, until at last Hogan pulled the Ford into the dirt parking lot in front of the embankment and got out.

Inside the cabin of his twenty-eight-foot workboat he would drop his lunch or dinner in the fridge and take a quick look around. Suntan lotion for his face, hand cream, a sleeping bag on the foam pad, a small cookstove if he had the chance to cook, a rifle for seals. The law allowed him to shoot at seals that were taking salmon out of his nets. He didn't use it much.

On a clear day, piloting his boat down one of the off-channel sloughs into the Columbia gave him a chance to look around at the islands passing by. As sun glinted off the water, a family of river otters might slink up onto dry land. A couple of great blue herons might rise out of some rushes into the sky, the silhouette of Mount Saint Helens forming a backdrop as they glided away. It was partly all these things that made him choose gill-netting; it was partly the work, too. Out on the river, Hogan had his favorite fishing spot at river mile 36, right about on the line dividing Washington's Wakiakum and Cowlitz counties. This was near the very spot where Hapgood and the Hume brothers set up the very first cannery on the river in 1866. Some pilings, all that was left of the buildings, were still visible along the shore.

An informal arrangement among the commercial gill-netters had given all the regulars a personal, though unofficial, spot on the river. Once a man had his own little piece of river it was up to him to design his net to fish that spot, come to know the river, the water, the air, and what the wind patterns forecast. Fishing wasn't just a livelihood to Hogan. It was one of the last ways a person could make a living close to the rhythms of nature, find himself a part of the flow of the river, know the movement of its creatures.

Hogan had found the basic techniques of gill-netting not hard to learn. He carried a couple of nylon nets wound up on large reels at the stern of his boat. He had designed his nets for his spot, thirty feet deep on the Oregon end and deeper, forty-one feet, on the Washington side. They had plastic floats along the top edge and lead sinkers along the bottom, and were fifteen hundred feet long, though they didn't stretch all the way across the river. Hogan's technique was to move the boat around, causing S-shaped bends in the net, so that the fish would run into another part of it when they tried to

go around. The diameters of the net openings corresponded to the size of the
salmon he was trying to catch. The mesh was smaller for coho, bigger for
chinook. The idea was a salmon would swim into the net and in trying to
back out would catch its gill openings in the diamond mesh.

To fish, Hogan turned on the boat's motor, which played a net out into
the river. He'd let the net drift with the current for as long as he could, until
it drifted toward someone else's territory, or a barge or freighter came up and
he had to pull the net out. "Picking" the salmon would have to go quickly
in that case; and Hogan, wearing his rain suit and rubber gloves, would strain
and sweat, freeing the drowned salmon from the net and dropping them on
the deck. Still, he knew he never worked as hard as the old-timers, who
pulled the nets in by hand. The old cotton and linen nets absorbed water by
the ton.

It was a way of life that the utilities and the power council people wanted
to lease back from Hogan. He had been lured to fishing in the beginning by
its independence, but it seemed that with each year he was much less
independent than before. The fishing seasons themselves were managed by a
whole list of agencies and agreements, starting with the international commission that allocated the catch between American and Canadian fishermen.
Then a regional management council, then state agencies, and now the power
council all had something to say about when Hogan could fish. It made his
head hurt just thinking about them all.

When the meetings with Duncan and the utilities started, Hogan came as
a representative of the Columbia River Fishermen's Protective Union. Along
with other gill-net representatives, he was wary. He didn't like charity, and
he didn't like the appearance of gill-netters being set up as scapegoats by the
more powerful industries on the river. Of the four stocks listed under the
Endangered Species Act, gill-netters had fished only the Snake River fall
chinook during the previous four years, and Hogan felt that harvest was
restricted to protect the upriver fish as much as possible. If saving endangered
species was the goal, lease-back didn't seem like it was going to help much,
he felt. Even if fishing was stopped altogether the problem of dam mortalities
wouldn't be solved.

Nevertheless, Hogan and the other gill-netters had realized that politically they had to put something on the bargaining table, and ultimately a deal was struck. Depending on their annual average catch over the previous five years, by leasing their licenses for the fall chinook harvest gill-netters would pocket between $1,500 and $16,000. The utilities would spend about $6 million if all Oregon and Washington lower Columbia gill-netters— about eight hundred licensees in all—participated in the program. Participation would be completely voluntary; each fisherman would make his own decision.

Hogan thought the deal for individual fishermen was probably fair enough, when he looked at his own costs. He knew that between his fees for fishing licenses, boat moorage, maintenance on the boat, the trailer, the boat itself, insurance, and his nineteen nets, when he sold the salmon he caught for one dollar per pound he needed to catch two hundred pounds to cover his investment for the day and have a take-home wage. Given the proposed season, and given his own history, he would probably do just as well in 1992 by accepting the lease-back program.

It wasn't only his decision, though.

Part of the deal had been that once the lower river arrangement was set, the mid-Columbia Indian tribes needed to agree to also let the fall chinook pass through their fishery. The logic was that the lower river lease-back wouldn't give a biological payoff unless the adults made it all the way back to the Snake River tributaries to spawn.

The plan was referred to the fishery committees members of the four mid-Columbia reservations—Yakima, Nez Perce, Umatilla, and Warm Springs—and they were given about one month to sign off so that the lower Columbia plan could be completed in time for the season opening in September. But the way the tribes worked, such decisions meant going back to the tribal fishermen to hear their views. And the Indians said there just wasn't enough time. They felt they should have been contacted sooner, but as it was they couldn't agree to the lease-back plan. Nevertheless, they said they were willing to reconsider it for 1993.

Back in Clatskanie, Jim Hogan greeted the news with continued mixed feelings. He did not, finally, have to decide whether to take himself out of fishing. That was OK. He was still thinking about what it meant. He, too, was willing to talk about the lease-back again in 1993. In the meantime he would go back to the river, to his spot, and try his luck.

In Portland, Angus Duncan was disappointed by the breakdown of the lease-back plan. But he was not discouraged. It seemed as if parties with divergent interests were at least willing to consider creative solutions that would both help the fish and support an industry most in danger of going belly-up. Communication and cooperation. This seemed to him the way to proceed.

In the fall of 1992, another creative solution was struggling toward fruition near the other end of the Columbia River in Oregon. The outward sign of that solution was a new pumping station up on the Umatilla plateau, not far from the Columbia. The pumps would keep water flowing into irrigation channels, and those channels would feed sprinkler systems throughout four irrigation districts in this farming country of northeastern Oregon. The manager of the irrigation districts, Bill Porfily, was happy to see the pumps on line. He had had a lot of heartburn along the way.

When he took the job as irrigation manager, Porfily never dreamed he'd get himself so tied up in fisheries disputes. He had been raised on a farm not far from these districts along the Umatilla River, and for him, farming was both livelihood and a way of life, just as fishing was for Jim Hogan downriver. But Porfily liked fish and fishing, too. He was president of the Oregon Bass Federation, the group dedicated to catching the warm-water game fish that had become more common in this region of the state. No matter that bass had become more common partly because of irrigation; that was the way things were, and the sport was still good. Many of the farmers Porfily knew felt as strongly about fishing as he did. Several were avid steelhead fishermen.

Porfily didn't think of himself as an opponent of environmental causes; he thought of himself as a farmer *and* an environmentalist. But WaterWatch, they were another kind of environmentalists altogether. Based in Portland, the water resources watchdog group just didn't seem to understand the northeastern Oregon that Porfily knew, not at all.

It was still Oregon, but the area between the town of Umatilla, where the

Umatilla River ran into the Columbia, and Pendleton, the county seat, seemed as different from the west side of the Cascades as places so close could be. Water was part of it. Fifty to one hundred fifty inches of rain was the rule on the Pacific Ocean side of Oregon and Washington, but the vast area east of the Cascades generally received fractions of those amounts. Fifteen inches of precipitation was a very good year in Pendleton. It could be killingly cold in the winter and so hot in the summer that farm crops would die quickly without water. Summer days over one hundred degrees were not uncommon, though lightning storms often would break them up with a light show that people could see just about anywhere in the county.

Partly it was the climate, then, but partly it was also the manners that grew up in such a climate that made northeastern Oregon different. This was good country, with great rolling hills and the ridge of the Blue Mountains off in the distance, really shining blue in the first rays of the morning. It was good country, but demanding, and the farmers who had settled it thought of themselves as friendly people. Good neighbors. You helped other people out, if you could. Making a living could be hard enough without adding conniving to it.

Porfily knew the area about as well as he knew himself, and many days he was optimistic about its future. For years, local farmers had grown wheat and alfalfa and the famous Hermiston watermelons. But more recently farmers had begun to see that the area was one of the best remaining places in North America for high-quality vegetable production. Enterprising new growers had begun planting sweet corn and cantaloupes and even specialty peppers and lily bulbs. At three dollars apiece retail, a farmer could do well growing lily bulbs.

Pendleton was about equidistant from Seattle, Boise, and Portland. It had always been a trade center. Back in the 1880s, cattle were rounded up in Pendleton for drives to Idaho, Montana, and Wyoming. A hundred years later, Porfily had dreams of seeing new food-processing plants added to the three already in business along the Umatilla. He kept reminding himself that the area had fifteen more growing days than the San Joaquin Valley in California. When he drove out to the farmlands and saw the miles of center-pivot irrigation systems snaking over the hills, the fine spray making rainbows in the bright sunshine, the potential of it all seemed truly unbelievable.

But all of the farming was dependent on scarce water, and just about all the farms were irrigated with water from the Umatilla River. More than fifty thousand acres depended on water that was doled out by the four Umatilla basin irrigation districts. As long as the farmers had exclusive rights to the water they were sitting pretty. The problem, though, was that the federal government was giving away something it didn't own.

The Bureau of Reclamation helped establish irrigated agriculture just after the turn of the century with a series of dams and irrigation channels that sucked the river dry from summer through fall. Unfortunately for the irrigators, the federal government had earlier promised the local Indians that they would be able to fish for salmon. The government had actually not given the Indians that right; through a treaty the Indians had reserved it. But without water in the river that right was meaningless. At about the time Porfily began working for the districts, the neighboring Indians, the Confederated Tribes of the Umatilla Indian Reservation, began seeking a way to restore water for salmon and steelhead.

Many farmers felt blindsided. The way they saw it, their families had been encouraged to settle and develop the area. They had been told that farming there would be good for the state, good for the nation. But now, suddenly, out of nowhere it seemed, they didn't have the rights they thought they had. Reluctantly at first, they entered into discussions with the Tribes. Those discussions went on through the 1980s. They were sometimes difficult, but they had come to a conclusion everyone in the area seemed satisfied with. Congress had then authorized the Umatilla Basin Project, and just when it seemed that finally people could get back to business, in the spring of 1991 these couple of environmental groups from Portland had raised a stink.

WaterWatch, a group run by Tom Simmons, a former Texan who made his fortune in computers, was in the lead on it; and Oregon Trout had joined them. They had complained to the Oregon Water Resources Department about a practice called "water spreading," in which they claimed that the irrigation districts were marketing water outside their area, violating state laws and federal contracts. They charged that basin project flows intended for fish would end up going to irrigation.

Porfily and the irrigation districts steadfastly denied anything illegal or improper was being done. The charges and denials went on for months, with WaterWatch threatening to block the start of the second phase of the basin project unless their demands were met.

The last straw for Porfily was a newspaper story that ran in the Sunday *Oregonian* in October, just before an important meeting of the state Water Resources Commission. The multipage article thrashed the irrigation interests, letting WaterWatch say that the irrigators were "undermining" the project by diverting scarce federal water illegally, and also blaming the state water resources department, which "has been handing out new water permits like candy."

"Each summer, the Umatilla is a polluted sink of sewage and farm wastes": for Porfily that summarized what he considered the article's unfair tone. It made him mad enough to spit.

So when it came time in November for the state commission to try to resolve the dispute, Porfily and the irrigators were in a defiant mood. A couple of environmental groups were threatening to block an agreement that was supposed to benefit the local fish and the Indians. It didn't make sense. The way Porfily saw it, they were taking the basin project hostage, and one useful thing he had learned from the newspapers, you don't negotiate with hostage takers. He had spent ten tough years cooperating to develop the project, and the irrigators had spent a hundred thousand dollars in legal fees. And it seemed they were losing. Thanks to the complaining of the environmentalists, the Bureau of Reclamation and the state announced they would shut off the out-of-district irrigation deliveries.

The irrigators had given enough, Porfily thought. Let the commission have an administrative law judge settle the dispute. He was tired of it.

Out in the audience at that meeting in Bend was a middle-aged Indian, a square-jawed, quiet man wearing a business suit, tinted glasses, and his black hair in two long braids. As chairman of the General Council of the Confederated Tribes of the Umatilla Indian Reservation, Antone Minthorn was listening carefully.

For more than ten years, as a tribal leader and as cochairman of a steering committee that brought together all the various parties, Minthorn had labored to forge a plan that would restore the Indians' salmon. Now all of that effort was about to be jeopardized by a dispute that didn't even relate directly to the fisheries project. He wasn't happy about the strategy WaterWatch and Oregon Trout had taken, objecting to the state and federal permit applications necessary to start one portion of the basin project. It seemed that some environmentalists were like the missionaries that had opened churches and schools as soon as the Indians were put on the reservation out there. They always thought they knew what was best for the Indians.

He didn't like the situation, but Minthorn didn't see he had any choice. He must try to get the irrigators, the environmentalists, and the Bureau of Reclamation to sit down with the Tribes and negotiate. Timing was crucial. The Bureau of Reclamation was preparing to ask Congress for an appropriation for the fisheries project, and the disputed permits must be in hand before requesting the appropriation. The whole project could be derailed if the dispute went to a contested case hearing. Once started down that road, parties only tended to become more disagreeable, and any decision that was made could be appealed. Congressional support, which the Tribes had so carefully woven together, would surely come unraveled.

Before the meeting, Minthorn had approached a senior official with the Bureau of Reclamation and the leader of WaterWatch. Both men said they would enter into negotiations coordinated by the Tribes. When Minthorn asked him, too, Porfily was still feeling defensive. But the irrigation leader said he thought he would come to a meeting with the Tribes and the others.

Now, at the commission meeting, Minthorn requested, and was granted, the opportunity to attempt to resolve the parties' differences through negotiations. The date of the first negotiating meeting was set for December.

When the time for it came, Minthorn was relieved to see that the representatives of the Bureau of Reclamation, WaterWatch, Oregon Trout, and the irrigation districts all showed up on the reservation. Under the guidance of professional mediators, by the end of the afternoon the session had ended in what Minthorn considered a success. Not only had everyone showed up, none of them got into a fistfight. He felt they were on their way to resolving the dispute.

Minthorn could not accept any other outcome.

For him, ensuring that the Umatilla Basin Project was not upset by the disagreements between the environmentalists and the irrigators went beyond a protectiveness toward a project he had nurtured for a decade. He saw himself as a custodian of the Tribes' history and future, and he could not break faith with that responsibility.

Minthorn was an unusual sort of leader. He preferred to listen rather than talk. He usually seemed serious, even introspective, and it was the tribe that he inevitably emphasized, never himself. An Indian learned early about the importance of the tribe.

When Minthorn was growing up he had known some of the survivors of Chief Joseph's band. For Indians in this region, Joseph was a tragic hero, his treatment by the whites a lesson for all of them. The Nez Perce chief had led an uprising when his band was driven from their home in the Wallowa Valley, not too far from the Umatilla reservation. The band was hunted down as it tried to flee Canada, rounded up, and sent to the "Indian Territory" in Oklahoma, where many died. Ultimately, Joseph's eloquence on behalf of his people helped persuade the federal government to return the remnants of his band to the Northwest.

As a young man Minthorn appreciated the importance of the treaty of 1855 between the federal government and the Cayuse, Walla Walla, and Umatilla Indians. As he grew older, he understood more clearly what the chiefs who had signed it were doing. They had said the treaty was not for them but for their children and their children's children. Minthorn realized he was one of those children, and now the vision of those chiefs had passed to him. He considered it a sacred trust. He had to speak for those who were not yet born and make sure that their welfare was protected. There was no other way.

Unhappily, the circumstances in which Minthorn found himself in 1991 were not those his ancestors had negotiated for in 1855. Then, the tribes ceded nearly 6.5 million acres of land to the United States government. In exchange they kept a reservation of 290,000 acres, on which they had exclusive rights to fish. They also reserved the rights to fish "at all other usual and accustomed stations in common with citizens of the United States."

Fishing for salmon was important to the tribes. When Lewis and Clark passed by the mouth of the Umatilla River in 1806, they observed a large village where some seven hundred Indians were awaiting the arrival of the spring chinook. It was the largest Indian village the explorers saw between Celilo Falls and the mouth of the Snake River.

After 1855, the government and the settlers seemed to have forgotten the guarantees in the treaty. By the 1870s the settlers who homesteaded on the former Indian lands began a campaign to throw open the Umatilla reservation to farming. The reservation was "lying waste, and completely under the control of the Indians," as one publication of the time phrased it. A decade later Congress obliged settlers in Oregon and other states by passing the so-called Allotment Acts. Reservation size, the government now said, was based not on the 1855 treaty, but on the number of tribal members. Land was allotted to those members, and the "surplus" reservation was sold off at public auction. The size of the Umatilla reservation was reduced by about half.

Not only was the reservation reduced in size, it was also broken up into a checkerboard of mixed ownership. As they lost control over their land, the Indians also began to lose control over water. That process was complete in the early 1900s, when the Bureau of Reclamation built the five dams on the Umatilla River, diverting the water for farmers' irrigation needs and leaving the lower river bone dry during the hot months. By 1920, salmon were extinct in the Umatilla.

For a generation the Tribes seemed beaten, their treaty rights to fish on their home river overwhelmed by the powerful farming interests and by the federal government's limitations on the Indians' self-government. At the same time, their treaty rights to fish on the Columbia River were ignored and dismissed not only by the hydropower interests but by the state fisheries agencies themselves.

In 1958 three Umatilla fishermen, descendants of the original signers of the 1855 treaty, had had enough. They decided to challenge the status quo by fishing during a closed season. They were arrested, and for five years their case worked its way through the courts. Ultimately they were vindicated when a federal judge ruled that Oregon could not ignore the Indians' fishing rights under the guise of conservation.

The success of the Umatilla case ushered in a tumultuous decade of legal challenges to the management of the Columbia River and coastal fisheries by various Indian tribes. For the mid-Columbia tribes this era climaxed with the *U.S. v. Oregon* decision of 1969, which confirmed that the treaties guaranteed the tribes a "fair and equitable share" of the salmon. Five years later, another federal judge ruled that "fair and equitable" meant half the harvestable salmon destined for the Indians' traditional fishing places. The *U.S. v. Oregon* decision put everyone—the tribes, the irrigators, the management agencies of the state and federal government—into new roles. But in 1981 when Minthorn was first elected chairman of the tribal general council, the Umatilla was still empty of salmon.

Getting the fish back in the river was not as simple as building a hatchery and letting the fish loose; the irrigators had legal rights to the river's water. The options were pretty clear to Minthorn and the rest of the tribal leaders. They could go to court for the water that their treaty rights to fish appeared to imply, or they could figure out some way to obtain water for the irrigators to replace the water they would take. It seemed much wiser to develop a comprehensive plan to present to Congress for funding rather than spend a great deal of money in court. Even if the Tribes prevailed in court, courts did not appropriate project funds. The Tribes opted to negotiate rather than to litigate.

At the beginning, Minthorn found the irrigators not very receptive to the idea of sharing the river with the Tribes. He sensed an attitude among irrigators that if the salmon were meant to get up the Umatilla River, they could walk. But he was patient and persistent, and he made sure that the irrigators understood that times had changed. He cultivated as an ally the Bureau of Reclamation. The agency had a trust responsibility to the Tribes. But beyond that, the bureau's regional director seemed to understand that the old days were over, that dam-building was a thing of the past, and that the agency's survival meant finding a new mission.

Initially both the irrigators and the Tribes wanted to obtain the needed water for the salmon by building new reservoirs. But political support for the reservoirs had dried up, and they were told to find other means. If guaranteeing a supply of water was the problem, what more likely solution than borrowing some from the Columbia River which flowed millions of gallons past the Umatilla area each day? Gradually a two-phase plan was worked out around that simple theme of exchange: Pump water out of the Columbia and provide it to the irrigators so that they would leave water in the Umatilla for salmon.

The plan gained the support of the Oregon congressional delegation and the key endorsement of Mark Hatfield. Hatfield the politician had taken the line that he would seek congressional approval and funding for the project if local residents gave it broad support. They did and he did. He introduced legislation authorizing the project, and each year afterward he saw to it that there would be an appropriation to keep the project moving forward. The Tribes were grateful to Hatfield.

Probably none of the Indians knew that some of the motive for his being their benefactor came from Hatfield's childhood. His mother had been a schoolteacher, and her very first job, in the 1920s, was on the Oregon coast, up the Siletz River, at the school next to the Indian reservation there. In those days, a journey from the Willamette Valley, where the family lived, to the Siletz involved transferring from stagecoach to horse-and-buggy to boat. Apparently, Mrs. Hatfield saw teaching the Indians about the white world as a matter of importance.

As a boy, Mark came to know Indians of his own age at the Chemawa Indian School in Salem. Knowing about them seemed important to him, too, and he remembered vividly when he joined his parents traveling by car down the newly built Columbia Gorge Highway to see the Indians fishing on the platforms at Celilo Falls. He squinted in the brilliant sunshine as he watched the Indians throw the salmon they caught up onto metal roofs to dry in the sun.

While Hatfield saw to it that congressional authorization of the Umatilla Basin Project began in 1988, the Tribes had actually begun six years before to return salmon to the Umatilla River. It had been a bold, controversial move. They put salmon back in the river before they had agreements for the water that the fish would need for their return. But Minthorn and other tribal leaders were convinced that waiting, rather than acting, had gotten the Tribes nowhere with the government. Better to take the initiative and let others react to them.

The Northwest Power Act gave the Tribes the opportunity to begin planning for restoration, and starting in 1982, the Bonneville Power Administration funded restoration efforts called for by the Power Planning Council. The first juvenile chinook were released into the Umatilla in 1982. When the first adult salmon returned to the Umatilla in 1988, Minthorn went down to the river to see them, watching from the shade of streamside cottonwood trees as they passed upstream. They were the first salmon to return to the reservation in seventy years. He never liked to be rushed, and he stood next to the stream for a long time, happy to know that restoration seemed possible.

Gratifying as the first salmon were, Minthorn envisioned much greater returns for the Umatilla Basin Project. All of the initial salmon for rebuilding the Umatilla runs were imported from other basins by the state fish agency, but a centerpiece of the Umatilla plan was a hatchery for coho and chinook. That hatchery was begun in 1990. When all the pieces of the restoration project were complete, in the late 1990s, the Tribes expected to be adding more than one hundred thousand fish to not only the Umatilla River fisheries, but to the fisheries of the Columbia River and Pacific Ocean as well. The Tribes expected about one-fifth of the catch to come to tribal members, providing a much-needed economic boost. The value of the catch overall was pegged at about $8 million.

For the Umatilla Tribes, the siting of a hatchery to benefit their fisheries righted what they considered another historic wrong. This was the failure of the federal government to place hatcheries in locations where Indians would benefit. Only two of the forty federal hatcheries and other fish-rearing facilities on the river were above The Dalles Dam, the second main-stem dam from the ocean. Hatcheries placed farther upriver would have helped the runs most hurt by the dams and would have also helped the mid-Columbia and Snake River Indian tribes, whose reservations were there.

So many hatcheries downriver had hurt the wild fish, too. Because harvests were based on the populations of the numerous lower-river hatchery fish, wild stocks in both the lower and upper river were subject to higher harvest rates than would have been the case otherwise. The hatcheries had helped spur the decline of the Snake River fall chinook as well as the lower Columbia coho.

All of this troubled history, the promises made and forgotten, the hopes raised and dashed, stalked Minthorn as the negotiations went forward in December 1991 and January 1992. He made a point of sitting down with the parties to the negotiations and learning what they wanted. Minthorn made sure that they all understood what the Tribes wanted. At the sessions that followed, he rarely felt the need to speak, but when he did it was to remind people of the goal, to go beyond differences and find a solution. He did not preach. He was just firm and clear, and everyone recognized that Minthorn carried some kind of personal authority.

In February, after five negotiating sessions, the thirteen parties that were ultimately involved in the discussions agreed, by consensus, to a resolution of the crisis. By agreement, water appropriations for the basin project would be used only for the project, not for the alleged water-spreading. The irrigators would be allowed to request legal expansions of their water use, but they would have to ensure that fish were not harmed. The environmentalists would withdraw their objections to the issuance of the permits for the project.

The Tribes called the parties together one last time to sign the papers and to feast on smoked salmon. They met at the Yellowhawk Clinic on the reservation, where, in his remarks, Minthorn emphasized the constructive work accomplished by them all. He focused on the virtues of neighborliness.

"Friendship and good relationship has been at the heart of the Umatilla Basin Project from its initial development through the most recent negotiations," said Minthorn. "We feel fortunate to have the kind of cooperative and dedicated neighbors that we do. Together we have worked out solutions to the difficult situations in which we have been placed."

Porfily responded in kind. "The irrigation districts are very excited about the relationships between us and the Tribes. There's a dream out there I think we can achieve."

The statements seemed more than just good manners and good politics. The Umatilla Basin Project appeared that uncommon thing amid the salmon crisis. It seemed not only a successful project, but a successful process.

The project brought benefits to both the fisheries interests and to some customary opponents, the irrigation interests. The project promised to bring the salmon back from extinction, while it also promised to spare a vital industry from potential extinction.

As a federal water project, the Umatilla Basin Project seemed comparatively inexpensive. The total construction costs were $45 million for the pumping stations, aqueducts, and the related improvements that would take some 39,000 acre-feet each year from the Columbia and put it in the Umatilla. Meanwhile, the Bonneville Power Administration was investing some $30 million in the hatchery, and in fish ladders so the salmon could get over the Umatilla dams. The BPA money was also paying for screens in the irrigation canals, so fish wouldn't be sucked into farmers' fields.

The Indians probably could have forced the irrigators to their knees, if social retribution or mere fish restoration had been their goal. But they were interested in restoring the watershed as a place, and apparently they felt it did no good to alienate those who lived there. These attitudes were intimately bound up with tribal culture, personified in Antone Minthorn.

The Wáashat religion emphasized that the Indian was part of the land, literally. What was done to the water was done to the Indian. He was made of water—even the white people's medical doctors would say the same thing. The Indian was truly part of the land, and the sun, and the air of his place, and they were part of him. These things Minthorn knew to be true.

People who had come from elsewhere had to learn to commit to place. They said they loved the land, but when the land no longer produced money, Minthorn saw that they tended to leave. His people did not leave.

He believed that the treaties of 1855, which guaranteed protections for Northwest Indian peoples, could be of benefit to all Americans. The treaties promised the Indians the ability to fish, which required an environment good enough to produce them. If all Indian tribes in the interior Northwest came together and saw to it that non-Indians honored the treaties fully, then salmon would come back to the rivers again. If all the tribes went about this task in the way the Umatilla did, Minthorn believed that other users of the water did not need to be wrenched from their livelihoods. The Indian treaties could help heal the region.

Minthorn knew that such thoughts were dreams. Many would disbelieve them; others would not share them. He knew that much work was needed to make such dreams real. But those who thought they could defeat the dreams of salmon restoration by just modifying or destroying the Endangered Species Act were wrong. They would have to modify or destroy the fishing rights reserved by the Indian treaties as well.

Such changes were not impossible. But Minthorn hoped with all his heart that the trust between his people and the white people, once committed only on paper but now promised in practice, would be allowed to grow. To do otherwise would bring dishonor to the nation and deep loss to all the people. It also would almost certainly bring the end of the salmon.

A COMMON FATE

There is no final ecological truth. All knowledge is a current approximation, and each addition to that knowledge is but a small, incremental step toward understanding. For not only are ecosystems more complex than we think, they are more complex than we can think.

—JACK WARD THOMAS, "WILDLIFE IN OLD-GROWTH FORESTS," 1992

In November 1992, the election of Democrats Bill Clinton and Al Gore buoyed many Northwest environmentalists, giving them hope for an end to the struggles with the federal government to uphold environmental laws. Many believed they had allies steering the ship of state. In *Earth in the Balance,* Gore had certainly sounded like one.

"I have come to believe that we must take bold and unequivocal action," the forty-three-year-old wrote in his best-seller. "We must make the rescue of the environment the central organizing principle for civilization."

In Oregon, Bob Doppelt had not expected Clinton and Gore to win, but he recognized the opportunity their victory provided. In the period before the Clinton inauguration, he shifted into high gear. Ever since the decisive meeting with the river scientists in 1991, Doppelt had grown in understanding the importance of protecting watersheds and managing them as ecosystems. He led in the development of a Rivers Council book that would present the state of knowledge of watersheds and propose an action plan for their protection and restoration. The book became larger by the month, until the manuscript was more than three hundred pages. The staff at the Rivers Council called it "Godzilla."

It was all trailblazing stuff, new and important, as far as Doppelt was concerned, and he saw to it that key staff people for congressional committees received copies. In early January 1993, before the inauguration, Doppelt traveled to Washington, D.C., to brief the staff of a House committee about the book. They were concerned about the reauthorization of the federal Clean Water Act and the Endangered Species Act, which would be introduced in their committee. Doppelt found them receptive to approaches that looked beyond single-purpose remedies to more holistic ones.

The briefing was a great success, and Doppelt was asked to conduct another, this time for congressmen. He decided on the day after the inauguration for that event, which turned out to be a superb piece of timing. Without other pressing commitments, about seventy-five people showed up and stayed to listen for an hour and a half to Doppelt and the scientists he had brought with him. This briefing was in big contrast to the usual D.C. scene, where fifteen harried staffers might stick around for twenty minutes, and a congressman might drift through the room on the way to the next hearing.

The second briefing led to plans for formal presentations at congressional hearings in March, and Doppelt went back home to Eugene, bolstered again by the keen interest in the Rivers Council's proposals. He and other staff members developed a discussion paper, which laid out a rationale and framework for watershed legislation.

The signs from the new administration seemed positive. Clinton's nominee for secretary of the interior, the administration's leading advocate for endangered species, was Bruce Babbitt. The former Arizona governor had most recently been president of the League of Conservation Voters. In his confirmation hearings, Babbitt sounded themes that environmentalists liked. He told a congressional committee that the Bush administration had mishandled the forest crisis by allowing various federal agencies to go off in different directions. Because the Forest Service, the Bureau of Land Management, and the Fish and Wildlife Service were not coordinated at the top, the courts had to step in. That disarray would be corrected under Clinton, Babbitt said.

Words that high administration officials had not previously been heard to utter came out of the new secretary's mouth once he was in office. In a speech in February Babbitt told members of the American Mining Congress that it was "very important we maintain the biodiversity that supports the life systems of the planet . . . and the productivity of this country."

Not only the diversity of life—"biodiversity"—but also the protection of species was high on the new secretary's list of priorities. He spoke of applying "preventive medicine" for endangered species. Ecosystems, he said, were the key.

"We need to step back and look at entire ecosystems and intervene before the crisis," he told a congressional committee. He set as a goal to devise ecosystem conservation and recovery plans before endangered species listings became necessary. He proposed forming a National Biological Survey to help.

To Doppelt it all sounded quite too good to be true: What a difference a few weeks could apparently make to American government. What was more, Babbitt was by no means the only new administrator seemingly friendly to environmentalists. George Frampton, the former president of The Wilderness Society, was named assistant secretary of the interior, in charge of the National Parks. James Lyons, the former congressional staffer and Yale Forestry School graduate who had orchestrated the Gang of Four effort, was named assistant secretary of agriculture, in charge of the Forest Service.

The appointments appeared to reflect a new agenda on the environment, an agenda symbolized by the establishment of a White House Office on Environmental Policy. "We face urgent environmental and economic challenges that demand a new way of thinking," President Clinton said on that occasion. The environmental policy office represented a "commitment to confront these challenges in a new, more effective way, recognizing the connection between environmental protection and economic growth."

Confront the challenges. Connect the environment and the economy. From Doppelt's point of view, what Clinton said couldn't have been better for the Rivers Council if Doppelt had written it himself. Through "Godzilla," now called *Entering the Watershed,* and the legislative policy paper that followed, the council was preparing a plan that would deliver just what the administration said it wanted—environmental protection *and* new jobs. Although the council's plan grew out of its earlier reports on fishing jobs linked to salmon habitat protection, they were now thinking bigger, more comprehensively; regionally. They even changed their name to reflect the expansion. It was Pacific Rivers Council now.

Doppelt formally unveiled the legislative plan at hearings in the House in March.

Back east, perhaps, some people still thought the Northwest was a pristine playground of green forests and clear streams. Doppelt spoiled that illusion. He testified that Northwest rivers were in "alarming" shape.

"Not one river system in the region has been spared," he told the national parks, forest, and public lands subcommittee. "Fisheries, healthy water quality and quantity produced by watershed ecosystems, and entire aquatic food chains are at risk."

Existing policies had failed, he said. The forest problems now went way beyond the spotted owl. During 1992 the Fish and Wildlife Service had designated the marbled murrelet, a seabird, as "threatened" under the Endangered Species Act. Although a seabird, the murrelet required a nesting site in old-growth forests, and was known to fly forty miles inland to find one. Manuel Lujan's own spotted-owl recovery team had identified at least 137 other animals associated with streamside zones within the range of the spotted owl. These species were also at risk of extinction, as were, of course, salmon—dozens of stocks—because of failed management policies.

But, Doppelt emphasized, the problems went beyond other species to affect people directly. As just one example, over 90 percent of water for the Pacific Northwest came from federal forest lands. This water quality was declining.

To address these problems, Doppelt called for new laws for watersheds and salmon habitat on federal lands in Oregon, Washington, and northern California. The laws would provide protection first, then restoration. There were jobs in both, Doppelt told the committee members.

The principal dangers to the security of watersheds were the logging roads that snaked throughout the federal lands—one hundred thousand miles of logging roads in Oregon and Washington forests alone. This was more than double the road miles in the entire national Interstate highway system. Twenty thousand of the forest road miles were not maintained and stood as accidents waiting to happen—blowouts during winter storms, landslides, sediment dumps into streams. Watersheds needed to be "stormproofed" first, Doppelt said.

For the restoration work that followed, both professionals and skilled laborers would be needed; hydrologists, surveyors, computer technicians, and economists. Skilled heavy equipment operators, technicians, and erosion control specialists would also find work within the Rivers Council's plan.

In closing, Doppelt tried to tell legislators why rivers were important to America.

"Riverine systems are the life-support system of our nation," he said. "These systems offer important sources of food, timber, fiber, water, and many other products that provide both jobs and sustenance." They were also a storehouse of genetic resources for the future. And their beauty uplifted the human spirit.

"It is our self-interest to protect and restore the Northwest's and America's riverine systems and biodiversity," Doppelt said.

"It is also our moral responsibility."

As he traveled back to Oregon after the hearing, Doppelt counted up the successes of the trip. His committee presentations had gone well. Private audiences with select Northwest congressmen boded even better. Someone else might call him crazy, he knew; but as his plane began its descent, and he saw again the heavily logged mountainsides of the Oregon Cascades looking like a quilt from which pieces had been ripped out, he felt sure that a change was coming. The question seemed not whether, but how the Rivers Council's watershed strategy would be adopted. Congress could move it legislatively, or the administration could issue executive orders to achieve much the same purposes. Doppelt dared believe that the nightmare of the Northwest's forests and rivers might be coming to an end.

In late March when the list of those invited to speak at President Clinton's forest conference was announced, Doppelt was shocked to see he wasn't on it. He was told Clinton didn't want to hear from the "national" groups. The president wanted to hear from the "little people," he was told, the ones who were affected by the actions of the big players. Doppelt had to wonder why the administration would want to exclude the Rivers Council, which, he believed, was the only group offering a solution to the forest crisis. It seemed to him that despite what the administration might want people to believe, it had no plan for a solution. He did, and he was puzzled.

Doppelt and David Bayles decided that the Clinton conference was the best opportunity the environmentalists were ever going to have to argue for protection of the remaining old-growth forests and the salmon. The Rivers Council needed to be at the table, and so they began to use some of their political chips to get there. Oregon's Democratic governor put in a good word for them with the Clinton organizers, as did a half-dozen others, and ultimately the pressure worked. Doppelt was invited to be one of some fifty speakers—loggers, environmentalists, mill owners, Indians, fishermen, economists, and scientists. They would be grouped into three panels, and each would present remarks to Clinton, Gore, and members of the cabinet.

The buildup for the April 2 conference went on in Portland during the week before Clinton's arrival. Expecting crowds, police patrols were increased; special traffic routings were prepared. On Wednesday, two nights before the opening, the Oregon Lands Coalition held a candlelight vigil in front of the convention center where the talks would be held. A few dozen children of timber families clutched phosphorescent glow-sticks and sang "This Land Is Your Land" to the accompaniment of a guitar.

The next day was April Fools' Day, and Portland around the convention center began to get caught up in an atmosphere that mixed carnival with political rally. Starting in the afternoon and going into the night, the environmentalists and their supporters staged their own kind of party. Some fifty thousand people gathered in a park along the bank of the Willamette River for an "Ancient Forest Celebration." It rained, but the rain didn't dampen the enthusiasm of the crowd or of the musicians who performed for them. Up on stage, singing anthems for old trees and exhorting young hearts, were Clinton-generation soft-rockers Carole King, Kenny Loggins, David Crosby, and Neil Young.

Rumors flew around that the president might attend, though to him this probably did not seem the occasion for being a member of a band. Leaders of environmental groups did put in appearances, though, and in the middle of a downpour Bob Doppelt arrived. He went backstage, shook Carole King's hand and talked a few minutes with Denis Hays, an old acquaintance who organized the original Earth Day. But Doppelt was tired from a long day, and he still had some thinking to do before bed.

He had driven up to Portland early in the day to be part of the last-minute strategy sessions with other environmentalists. One of the scheduled events for all of them was a role-playing rehearsal, to prepare for what some believed would be an intense cross-examination in front of Clinton. Doppelt recognized that, with three panels, each with about eighteen panelists giving talks of three minutes apiece, there was no way that the president was going to encourage a freewheeling, around-the-table debate—not if he expected to leave Portland at a reasonable hour. Even more to the point, he clearly wanted to avoid confrontations at his conference. Andy Kerr had only finally been invited on Tuesday.

Doppelt quickly ducked out of that role-playing session with environmentalists, but he was immediately besieged by journalists looking for news angles to fill the day before the main event. About eight hundred reporters and photographers were on hand for the conference, some of whom certainly would not have been along if Russian leader Boris Yeltsin were not meeting Clinton in nearby Vancouver, British Columbia, on Saturday. Doppelt gave interviews until he was worn out, missing a press conference where Willa Nehlsen was speaking. Nehlsen was on his team now, which made Doppelt happy. She had resigned from the Power Planning Council and had been working for the Rivers Council since the beginning of the year, helping them plan their salmon strategy.

The next morning, the day of the conference, a reporter woke Doppelt and his wife at 5:30 with a call to their hotel room. Out on the street it was still quiet, but by the time he had dressed and was ready to drive to the staging area for the conference, the traffic had begun. Mills, logging companies, and other timber businesses all over the region had closed for the day to allow workers to go to Portland. Environmentalists planned their own vigil in front of the convention center. Thousands of cars, buses, and vans were converging on the building across the spiderweb of bridges spanning the Willamette River.

When Doppelt arrived inside the hall to take his place in the gallery, he was still debating the best approach to take for his three minutes of the president's attention. One way was to concoct memorable sound-bites that might distinguish the Rivers Council among the pack of presenters. White House staff had urged that approach, saying the conference was a "TV event"; it was going to be covered live on C-SPAN and public television and radio. But the more he sat in the hall, the less comfortable he felt about playing to the media audience.

It was more important, Bayles had counseled him, to capture the president's interest and that of Interior Secretary Babbitt and Secretary of Agriculture Mike Espy. It was better to lay out the principles of the Rivers Council's proposed solution, better to lay a solid foundation for further discussion than to make a splash. Doppelt had already rewritten his comments six times, but sitting in the gallery he began penciling over them again.

Just before eleven o'clock the president, the vice-president, and all the cabinet members quickly came out into the hall and took their seats around the massive, oblong wooden table. The nervous chattering in the room suddenly dropped to a hush. Doppelt, scores of other guests in the convention hall, hundreds of journalists consigned to a media room downstairs, and no doubt thousands of others watching TV abruptly snapped to attention.

It was a remarkable moment. The highest elected officials in the nation and all their top advisers were devoting a day to a single environmental issue. Without saying a word, Clinton and Gore and the cabinet had made a statement of interest and intention that seemed altogether appropriate to the circumstances. Yet it must have struck many as extraordinary to see all the decision makers of the government in one place and ready to engage in discussion. Would this have happened under Bush or Reagan? Could it have?

Doppelt thought the session began well. Clinton, looking relaxed, sounding confident, read from a prepared statement in which he said, "If we destroy our old-growth forests, we will lose jobs in salmon fishing, in tourism, and eventually in the timber industry as well."

The vice-president sounded right on the Rivers Council's track, too.

"The days when this debate was defined by either/or choices are over," Gore said. "This isn't about saving jobs or saving the environment. It's about saving jobs *and* saving the environment—because we can't do one without the other, certainly not in the long term. A healthy forest economy demands healthy forests."

Once the invited speakers began, however, Doppelt began to worry. For the first couple of hours the discussion was dominated by people from the timber industry lamenting how times had changed. Much of it was emotionally wrenching—about people out of work, communities out of hope—and Clinton looked sympathetic. Doppelt was concerned that the environmentalists' points weren't getting across.

He breathed easier in the next session, when Charles Meslow, leader of the fish and wildlife research station in Corvallis, fixed the discussion on science and solutions. "The problem with forest management in the Northwest is not that we are running out of trees," Meslow told the president. "Professional forest managers have become quite adept at replacing cutover areas. What is becoming an increasingly scarce commodity in the Northwest are forests—especially old forests," said Meslow.

"What most scientists are advocating is an ecosystem approach to the management of *all* old-forest-associated resources."

As Meslow—and no doubt Clinton—knew, five months earlier the chief of the Forest Service had in fact unilaterally declared that the national forests would be managed by the new principle of "ecosystem management." Since then everyone had been trying to find out what that meant—or to influence what it would mean.

Doppelt knew this background, and so he was struck when a timber industry spokesman said the industry was ready to "embrace the exciting and innovative concept of ecosystem management." But Jim Geisinger, president of the Northwest Forestry Association, added a "stipulation"—"that we manage broad landscapes rather than applying these new techniques to just the small amount of land that is currently available for timber management."

This sounded like clever public relations to Doppelt, a bid to open up even parks and wilderness areas to development. He hoped someone would take it on. Andy Kerr was next on the agenda, and he did indeed question the new perspectives of the timber industry. Kerr cautioned the president against becoming too enamored of "ecosystem management."

"I hear 'ecosystem,' " said Kerr, "while a forester hears 'management.' "

Kerr's skepticism went deep, he told Clinton.

"Environmentalists like myself were very wary about the forest conference, because in a situation like this, everyone is called upon to compromise. Then everybody splits the difference and says there's a deal.

"But when so little of the virgin forest is left, about ten percent, environmentalists are not in a position to compromise the forest any further.

"We're not in a position to compromise any more," said Kerr, trying to sound reasonable, "because the scientists, the economists, and our own eyes tell us that if we continue to log out the last of the big trees, the extinction of species, the extinction of ecosystems, and the extinction of jobs and economies that depend on the sustainable use of those ecosystems will be the inevitable result.

"So the forests have already been compromised all they can stand."

"No compromise" and no proposals was not a message Clinton was eager to hear, and when Kerr was done, the president gave him no reply. Doppelt felt all the more keenly that he must lay out something substantive for the president.

Finally, nearing the end of the conference, his chance arrived.

Up at the big table under the television spotlights, however, Doppelt became nervous. Suddenly he thought of all the people all over the country who were watching him. It was hotter than a pistol. He felt that his long hair wasn't well combed. His eyeglasses sat heavy on the bridge of his nose. He felt flushed and his mouth was dry. Then the president called on him.

He went to work. As he began talking, his confidence returned.

"Any resolution to the Northwest forest issues must involve a comprehensive and regionwide watershed protection and restoration program," Doppelt told the president.

The basic principles were straightforward, he said.

"Treat the problems in these systems, not the symptoms. Second, protect the best remaining areas, and then restore the rest with the help and involvement of local communities.

"We are down to ten percent or less of our native salmon," Doppelt said, his voice sounding urgent. "How would our society respond if our agricultural output was reduced to ten percent or threatened with elimination altogether?

"I believe we would marshall large-scale forces and invest whatever was needed to stop the hemorrhaging and reverse the trend. And that is indeed what is needed now. A long-term significant federal investment is going to be required."

Doppelt said that at least $720 million would be needed to implement the Rivers Council's protection-and-restoration program on federal lands. But thousands of jobs would be created.

He had handed the president a gift package, the way he saw it. He ended quickly, as if to leave opportunity for a comment about jobs and the environment.

But the president was cool in response.

"Thank you," was all he said.

As Doppelt sat back, his face cooling off, his shoulders relaxing, he thought maybe he had overstepped his bounds. Maybe the Rhodes-scholar president, the fabled "policy wonk," didn't like other people suggesting federal policy to him.

Or maybe, he thought, the president was just tired from listening all day. He decided not to judge, not just yet.

The conference was almost over. At the end, the last word was given to a representative of the Indians. The speaker was Ted Strong, of the Columbia River Inter-Tribal Fish Commission.

"The natives of this land have existed for more than thirty-five thousand years, an estimated seven hundred generations," Strong began in his rich, sad voice, looking directly at Clinton.

"Present-day America is approximately ten generations old. For six hundred and ninety generations 'ecosystem management' was defined, illustrated, and scientifically concluded by each generation of American Indians living on this land.

"In the ten short generations, one broad sweep of the geological second hand, America has reduced its life-forms to struggling endangered species."

Strong kept his eyes on Clinton and Gore.

"I was asked to address the question, 'Where do we go from here?' And Mr. President, there are an estimated five million American Indians, and they may be tempted to quote an old Hollywood Indian and say, 'What do you mean "we," Kimosabe?' "

Clinton and Gore let out big guffaws. The audience laughed right along, in a mixture of acknowledgment and relief that the criticism was not harsher.

Strong continued, deadpanning. "But Mr. President, quoting fictional characters and Hollywood characters belongs to another administration."

Laughter again, all around the room. Strong now had Clinton and Gore's total attention. They were watching him closely. He continued.

"You have elevated our relationships to a very respectable place, and we appreciate that.

"So, in all seriousness, where do we go from here? Well, we go home to worried families and stressed ecosystems. In actuality, tomorrow we go out to build coalitions across all ideological lines. We unite as family. And we begin to do the work that lets us leave behind a legacy of love for our natural resources to be enjoyed in perpetuity by all humans yet to walk this earth."

He was almost done. Strong's gaze zeroed in on the president.

"Mr. President Clinton, you have been chosen to write one page on the book of American history. American Indians, natives to this land, hope and pray that the pen you wield will be guided by the sacred beings who created and authored the perfect laws of nature by which all mankind has existed since the beginning of time."

The room was very quiet. Clinton did not take his eyes off Strong.

The sacred beings. The sacred beings who authored the perfect laws of nature. In all the long day of passion and persuasion, no one has said such a thing.

The president looked thoughtful, and he said nothing for a long moment.

"I'd like to say I had heard him speak before, when I invited him to be the last speaker," said Clinton finally, sounding genuinely moved. "I hadn't. It was just the hand of Providence."

It remained only for Clinton to say what he would do next. He promised to begin work immediately to prepare a "balanced and comprehensive long-term policy." He directed the cabinet to report to him in sixty days with a plan that would "end this stalemate." He laid out five guiding principles for any plan that he would endorse.

At the table, Doppelt strained to listen carefully as Clinton touched on the principles.

The government would speak with one voice, Clinton said.

A predictable and sustainable level of timber sales would be developed.

The needs of timber communities would be addressed. "Where sound management policies can preserve the health of the forest lands, timber sales can and should go forward. Where this requirement cannot be met we need to do our best to offer new economic opportunities for year-round, high-waged, and high-skilled jobs."

Bob Doppelt's eyes opened a notch. This was sounding very good.

The president continued.

"We need to protect the long-term health of our forests, our wildlife, and our waterways. They are, as Ted Strong said, a gift from God that we hold in trust for future generations."

Doppelt nodded quietly.

"Our efforts must be," the president was continuing, "scientifically sound, ecologically credible, and legally responsible."

What was this? Doppelt struggled to remember the phrases. *Scientifically sound. Ecologically credible. Legally responsible.*

Well, if Clinton held to those principles, the doubting was mainly over. Doppelt sensed there wouldn't be much wiggle room if the plan needed to be all three of those things. The old forests would have to be substantially protected. But maybe Clinton himself didn't know what strong medicine he was prescribing. As Doppelt continued to listen closely, the rest of what the president said had that peculiar decency that marked him—"You don't have to fight in a court of law anymore . . . You can work with us for long-term solutions"—but it also sounded woolly headed somehow, as if he didn't really understand how deep the divisions were between the parties.

As the conference ended and Doppelt waited around the table to shake the president's hand, he felt both hopeful and anxious. *Timber sales can and should go forward.* He remembered that the president had said this, too. What the outcome would be was by no means certain.

To develop a plan that would be "scientifically sound and ecologically credible," Clinton established a scientific committee. Gordon Reeves was named a member of that committee. He was not surprised.

Back in 1991, the Gang of Four report had represented for him the unexpected once-in-a-career chance to influence national forest policy. Little did he know when that report was finished that such efforts were only beginning for him. Reeves could thank Judge Dwyer.

When Dwyer had ruled for environmentalists in 1992 and required the Forest Service to update its final environmental impact statement concerning management of the spotted owl, Jack Ward Thomas had again been asked to lead a scientific team that would respond to Dwyer's concerns. Thomas had asked Reeves and Jim Sedell to serve on the team. Work had begun in July 1992.

In March 1993 this scientific assessment team's report, more than five hundred pages, was presented to Dwyer. Not only was it lengthy, Reeves and the others felt it was an advance on all previous such work. Along with updating management plans for the owl, Dwyer had required them to specifically consider whether other species associated with old-growth forests would be placed at serious risk by the Forest Service's owl plans. In response to the judge, Thomas, Reeves, and the others had, for the first time, collected the state of knowledge about all species believed to be associated with old-growth forests within the owl's range.

The numbers were staggering, going far beyond the 137 streamside species identified earlier by Lujan's recovery team. The scientific assessment team described 667 species: 35 mammals, 38 birds, 21 reptiles and amphibians, 112 fish stocks, 149 invertebrates, and 312 plants. In the report, they evaluated the likelihood of maintaining viable populations of these species under various management alternatives. Finally, they laid out measures needed to prevent the demise of the species. The measures depended heavily on the conservation strategy described first in Thomas's owl report.

During much of the time that Reeves was working on this report for Dwyer, he was also involved in another Forest Service working group. This one was supposed to define an ecosystem-based approach to restoring and maintaining the natural production of salmonids on federal lands in all the western states, including Alaska. This effort, which went by the name PACFISH, had arisen under warnings from the Pacific Rivers Council and other groups that the agency's official forest plans were deficient. They didn't take the salmon information from the "Crossroads" paper into account.

The environmentalists were right. The forest plans were inadequate, and Reeves knew that his efforts to better direct the Forest Service were essential. Part of him, though, was beginning to seriously dislike all the meetings. He felt he was losing touch with the fish. He longed to get back in a river.

In the days before Clinton's forest conference, the scientists who would work after the conference was over were quietly named. Reeves learned that Jack Ward Thomas would once again lead, directing the Forest Ecosystem Management Assessment Team—or, in the inevitable way of these activities, the FEMAT. Two other members of the Gang of Four, economist Norm Johnson and ecologist Jerry Franklin, were expected to participate. Reeves and Sedell took it as a foregone conclusion that they would be part of it, too, and in the final days before the conference the two of them were indeed asked to be ready to brief members of Clinton's cabinet, if needed. Reeves lived alongside the telephone. He was not surprised when the call came finally, the day before the conference. No, he did not need to rush to Portland to brief the politicians, the caller said. Reeves just needed to report to Portland the following week. There he would start working for the White House.

When Reeves learned of Clinton's intent to have a plan in sixty days he knew what he needed to do first. He had a pretty good feeling for what those sixty days would involve. So he quickly assembled a vacation with his wife.

It was over too soon, and one morning he found himself coming out of the elevator on the fourteenth floor of the U.S. Bank building in downtown Portland. There he was assigned a cubicle in a big open room divided into partitions. This was the beehive, and he was to be one of the drones.

He was chosen the coleader, with Sedell, of the fifteen-member "aquatic group." There were other groups, too, focused on terrestrial ecology and on the resources themselves. Once, when most of them were together, Jack Ward Thomas explained what they would be doing.

"We're not doing science," he said. "We're doing science *assessment.*"

Thomas wanted the scientists not to be confused. They weren't being asked to design a plan that would be "best" for the forests. They were asked to apply their knowledge within a set of constraints. Specifically, the mission statement from the administration asked the FEMAT to "identify management alternatives that attain the greatest economic and social contribution from the forests of the region and meet the requirements of the applicable laws and regulations."

As the Gang of Four had done, the FEMAT scientists would prepare options, describe the environmental risks and benefits—and leave the policy decisions to the policymakers.

The sixty-day clock began to tick.

Reeves began putting in ten hours daily, or more. Before work started and in the off hours during the day when the tension became too much, he'd escape to the athletic club in the bank tower and work out, or just collapse in the hot tub.

The tension was partly caused by the way the effort was set up. This was not like the Gang of Four or the scientific assessment team, where the main work was done by a core group of fifteen people or fewer. The FEMAT was a much larger assembly; one hundred top scientists from different agencies were directly involved. Besides the forest scientists, the planning effort also included a group of policy people working to coordinate the federal agencies, and a labor and economics panel. A final group was specifically charged with turning the science team's proposals into a formal environmental impact statement that the Department of Agriculture and the Department of the Interior could submit to Judge Dwyer. Overall, more than six hundred people, including technicians and support people, were connected to the process.

For the scientists, a lot of time at the beginning was spent in ritual dances, people throwing their weight around, establishing their territories. Reeves found it comical but also annoying. The irritations of the work were sharpened by the lack of relief. As he had on the Gang of Four project, Reeves often worked six-day weeks, getting home frazzled for one day, seeing his wife and two sons, and then turning around and driving the hour and a half back up to Portland. He worked most weekends, but made a point of getting home for every soccer game his boys were playing. He had to wonder whether what he was concocting was going to wind up being another well-intentioned casserole pronounced indigestible by Congress.

Congress could try to drop the plan in the garbage, but the team wasn't working to serve them. Bill Clinton wasn't even the man they had to please. Judge Dwyer was. Whatever option Clinton selected would need to pass muster with the judge, if the administration was going to free up some lands for logging. Dwyer would have to be convinced that the plan would not harm the listed species, the owl and the murrelet, and the other species, like the salmon, that were associated with the old-growth forests. The team assumed that legal challenges from environmentalists and the timber industry were likely.

As the deadline came ever closer, the FEMAT members turned from needling one another over intellectual turf to hovering over what needed to be preserved in the forests. There the magnitude of their task became clear. All of them felt that this might well be the last chance to put the management of these forests and their wildlife on a basis that recognized the forests as complex ecosystems. It was likely to be the last chance these scientists would have. It was likely to be the last chance the forests would have, too.

No one needed to be reminded that the outcome of their process had to be usable by the administration. Reeves watched closely as Bruce Babbitt and Jim Lyons came to the beehive. They asked questions, uttered words of encouragement, but never said, "Thou shalt give us 'X' board feet of timber to log" or "Thou shalt set aside 'Y' acres in wildlife preserves." The political pressure was more subtle.

Reeves was irritated by one apparent pressure tactic when he heard it first, and it eventually annoyed him enough that he made an issue out of it. Some of the lower-level policy types, some lawyers, kept saying the scientists were *responsible* for determining what prescriptions would be "legally acceptable" to the judge. Finally, at a general meeting, Reeves said that wasn't his job. If he had wanted to be a lawyer, he said, he would have gone to law school. The scientists didn't know what would be "legally acceptable." As far as Reeves knew, no one had bothered to go through Dwyer's previous decisions and try to determine what measures of species protection the judge would apply to Clinton's proposal.

Another continuous pressure throughout the period of April to July came courtesy of the news media. The media seemed to be feasting on stories about apparent Clinton miscues, of his mishandling Congress over his economic stimulus plan, of difficulties in saying what he meant and sticking to it. Reeves kept wondering whether the FEMAT report, however good the options, would just be too prickly for Clinton himself to swallow. Maybe the president just wouldn't have the stomach for another fight with Congress, wouldn't have the guts to follow through on what he'd promised. No one really knew. So the undercurrent of the talk every day on the fourteenth floor was, is this a waste of time?

Sometimes he had to remind himself why he was there. He wouldn't say it to others, but he admitted it to himself that he liked the chance to be influential. It made him feel good that his abilities were recognized. But that wasn't why he was there. He thought of his sons a lot. And just for a few moments, standing in the beehive of offices, studying a forest map, it would come over him again: *What forests these were.*

The stillness.

The immensity.

The feeling of awe at the richness of life.

Reeves would stand there and smile. No words could capture the feelings. Words went straight ahead, one way; but these forests went every which way, in layers, upon layers, up into the sky and down into the water.

Whatever he could do to ensure that this world would persist, he must do.

Jack Ward Thomas had a saying borrowed from Aldo Leopold. It was almost mystical, and it captured the way many of the biologists felt. "Ecosystems are not only more complex than we think," Thomas would say, "they're more complex than we *can* think."

To construct their alternatives, the team members began by sifting through everything that had been developed before: the Thomas owl plan, the owl recovery plan, the Gang of Four report, the scientific assessment team report, the PACFISH project. They took the best, slowly cobbling together the options. By late May they had produced seven of them.

At least two of them would be legally acceptable, as they all knew. Option one—which many referred to as the "Green Dream"—allowed only very limited logging. It also offered the highest levels of protection for old-growth forest animals. Option four was very good, too, as it protected the most ecologically significant forests. But some FEMAT members worried. They questioned themselves whether their options presented ecosystem management the best way possible. They worried, too, about meeting Clinton's expectations of incurring the least social costs. They worried about what they called "duplications"—they didn't want to be criticized for setting aside a certain acreage for owls, another for marbled murrelets, and additional acreage nearby for salmon protection, if by adjusting those separate areas they could find an acceptable single area that would protect all.

One Friday night at the end of May, a group of about fifteen of them met and decided to produce yet another option, something better, that would place management into a different geographic frame.

After some discussion, Jerry Franklin proposed that they go back to the "key watersheds" concept first identified by the Gang of Four. The organizing framework would not be the landscape sections required by spotted owls or marbled murrelets, but instead the land-and-water framework of watersheds. The key watersheds would include much of the landscape important for the owls and the murrelets, and where they did not, more habitat outside the watersheds could be incorporated for the birds.

Once they laid out the approach, the questions began, and Reeves felt suddenly as if all the intellectual firepower in the entire forestry profession was focused on his knowledge.

Someone in the conference room said, "If we're going to use watershed as the basis of this option, you guys better be damned well sure you know what those watersheds look like."

Reeves swallowed hard. He said they did. Sedell did, too.

Watersheds became the organizing principle of the new option.

For about ten days this core group went over, one more time, just about every square mile of the forests, arguing once more over the management of each National Forest and Bureau of Land Management district within the range of the northern spotted owl. Reeves knew many of the watersheds firsthand, knew where the good fish habitat was on these lands, and he was determined to see the good places included in the option. Give-and-take was the game, but Reeves had learned a crucial lesson from Thomas during the Gang of Four deliberations. Thomas had said, "You decide what your bottom line is. Then you don't blink."

By the end, the scientists had kept most of the 137 key watersheds from the Gang of Four report and added to them additional watersheds on Forest Service and BLM lands, for a total of 162 watersheds, covering one-third of the total acreage of the owl forests, nearly 9 million acres. In the process of their reevaluation, they also found more acreage that could be freed up for logging than they previously had believed possible.

In early June, the scientists finished their report, and in about a week of feverish work, the group charged with assembling the formal *Draft Supplemental Environmental Impact Statement* required by Dwyer also finished their task. On July 1, Clinton was scheduled to announce his intentions from the White House.

In Oregon, Reeves had worked seventy-two straight hours in the last days of June, tidying up loose ends of the FEMAT document, and then he had gone back home to get some sleep. When the president made his announcement, Reeves stumbled out of bed and switched on the broadcast.

Under the television lights, flanked by cabinet members and by Vice President Gore, the president said that his solution to the forest crisis was option nine, the plan based on key watersheds and old-growth forest reserves advanced by Reeves, Sedell, and the other insiders.

"This plan offers an innovative approach to conservation, protecting key watersheds and the most valuable of our old-growth forests," Clinton explained. "It protects key rivers and streams while saving the most important groves of ancient trees and providing habitat for salmon and other endangered species.

"I believe the plan is fair and balanced," the president said. "I believe it will protect jobs and offer new job opportunities.

"We know that our solutions will not make everybody happy," he said. "Indeed they may not make anybody happy. But do understand that we are all going to be better off if we act on the plan and end the deadlock and divisiveness."

To Reeves, Clinton did not look or sound like a happy man. He seemed chastened by the unenviable job he had, of coming into a home after the big party is over and trying to clean up the mess. The party had gotten out of hand, and now some of the party-goers were a bit hung over, not quite believing that things were as bad as they looked. They might be belligerent.

The details of the plan were not made public for a few weeks, when the eight-hundred-page scientific report, *Forest Ecosystem Management,* and the slightly shorter *Draft Supplemental Environmental Impact Statement* were published. The two documents collected absolutely the latest scientific information about old forests, laced with enough numbers to make probably any reader dizzy. But the major points were not hard to see.

The timber-cutting in the owl forests would continue, but would be substantially reduced. Instead of timber harvesting, protection would become a priority on most of these national forest lands. Management would be redirected to concentrate on watersheds and old-growth refuges.

The draft impact statement presented ten management alternatives, including Clinton's chosen option nine. "All of the alternatives reverse the management trend of the last fifty years on federal lands," the authors wrote. If those trends continued, they said, they "would have resulted in a steep decline in the quantity and quality of late-successional ecosystems and the eventual loss of those ecosystems in many federal planning areas."

The estimated levels of logging for the various options did certainly seem to "reverse the management trend." While the clearly unsustainable harvests of the 1980s had averaged 4.5 billion board feet per year, and those of the court-restricted period of 1990–92 had averaged 2.4 billion board feet, the impact statement said that during the first decade of operation, on an annual average, all ten options would have "probable" sales below the 2.4 billion level. They ranged from only 200 million board feet, for option one, to a high of 1.6 billion board feet. Option nine logged an average of 1.2 billion board feet.

A certain reduced level of logging was only one element of option nine. Like all the other alternatives, Clinton's chosen option divided all the forest lands into two broad classes and then into finer classifications. The broad classes comprised lands protected to one degree or other in "designated areas," and the mainly unprotected forest "matrix," the lands designated primarily for logging.

Of the 24 million acres in the owl forests, almost 7 million acres—29 percent—were already receiving some degree of long-term protection as congressionally reserved Wilderness Areas, Wild and Scenic Rivers, and National Parks. Under option nine an additional 7 percent was in recreational areas or other forest lands "administratively withdrawn" from logging. Option nine placed another 29 percent of the land in "late-successional" reserves; and 9 percent more—some 2.2 million acres—was dedicated to streamside protection or "riparian reserves." The protections on fish-bearing streams would represent a significant improvement over previous practices; the no-logging buffer would be no less than three hundred feet wide.

The largest remaining chunk of option nine—20 percent of the forest, or nearly 5 million acres—was the "matrix." Logging would also be carried out in some of the "adaptive management areas," the final 6 percent of the forest acreage under the option.

These adaptive management areas were a novelty of this particular option.

The idea behind them seemed to be to give local interests greater control over management of federal lands. Depending on one's point of view, such a long-range social experiment in management of resources was either a progressive idea worth trying, a quixotic miscalculation of rural community sophistication, or merely a cynical way of increasing the timber harvest. The most anyone could say for sure when the Clinton plan was released was that time would tell which interpretation was correct.

As Reeves looked back over the FEMAT report, he tried to assess what had come of the weeks of tension and long hours. He knew the outlook for the salmon and the sea-run trout under Clinton's plan was decent, but not as good as it could have been. Reeves might have wished that Clinton had chosen options one or four for his plan, because the aquatic scientists considered them more likely to provide habitat conditions that would support more salmonids, more widely dispersed, during the next one hundred years. By comparison, the team rated option nine as providing only about 65 percent likelihood of attaining such habitat conditions. The likelihood would increase to 80 percent or better, they said, if no logging were permitted in the key watersheds. Such a change would reduce potential timber sales under the plan by some 15 percent.

Reeves knew what compromises had gone into option nine, but he could not be unhappy with it. If the plan was followed to the letter, its effects would go beyond what he and his colleagues had ever dreamed possible on federal lands only a couple of years before. In simple terms, he thought it would indeed halt and reverse the degradation of aquatic ecosystems on westside federal forests, from northern California to Canada. Where else in the United States, in North America, or for that matter in the world, had such a sizable thing been done?

The fate of Clinton's plan was nearly impossible to tell. But, Reeves felt, if it was accepted by environmentalists and loggers, blessed by Dwyer, not damned by Congress, and followed scrupulously by the agencies over an extended period of time, the fish would benefit. These were very big political "ifs." It seemed unlikely that so much forbearance would be shown where so little had been before.

Beyond the plan, though, he believed that the conservation strategy that his group developed for the FEMAT report could be a model for management of aquatic ecosystems. It would be a shame if the group's strategy was overlooked in the struggle over Clinton's chosen option. The strategy offered much that could be put to good use not only on the federal lands but on any forests and streams.

The group had tried to make it impossible to ignore the urgency for change. In the introduction to their chapter, they presented many indications of river decline in the United States, including:

> The Nationwide Rivers Inventory, completed in 1982 by the U.S. National Park Service, found that, of 3.25 million stream miles examined in the lower 48 states, less than 2 percent were considered of "high natural quality."

> (As of 1990) 57 percent of the freshwater native fishes of California were extinct or in need of immediate attention.

> Approximately 55 percent of the 27,000 stream miles examined in Oregon are either severely or moderately impacted by nonpoint source pollution.

The geographic basis for forest management needed to change, they said. It made little sense to manage forests by administrative units such as ranger districts or by topographic units such as townships. The aquatic group argued that watersheds of twenty to two hundred square miles were the appropriate geographic units for forest management. Among their several supporting arguments, they said:

> *Watersheds link physical processes.* "Many key physical processes are best understood on a watershed basis, such as the movement of water, sediment, and wood. Many processes are linked in time and space and tend to propagate downstream."

> *Watersheds provide a sound basis for managing key species.* "Some organisms are strongly tied to watersheds and associated channel

networks, such as fish; others that are not, such as owls, can be accounted for by including trans-watershed habitat and migration areas."

Watersheds make sense for agencies. "Both management and regulatory agencies could coordinate planning and implementation across multiple ownerships, and efficiently deal with complex and interconnected resource problems."

Watersheds make sense for involving communities. "A watershed basis for planning insures that those communities and individuals most directly affected by decisions have a role in decision making."

Actually managing watersheds, they went on to say, meant addressing protection and restoration together.

"We advocate an approach to watershed and riparian ecosystem restoration that emphasizes protecting the best habitats that remain," they wrote. "Restoring watersheds that are currently degraded is also important in the long term, to bring all public land ecosystems to full productivity and function."

They identified the three most important restoration opportunities that could benefit fish—controlling and preventing road erosion and sedimentation, planting bushes and trees on eroding streambanks, and improving stream channels with structures such as logs and boulders.

Plenty of work needed to be done, the group pointed out. Of the 29,000 miles of roads in the key watersheds, they estimated that one-third of them needed to be taken out and one-third needed to be upgraded.

Of the total estimated streamside acreage throughout the owl forests, they figured that more than 100,000 acres were both in need of streamside vegetation improvements and could be operated in successfully.

Finally, of the nearly 25,000 miles of streams within these forests, they estimated that more than 1,200 miles of stream sites would be appropriate for in-channel improvements.

The strategy went on like this for pages. Reeves knew that the level of detail in the report would be daunting for many readers. But the aquatic group wanted to be sure that no one would mistake the depth of the problems, the need to act to solve them, or the approaches that could be taken.

Taken as a whole, the boldest recommendation of the entire aquatic conservation strategy, the one most likely at first to surprise or confuse readers, was its staged goal of "maintaining the 'natural' disturbance regime." The statement probably sounded contradictory to anyone who believes that, without humans, nature rests *undisturbed*—pristine, unchanging. The language that environmentalists sometimes used could create that impression. But Reeves and the others wanted to retain disturbances—landslides, floods, fires, logs falling into streams. Nature, they understood, is messy. They wanted to restore and maintain that productive, natural mess, which had been exaggerated and compromised by people. They did not want that kind of distortion. But they also didn't want the distortion of a biosphere under glass.

At the end, Reeves was happy enough with his work. But he was also relieved when his stint working for the White House was over. He was intellectually and physically exhausted. He didn't want to have anything to do with scientific assessments, with panels, committees, or *anything* in a big room. In his wry moments, he thought of himself as some "damned intellectual-exercise groupie." People might say that by being a part of the Clinton forest team he had it made in his career in the Forest Service. He doubted it. Maybe while Clinton was in office he did. *Maybe.* He couldn't worry about it.

All he wanted to do was to get outside and stick his head in a stream. He wanted to get back to his research. He planned to keep working on a research project in the Elk River and in Alaska that he had started the year before. The coastal cutthroat trout were probably not doing so well—but no one was really sure. Reeves was determined to find out.

The scientists who developed Clinton's forest plan might have been pleased by their report and resigned that the president's choice was as good as politically possible. But as Clinton has predicted, the plan did succeed in making both the wood-products industry and environmentalists unhappy.

Some were very unhappy. The sentiments played themselves out in the daily newspapers as soon as the plan was released, and the debate about the plan continued for months, ultimately revealing major differences within the environmental community itself.

On the day of Clinton's announcement, the spokesman for the Western Council of Industrial Workers, the union that represented thirty thousand wood-products employees, said, "President Clinton has thrown sand in the nation's economic engine."

"Not only is he putting tens of thousands of workers in the unemployment lines," said the union's Mike Draper, "he is increasing lumber prices, preventing more Americans from buying a new home."

Draper accused Clinton of caving in to environmentalists.

Andy Kerr said just about the opposite.

"The timber workers of the Pacific Northwest are getting a much better deal," said Kerr, "than fishing, tourism, and recreation interests, whose jobs may also be lost because of the plan's loopholes that allow logging in old-growth forests."

The provisions for logging old-growth forests prevented some environmentalists from seeing anything else in the plan. In option nine more than 40 percent of the total late-successional and old-growth forest were part of the "matrix" and subject to logging. In addition to this expected logging, the plan also contemplated more selective logging even in the areas designated as "reserves." Logging would be permitted in order to control and prevent fires in old-growth reserves, to "salvage" trees after fires, disease outbreaks, and other catastrophic events, and to "thin" the forest of some younger trees.

The FEMAT scientists had recognized that logging in reserves would be controversial, and at least with respect to thinning, they had taken some pains to explain that west of the Cascades no stands older than eighty years would be thinned. If some younger trees were removed, so the theory went, the remaining trees would grow faster, thereby producing the habitat characteristics of old-growth forests sooner. The scientists conceded that whether such a goal would be attained was unknown.

Groups like Kerr's Oregon Natural Resources Council pointed to the uncertainty expressed by the FEMAT scientists. ONRC's staff ecologist wrote:

> A major fear of many scientists as they learn more about Op-
> tion 9 is that at some point our westside forests will have lost so
> many young trees to thinning, so many older trees in disturbed
> sites to salvaging, and so many forest floor logs to removal that
> the forests will cease to be virgin, old-growth ecosystems, and
> will instead become managed tree plantations.

No further logging of the precious remaining old-growth forests could be condoned, the ONRC said. As Kerr had argued at the forest conference, the Clinton plan seemed doomed to be another "balancing" deal, and the old-growth forests had long before been balanced just about into oblivion.

Other environmental groups took a more conciliatory position on the Clinton plan, trying to assess the political risks and trying to make the most of what was offered. Some leaders, including Vic Sher of the Sierra Club Legal Defense Fund, argued that the appearance of intransigence by environmentalists on the plan might only aid and abet those in Congress who sought to weaken the Endangered Species Act. Intransigence would also anger the administration, which might then backtrack on the plan or go soft when met with congressional resistance.

Bob Doppelt was one who was willing to be accommodative.

Doppelt knew firsthand that many environmental groups were at the point of bolting from the plan, but he was just as worried about Congress and the land-management agencies. In many ways they seemed to be prepared to scuttle or at least cripple the plan themselves, for their own reasons.

During the development of the plan, support in Congress and the administration seemed to be growing for the sort of watershed jobs outlined by the Rivers Council. A budget of more than $700 million was being talked about for a five-to-ten-year program; a $70 million appropriation for the federal year beginning in October 1993 seemed possible. The Rivers Council projected that "tens of thousands" of "person-years" of employment could be created by the ten-year program. But when the logging reductions in option nine became known to them, key Northwest Democratic members of Congress, led by House Speaker Tom Foley, began to distance themselves from the plan.

After Clinton released the plan, the watershed-jobs agenda seemed to falter. Funding in Congress looked uncertain. Mark Hatfield, still the ranking Republican on the Senate Appropriations Committee, initially balked at any appropriations at all for watershed work.

It was hard to gauge Hatfield's purposes. Before the forest conference, the senator had told reporters that "science must be the cornerstone of any real solution." When the plan was released, however, Hatfield looked to discredit the science, saying, "It appears as if the ratio of common sense is inversely proportional to the number of scientists and bureaucrats involved in the process." Some environmentalists leaped to the conclusion that Hatfield was so entrenched in old ways of thinking about the forest economy that he was unable to see the inevitability of change.

Appearances certainly conspired against him. In the 1990 campaign, Hatfield reportedly received more money from political action committees of the timber industry than any other legislator, some $87,000. For the many Americans who believed that substantive change in American governance was dependent on reform of campaign financing, Hatfield appeared to make a tempting case in point.

But campaign finance reform was another battle, in Doppelt's view. "The Six Phases of a Project," taped above his desk, reminded him of the ways big projects could go astray. The phases were:

1. Enthusiasm
2. Disillusionment
3. Panic
4. Search for the Guilty
5. Punishment of the Innocent
6. Prizes and Honors for the Nonparticipants

It was supposed to be funny, of course, but the point was: Don't get diverted. He wanted to stay focused on developing a watershed program. In a letter to

Pacific Rivers Council members, Doppelt argued that Clinton's plan *"could usher in a new age of watershed restoration.*

"But it needs improvement," he added.

The plan, Doppelt noted, "is built upon the watershed and salmon-habitat protection proposals that the Rivers Council, working with some of the best scientists in the nation, helped develop and advocate."

Doppelt believed—had to believe—that the science was "sound." The problems, he told members, were "with what I call the 'political and implementation overlays.' "

The Rivers Council didn't see how environmentalists could prevent the logging of the old-growth timber contained in the "matrix." But they were not prepared to allow the experiment of logging within reserves. Doppelt urged members to write President Clinton, telling him of their support for "inviolate" old-growth reserves and for complete protection of key watersheds. Enactment of those measures, he thought, could satisfy environmentalists.

Doppelt really believed that the Clinton plan could be a "watershed," in the common use of the term as a dividing line, or, by extension, a turning point. The best of the plan made the case for ecosystem management more persuasively than any other government document so far. It went far beyond anything developed by the Power Planning Council or the National Marine Fisheries Service, even. It was worth its faults.

Still, other environmentalists argued that the Rivers Council's hopes for a restoration agenda were doomed by a naivete about Congress and the federal economy. *Where was the money for watershed restoration really going to come from?* they asked. *What would be the cost of obtaining such funds?*

Because passions ran so high in the Northwest over logging or protecting the forests, and because the fate of the forests had been analyzed and discussed for years, many people involved in the issue had attuned themselves to the labyrinthine ways of politics, money, and land management. Quite in vogue by 1993 was the "iron triangle" analysis, which explained how legislators, special interests, and bureaucrats were mutually linked. They were joined, so the argument went, by a desire to fund federal projects that would enlarge bureaucracies, profit the special interests, and help keep the legislators in office. To those who held this view, the Clinton forest plan looked like just another dodge to keep employment levels up in the Forest Service, to put money in the pockets of the timber industry, and to ensure campaign contributions for the reelection of the timber-oriented congressional delegation.

Such disenchantment with the administration's plan and the Congress, coupled with terminal despair over the industry, fueled a growing belief among some activists that the only possible place to make progress was in reforming the land-management agencies themselves. The Forest Service was a great disappointment to a great many conservationists. The service had been established during the Progressive era, in 1905, in the wake of the nation's first major conservation movement. The Progressives' hope had been that scientific principles would guide the management of the nation's resources for the long-term benefit of the public. Over time, however, the Forest Service had lost its Progressive bearings and become reactionary.

Reform of the agency, a growing number of critics believed, required a change in incentives. Agencies, like individuals, were ruled by incentives, particularly by financial incentives. Change these incentives and the agencies would act differently. Maverick forest economist Randal O'Toole had written a book published in 1988 called *Reforming the Forest Service,* which claimed just that. O'Toole, an Oregon State University forestry graduate but a consultant to environmental groups, was one of the Forest Service's most knowledgeable and provocative critics.

O'Toole was the first to point out that the vast majority of national forests lost money on timber sales, once all the costs of administering the sales were taken into account. He argued forcibly that reforming the Forest Service meant changing its budget, which encouraged such wasteful expense of taxpayers' money. He liked to tell the story about how he had come to the unromantic conclusion that the agency's budget was its underlying problem. He had been a bike-riding, train-loving, "living-lightly" do-gooder, inclined to the idea that the problem with the Forest Service was seamy *corruption.*

"Ten years ago," O'Toole wrote in 1992, "I believed that national forest problems were due to ignorant, incompetent, or corrupt Forest Service officials."

> But in the past ten years, I have visited over half of all national forest supervisors offices, all but one regional office, and numerous district offices. I've met hundreds of Forest Service employees and haven't found one who was ignorant, incompetent, or corrupt.
>
> Indeed virtually all Forest Service officials genuinely love the forests and want to manage them the best way they can.
>
> So it gradually dawned on me that there must be some other explanation for all the money-losing and environmentally destructive timber sales on the national forests. Strangely enough, I was given the answer by the Chief of the Forest Service, Dale Robertson. [At a meeting] Robertson said, "We can talk a lot of philosophy about how the national forests ought to be managed. But let me tell you, it's the budget that energizes the Forest Service."

"This has become abundantly clear to me," wrote O'Toole.

> Forest managers don't sell trees because they like clearcuts, because they are in the pockets of the timber industry, or even because Congress tells them to. Instead, they use timber sales as a fund-raising tool.
>
> Timber is responsible for half of the national forest budget . . . A little over half the money comes from congressional appropriations. The rest comes from receipts retained under the Knutson-Vandenberg Act and similar laws . . .
>
> An important key to this system is the fact that forest managers can keep timber receipts for recreation, wildlife, and watershed resources. Since Congress normally underfunds these

resources, managers end up promoting timber sales as a way to manage other activities.

Such a system, in which wildlife enhancement was funded by cutting down the trees that wildlife depended on, obviously made no sense. O'Toole argued that if the Forest Service were allowed to charge fair market value for the use of forest resources and if managers were allowed to keep the income to support those resources, the forest would be better managed.

Recreation, for example, was one of the prime "resources" of the forest, and yet it was chronically undervalued in the budget. If campers, hikers, and boaters paid market-value fees for recreation, O'Toole argued, and if managers could keep those fees to enhance recreation opportunities, then recreational assets would be better cared for. Indeed, the management of the national forests would become more oriented toward providing recreational opportunities.

If a new approach to the Forest Service's budget was required for real change to come to the agency, it followed that new funding for the agency that played into the existing budget structure would just make the existing problems worse. Therefore, although watershed restoration jobs might sound good to those who, like Doppelt, wanted to provide a politically attractive response to the "jobs versus the environment" argument, O'Toole saw taxpayer-funded restoration jobs as just another counterproductive example of congressional "pork barrel" politics.

"Pork," the largesse that is bestowed upon a certain area of the country and certain businesses thanks to a powerful legislator, was familiar to environmentalists. In the form of defense contracts, dam-building, and public works contracts of all sorts, pork was as American as apple pie. But O'Toole's claim that pork was *always* bad, not only when it was feeding military bases and giant hydroelectric dams, was something new.

"Because pork is inevitably wasteful, it reduces America's overall wealth," O'Toole argued. "On the average, people will make environmental protection a higher priority when they are wealthier. If pork reduces our wealth, the environment will be a lower priority."

The forest economist urged environmentalists not only to refuse federal pork but also to crusade against it. His disturbing vision of the future required no less:

> With a $4 trillion debt, a sluggish economy, and a growing competition from Europe and Japan, U.S. citizens are facing the possibility that their country will become another England, a has-been rather than a world leader. If this happens, the environment will be sacrificed in frantic efforts to catch up. A Congress in the pork barrel habit, released of environmental constraints on the part of the voters, will start to declassify wilderness and rapidly give away timber, oil, and even land to those who promise economic growth.

In May 1993 O'Toole's magazine began selling a new bumper sticker. "Pork Kills Salmon," it read.

But would "pork kill salmon"? Or would congressional spending, both in the forests and on the Columbia River, save the salmon? Doppelt, for one, believed that watershed "pork," if that's what it was, would restore the productivity of streams and forests, and ultimately produce more fish and timber. Viewed this way, federal spending would increase the nation's wealth. Doppelt saw danger in waiting for O'Toole's style of reform to enlighten Congress and the Forest Service. He decided to deal with the institutions as they were, not as he wished them to be. He committed himself to working with Mark Hatfield and whoever else was necessary to secure funding for a watershed program.

If divisiveness continued to hamper resolution to the salmon crisis in the west-side forests in 1993, divisiveness was only increasing in the Columbia and Snake river basins, and resolution there began to appear more and more remote. Increasing numbers of legal challenges were being filed.

The first shots in what looked to become a protracted legal battle were fired in February, when environmentalists forced the National Marine Fisheries Service to reevaluate a decade-old practice. In the spring, in every year since 1981, the Army Corps of Engineers collected juvenile salmon at Snake River dams, removed them from the river, put them on trucks and barges, and transported them downriver, finally returning them to the Columbia below Bonneville Dam. The program was not cheap. During 1992, the Corps spent approximately $31 million on it.

In 1993, the Corps proposed to transport the juveniles again. Since juvenile sockeye and chinook would be involved in the transport program, and wild stocks of those species were listed under the Endangered Species Act, the proposal required a permit.

The permit could be granted by the Fisheries Service under section 10 of the ESA, which allows exemptions to the law's protections if certain conditions are met. But Idaho fish advocate Ed Chaney considered the transport program a menace to the fish, and he sent a notice to the agency of his intent to file suit under the ESA to prevent the agency from issuing the permit. When the issue came to a hearing in Portland, the Corps of Engineers argued that the permit for them to transport the fish was warranted because— essentially—the dams, which they built and operated, kill fish.

The Corps noted that recent studies showed that 98 percent of fish transported from Lower Granite Dam, near Lewiston, Idaho, survive to below Bonneville Dam, near Portland. By contrast, other studies showed that about 50 to 80 percent would be lost during in-river passage.

"If transportation is not allowed," the Corps said, "Columbia River salmon and steelhead populations would be diminished severely by dam and reservoir mortality, and segments of the wild populations could become extinct."

Opponents of the permit request argued that the agency was not limited to the choices of transporting the fish or watching them die at the dams. At the hearing Andy Kerr tried to inject some humor in the discussion in making that case.

"When I was a boy, the fish were in the river," Kerr told the hearings officer. "Commodity traffic went by rail or truck.

"Then the Army decided it was a great idea to start trucking fish, and the fish went up and down river by truck on the roadside. I'm glad that they've finally gotten to the point that the fish are back *on* the river. Now we have to go the next step, and put them back *in* the river.

"It's not hard.

"They're used to it," Kerr chuckled.

"Call me a radical, but that's the way it's always been done."

Kerr dismissed arguments that no one knew how the wild fish would be affected by a change in the Corps' operations.

"Opponents say the experiment is in running the river like a river," he said. "The fish have thousands of years of experience, and did just fine. Now the fish have continued to decline as we have made the river into a series of slackwater ponds.

"It's logical and obvious that if we went back more to the way the river way, it would be beneficial for the fish."

Lawyer Dan Rohlf put the conservationists' argument in legal terms. "The permit must be consistent with the statute's purposes," Rohlf said, "and the purpose of the ESA is not only to conserve species but also the ecosystems on which they depend."

Taking the fish out of the river ignores the law's ecosystem goals, he argued. Supporting his claim, Rohlf pointed to the Bureau of Land Management's request in 1992 for an exemption from ESA provisions so that the agency could allow timber cutting in spotted-owl habitat.

"Why didn't the BLM just figure," said Rohlf, " 'Hey, we can just cut this habitat, then we can go capture a few juvenile owls, put them in a car, drive them over to the next habitat conservation area, and let them go'?

"It would have been a lot cheaper, but the BLM would have seen it was a ludicrous idea," Rohlf said. "The Corps is proposing pretty much the same thing here."

Section 10 of the ESA gives the Fisheries Service authority to permit "takes" of the fish if such actions will enhance them. "Take" is a term of law that has a broad meaning, including harass, harm, capture, and collect. However, Rohlf argued, "the clear bottom line under the ESA is that NMFS can permit 'taking' *to enhance* only when the agency has taken all possible steps to conserve the habitat of the species."

Rohlf contended the agency had not done that.

In April, however, the Fisheries Service issued the permit to the Corps, and the agency began barging the juveniles. In quick reply, the Sierra Club, the Oregon Natural Resources Council, Chaney's Northwest Resource Information Center, American Rivers, and the Confederated Tribes and Bands of the Yakima Indian Nation went to court to try to stop the barging.

The environmentalists and the Indians lost.

A federal judge denied both a temporary restraining order and then a preliminary injunction, saying that while the barging of fish didn't enhance the fish runs, he was not convinced the practice harmed them.

If Chaney, Rohlf, Kerr, and others felt that the Fisheries Service was often not on their side, they were not alone. A recurring complaint with the agency was that it seemed more concerned with, in effect, the letter of the ESA rather than with its spirit.

Rollie Schmitten, the agency's regional director, had gone out of his way to make the ESA what he called "more user-friendly." Schmitten, a former lumber company owner, had been appointed to the fish-agency post in 1985 by President Reagan. A former Marine Corps officer, Schmitten was keenly attuned to process. He wanted to avoid the uproar caused by the spotted-owl listing, and he thought that might be accomplished by making the process of the ESA listing more open to the public. For example, he had opened the deliberations over the biological merits of the Columbia and Snake petitions to scientists representing affected interests, including economic interests. He had also made sure that the scientists whom he later appointed to prepare the mandated species-recovery plans were independents, rather than members of his agency; and he had insisted that this recovery team meet with concerned parties throughout the region.

Such openness was a departure from the way the Fisheries Service and the Fish and Wildlife Service had handled ESA petitions in the past, and was certainly welcome in the region. But many fish advocates complained that procedural improvements were not a substitute for aggressively prosecuting the ESA, and they complained repeatedly that the Fisheries Service was not as forceful as it might be in its relations with other agencies.

One new test of the Fisheries Service's commitment would be its handling of Forest Service and BLM land-management actions within the critical habitat of the listed salmon species. The Fisheries Service began an ambitious program of consulting with these agencies in 1993.

As the Columbia and Snake fish advocates looked for legal support to end barging of fish and provide more water for them, industrial users of the rivers were taking legal action of their own, supposedly also to benefit the fish. In March, several lawsuits by utilities, aluminum companies, and irrigation districts were heard by a federal judge in Portland. The thrust of the suits was to ban all commercial and sport fishing on the listed Snake River stocks of salmon, on the grounds that such fishing constituted a violation of the Endangered Species Act.

Although the various state and federal fish agencies that were defendants in the suits indeed allowed and regulated limited fishing on the endangered stocks, fishing accounted for only a tiny fraction of the deaths to those salmon compared to other deaths caused by the dams. Moreover, all the plaintiffs benefitted from the operation of those dams, either for hydropower, irrigation, or river transportation.

In his sharply worded ruling in the case, Judge Malcolm Marsh scornfully questioned the motives of the industries.

> By invoking the ESA, they purport to represent the interests of the listed species. Yet, when push comes to shove, if the resources become so scarce that truly hard choices must be made, plaintiffs' asserted interests in the listed species may yield to . . . their interests in power and water for hydroelectric use.
>
> If plaintiffs' ultimate goal was protection of the listed species . . . then conspicuously absent is a claim for a reduction in hydroelectric activity or correction of those aspects of the dams which overwhelmingly destroy more juvenile migrants in each of the three listed species than all harvests combined.
>
> To permit these plaintiffs to proceed with their claims under

the ESA would be akin to permitting the fox to complain that the chickens have not been fed. . . .

The judge may have considered the industries wily foxes, but the industries did not think of themselves that way. Underlying this lawsuit and others filed by other industrial interests was an anxiety over the cost and availability of Columbia River system hydropower and water. The anxiety was, in fact, well placed. The Bonneville Power Administration was having serious financial troubles, and when the giant power wholesaler teetered, its customers could be expected to feel anxious.

In January 1993 the administrator of the BPA, Randall Hardy, had proposed an electricity rate increase of just less than 12 percent. This increase would raise power rates to Northwest customers to something less than three cents per kilowatt-hour. Power in the Northwest was still a bargain, relative to other regions of the country, such as New England, where rates averaged about eleven cents per kilowatt-hour, or even the Midwest, where the rate hovered under nine cents. However, the BPA increase, the first double-digit hike since the early 1980s, alarmed the agency's utility customers.

The proposed rate hike had three main causes. Hydroelectric energy production was reduced as a consequence of a six-year-long drought in the Columbia Basin; programs for fish and wildlife were costing more; and revenues from the aluminum industry were down. Aluminum continued to be the customer for about 30 percent of BPA power, and because the industry's electricity rates were pegged to the world market price of the metal and aluminum was in a protracted slump, BPA revenues from the industry were down, too.

When the drought continued into the late winter of 1993, the BPA needed to buy energy from other suppliers to supplement its own sources, at a cost of $175 million. The additional expenditure immediately raised the specter of a rate increase perhaps double the 12 percent proposed just months before. The BPA was clearly worried. The agency had gone from the comfortable position of having $1 billion in reserves in October 1991 to the distinctly uncomfortable position of projecting reserves of less than $100 million in October 1993—a 90 percent drop.

If the proposed 12-percent increase had alarmed utility and industrial customers, an increase of maybe twice that much put them up in arms. These power customers fretted about the cost of the BPA's responsibilities to fish and to conservation, forgetting that when the utilities had dominated regional energy planning in the 1970s and pushed for nuclear power plant development, rates had skyrocketed some 500 percent. Now they pressured administrator Hardy to hold the rate increase down by cutting back on programs and by making the agency more efficient. In due course "competitiveness" became the battle cry of the agency. The BPA's own fear was that independent producers, selling low-cost power produced by new natural-gas-fired turbines, might take customers away from the federal agency.

In looking for ways to cut the BPA budget and placate major customers, Hardy proposed taking funds from two program areas mandated by the Northwest Power Act—fish and wildlife, and energy conservation. From the fish and wildlife budget, much of which was dedicated to the Power Planning Council's salmon strategy, the BPA proposed to cut about $15 million to $20 million from a budget of approximately $90 million. The savings for the BPA were not much. Fifteen million dollars represented only about one-half of 1 percent of the BPA's revenues. But the proposed cuts gained the attention of members of the council and of every salmon advocate in the region.

Angus Duncan and Ted Hallock were particularly concerned about the hedging on the commitment to fish. Duncan noted that among the measures that the BPA slated for cuts were ones that he considered critical for salmon recovery. The salmon strategy had called for information that no management authority—not the council, not the Fisheries Service, not the state agencies—had ever possessed before. But the BPA was planning on cutting the development of comprehensive data on the region's wild and naturally spawning populations. The power agency also proposed to cut both the establishment of rebuilding "targets" for weak stocks and the performance standards and monitoring efforts that would determine whether those targets were being hit. Without better information about wild salmon and the condition of weak stocks, the council's stated commitment to rebuilding the salmon runs "without further loss of biological diversity" rang hollow. To Duncan, it certainly seemed as if the BPA was planning to sacrifice the council's long-term salmon goals on the altar of short-term energy savings.

The inevitable discussions between the council and the BPA began in the spring and continued into the fall in an effort to resolve the budget dispute. The council ultimately acquiesced in some $15 million of cuts, deferrals, and what the parties called "efficiency measures." However, the council was not willing to acquiesce to the BPA's peremptory handling of the fish and wildlife budget. As Duncan saw it, the BPA had taken the position that it would spend $80 million and no more on the salmon, regardless of the merits of the activities that would be excluded. The Power Act, however, directed the BPA to fund the council's program. In righteous indignation, the council appealed to members of Congress for language in appropriations bills that would require the BPA, the Corps of Engineers, and the Bureau of Reclamation to fully carry out the council's fish and wildlife program on the existing schedule.

Just as the BPA's rate plans had galvanized the utilities, so the cutbacks in BPA funding for salmon measures naturally prompted reactions from salmon advocates. If the BPA really needed to find an extra $10 million or so in its budget, some argued, why not just eliminate the approximately $13 million subsidy that irrigated agriculture enjoyed? The BPA provided irrigators with a discount of about that much annually on the electricity used to pump water. The agency then needed to make up this lost revenue by charging other ratepayers more.

Other BPA special expenditures drew the attention of the Indians. The innovative idea of keeping the lower Columbia gill-netters from fishing by leasing their permits required some BPA funds, and when the idea came up again in 1993, the Columbia Indian tribes scotched it. They didn't want to give up their rights to catch the fish passed up by the gill-netters, fearing that it would make their treaty rights seem negotiable. Furthermore, when the BPA was cutting salmon programs that affected the tribes because the agency said it did not have enough money, it made it hard for the Indians to cooperate on a salmon project that the BPA said it *did* have money for and which would benefit others.

What guidance the Congress might provide to the council and the BPA on budgetary matters was uncertain. But more certain was that both the council and the BPA were liable to some institutional fine-tuning. An Oregon congressman and member of the House Committee on Natural Resources, Peter DeFazio, began conducting oversight hearings into BPA operations in 1993, while at the same time the BPA was named by Vice-President Gore as one of seventeen federal "reinvention laboratories." Such agencies were chosen to develop recommendations that would, as the BPA described it, "remove barriers to efficiency."

Mark Hatfield was doing his own ruminating about how to improve the Power Planning Council and the BPA. Hatfield had watched both institutions over many years, and he had felt clearly that the council's programs were moving in the right direction. He considered the council in the vanguard of a governmental restructuring that was needed in order to put environmental planning on a regional basis. Hatfield was sympathetic to the concerns of council supporters, and members such as Angus Duncan, that the economic interests in the region, and now the BPA, were picking and choosing what they wanted to implement in the council's salmon plan. The question was, what could be done about it?

Certainly, the council had reached the limits of its current authority and power; it was predictable that members such as Duncan would be frustrated. But Hatfield preferred to look at the council as a work in progress. He did not know quite what the final form would look like yet, but he favored the idea that some new government "structure" was needed, something that would be able to both develop and carry out coherent environmental and economic policies on a regional basis. The Northwest Power Act might be able to be expanded or refined to let the council achieve this greater role; or some other entity might be needed. Hatfield did not know yet.

As if there were not already enough arenas of the salmon crisis, a new, though not unexpected one, was added during 1993. Coastal stocks of salmon were petitioned for protection under the Endangered Species Act.

Ever since their meeting in Portland in February 1992, environmental groups had been considering coastal petitions. But they had decided to wait for the outcome of the Rivers Council's priority-setting process and for stock-protection proposals that might come from government. A year later, many of the same groups met again to reassess their petitioning strategy.

The Rivers Council conceded that its scientific consultants were finding the task of setting stock priorities much more difficult than they had ever anticipated, and that definite recommendations were still somewhere off in the future. Under the renewed urgings of Andy Kerr and Vic Sher, the groups decided that petitions could no longer be delayed.

Kerr was first to petition. In March the Oregon Natural Resources Council, the Wilderness Society, and one local conservation group petitioned on behalf of the sea-run cutthroat trout that spawned in the Umpqua River, one of Oregon's celebrated fishing rivers. In July the Fisheries Service announced the petition had merit, and it was undertaking a review of the status of the cutthroat. All harvest of the cutthroats had been banned since 1986, but the fish were thought to be near extinction in 1993.

Bill Bakke petitioned next. In July, Bakke led Oregon Trout and two other organizations in filing a petition for protection of forty separate populations of wild coho salmon on the Oregon coast. Here seemed that dread event which environmentalists and their detractors had been conjuring for the better part of three years—a petition that spanned a broad area and would, presumably, therefore have correspondingly broad implications, if protections were granted.

Even so, the Oregon Trout petition really only addressed part of the still-larger regional decline of coho. Fish advocates had known since the "Crossroads" paper that coho were in serious trouble not only in Oregon but also in coastal California and parts of Washington. The causes included the litany of habitat loss, overharvest, and ineffective and sometimes harmful hatchery practices. Dams were not a main cause at the coast. A good deal of popular attention was given to seals and sea lions, whose populations themselves had rebounded thanks to the Marine Mammal Protection Act. Any visitor to the coast could see the big mammals visibly feeding on salmon, but researchers did not agree about how big a bite the mammals were taking out of salmon populations as a whole.

One other factor which scientists had long suspected did seem to be contributing significantly to coho's problems: Ocean conditions appeared to be moving through the bottom of a cycle.

Since the mid-1980s evidence had been accumulating that oceanic food supplies for salmon go through cycles of abundance, which appeared to last about forty to sixty years. These productivity cycles were linked to large-scale and imperfectly understood oceanic and atmospheric phenomena. The productivity cycle off Washington, Oregon, and California, moreover, appeared to be opposite to the cycle off northern British Columbia and Alaska. When production slumped in the south, it crested in the north.

Such a shift from high to low productivity had occurred off the Oregon coast about 1976, and the trend in Oregon natural-spawning coho since then had been steadily down. The exemplary bad year was 1983, when an episode of the ocean-warming phenomenon known as El Niño sent coho populations plummeting. A warmer ocean meant reduced food supplies for salmon. A recurrence of the phenomenon in 1992 and 1993 had even more devastating consequences, at least partly because of the continued paucity of adult spawners in the intervening decade. The total returns of coho to Washington, Oregon, and northern California were the worst on record in 1993, and were predicted to be worse still in 1994. Meanwhile, the salmon catch in Alaska generally increased throughout the 1980s and in 1993 hit a record high.

What were managers supposed to do about the unfavorable ocean conditions? The prevailing wisdom seemed to be that conditions in the ocean could certainly harm salmon, but nothing could be done about them. They had been bad before but had apparently never placed whole species at risk of extinction. Although it was foolish to be unaware of the potential significance of ocean conditions on abundance, it was best to concentrate on rivers, streams, and related lands in salmon management. People could do something about conditions there, but nothing about the ocean.

In 1993 the coho indisputably needed help, coastwide, and the environmental groups had informally decided that a regional organization should address the regional aspect of the problem. The Pacific Rivers Council considered itself that organization, and Doppelt and Bayles filed that petition.

Few doubted the merit of the two coastal coho petitions. In Oregon, the state fish agency itself acknowledged that the forty coho salmon populations were at risk of extinction. The productivity of wild coho salmon had fallen to less than 5 percent of historic levels. Bakke knew that the Oregon petition had been needed for a long time, and he was relieved to finally be getting on with it.

He took the public position that an ESA listing was the coho's best chance for recovery. The state of Oregon had begun its own coastal salmon recovery strategy, after considerable public discussion and a commitment from the governor. That was fine and very welcome. The Clinton forest plan would also, at best, help the coho on federal lands. But no program addressed all the coastal watersheds outside of federal lands or the private landholdings that affected the coho. The great majority of coastal coho streams were not on federal land.

"Oregon Trout is filing this petition as a tool, not a weapon," Bakke said at the filing.

Underlying Bakke's concerns was an awareness of how the Oregon coast was changing. He didn't need a crystal ball to see how those changes might well affect the coho. This often rainy and comparatively unpopulated coast was rapidly becoming more populated, and the pressure of more residents on local resources was only likely to compound the problems the fish were already facing.

Bakke always remembered the lesson he learned as a child, when he and his dog raided the neighbor's goldfish pond. Once the goldfish were gone the neighbor removed the pond. Bakke, the kid, felt awful. The lesson was that the habitat that supported fish could no more survive the loss of the fish than the fish could survive the loss of the habitat. Now Bakke, the adult, knew how convenient it was for those who had other designs on the undeveloped coastal habitat to not be troubled if the fish went away.

So Bakke's goals—Oregon Trout's goals—were a refinement of his longstanding concerns. He hoped that a listing of the coho would force state and federal resource managers to protect and restore streams so that they could produce salmon. He also wanted a listing to control salmon harvests so that proper numbers of salmon were allowed to spawn; and he wanted to reform hatchery programs so that wild coho would be protected.

For anyone keeping score, the number of legal actions—petitions, lawsuits, countersuits, legal briefs—that were advanced in 1993 promised a salmon crisis that was likely to become more contentious, not less. It was commonplace to read in newspapers and organizational newsletters the opinion that disputes over salmon would soon make the battle over the spotted owl look like a walk in the park. It seemed to many people in the Northwest that protection and restoration of the salmon, both in the Columbia Basin and along the coast, would be a long and difficult journey upstream against the current, if indeed it could be negotiated at all.

Nevertheless, those embarked on the journey were probably better prepared than any others attempting so formidable a task before. As a group, fish biologists, ecologists, and other natural resource scientists were coming to think about their own history and professional practices more critically than at any previous time. They were talking among themselves in a productive way. Perhaps just as important, what they said was also absorbed by others; environmentalists were listening closely.

Since the late 1980s, the contradictions between their professional responsibilities and the condition of the resources for which they were responsible had clearly spawned a new professional activism. Underneath the activism, supporting and urging it on, there was by 1993 a new outspokenness in scholarship. Gordon Reeves and Jim Sedell were prominent in using scientific data to reform forestry policies, for example, while others used the history of other fisheries to bolster their case.

Dan Bottom, a research biologist with the Oregon Department of Fish and Wildlife and the president of the Oregon chapter of the American Fisheries Society the year after Reeves, became particularly interested in what the Northwest might learn from the salmon history of New England. Bottom wrote a scholarly three-part study of the origins of American fisheries management, its adoption in the Northwest, and new ideas for management that had been emerging from the Northwest salmon crisis. As the parts were completed, Bottom circulated them to colleagues and gave public talks about them. He planned a book when all three parts were complete.

Atlantic salmon had once been plentiful throughout New England, but by the latter part of the nineteenth century they were virtually extinct. Bottom had researched the causes of the decline and had unearthed some revealing documents. In 1857, George Perkins Marsh prepared a report for the Vermont legislature, in which he described the causes of the Atlantic salmon decline: overharvest, obstruction of fish passage by dams, water pollution caused by sawdust and other industrial wastes, and stream habitat alteration by the logging of the New England forests.

If it were not for Marsh's ornate prose, Bottom might have thought that the stream conditions Marsh was describing were not those of Vermont in the 1850s but of Oregon in the 1990s. Perkins wrote, for example:

> The clearing of the woods has been attended with the removal of many obstructions to the flow of water . . . The general character of our water courses has become more *torrential* . . . [so that in] inundations, not only does the mechanical violence of the current destroy or sweep down fish and their eggs, and fill the water with mud and other impurities, but it continually changes the banks and beds of the streams, and thus renders it difficult and often impossible for fish to fulfill that law of their nature which impels them annually to return to their breeding place to deposit their spawn.

Bottom saw in Marsh much more than an acute observer of the effects of human disturbances on nature; Marsh saw the need for human self-control to avoid destroying nature. But he also promoted the idea of privately owned fish hatcheries as a way to compensate for the loss of those conditions that the fish needed.

"When viewed as alternatives," Bottom wrote, "it is little wonder which message would have the greater popular appeal."

Over time Americans consistently chose hatcheries over habitat. Bottom saw that hatcheries were more than just a technological fix; they were also a psychological fix. "Fish culture complemented the romantic vision of an earlier age, when nature was unspoiled by human hands," he wrote. "The possibility of recreating plenty from scarcity—whether for profit or from remorse—was a powerful force."

The New England experience, Bottom came to believe, was important not because it showed that the salmon's history was repeating itself, but because it provided an opportunity for the salmon's history to not repeat itself entirely. If Oregon and the Northwest were going to be able to think afresh about fisheries science and management and solve long-festering problems, it was crucial to expose how the accepted biases in the profession had originated.

At the same time that Bottom was exploring the past to set a better course for his colleagues, Jack Williams was attempting to use his current influence to move not only fisheries colleagues but an entire federal agency. Williams had been elevated from fisheries program manager of the Bureau of Land Management to the high position of science adviser to the agency's director. During his tenure in that position he wrote openly about aquatic ecosystem decline on federal lands and the need for agency reform. In an essay written for the conservation magazine *Trout,* Williams recommended new goals for land management to replace "commodity production."

"Restoring and maintaining ecosystem health should be the primary goal in management of public lands," Williams wrote. "Commodity targets should be abolished."

Continuing in this radical vein, Williams urged that ties between commodity production and agency budgets should be severed and that measures of performance appropriate to the new goals should be established. One good measure of agency performance, he said, would be a change in the amount of habitat that met the desired conditions for ecosystem health. "Ecosystem health" itself, he argued, need not be a mysterious concept. As with human health, ecosystem health was demonstrated by how productive the ecosystem was and by how resilient it remained.

Williams had also been part of the FEMAT aquatic ecosystems group, and for him, watersheds needed to become the focus of action. "Healthy" watersheds, he understood, bounced back more quickly after natural disturbances such as floods, drought, or fire than unhealthy ones could. However, when people "stressed" watersheds by road-building and a hundred other activities, they reduced a healthy watershed's capacity to recover from such disturbances.

Williams certainly advocated changes in management. Habitat could be restored, hatcheries and hydropower operations could be refined, harvest could be managed better. But he issued a warning that there were "no technological quick-fixes to the Pacific salmon problems." Reforms would all take time and the institutional commitments to taking the time.

By the end of 1993 it was apparent to the biologists and managers who were absorbed in the salmon crisis that a rare event in the practice of any scientific profession was occurring in their midst. Their profession was going through what philosopher of science Thomas Kuhn called a "paradigm shift," a major reorientation of the operating assumptions and values of a profession—its worldview. For salmon specialists, the old worldview of species production and ecosystem consumption was giving way to a new one of species conservation and ecosystem restoration.

Among dozens of signs, this shift was perhaps most clearly heralded by a professional conference announced for Seattle in January 1994. The subject of the conference was "Pacific Salmon and their Ecosystems," itself a linkage that not long before would not have commanded primary attention. Furthermore, the committee that established the agenda for the three-day program included a who's who of the professionals that, only a year or two earlier, had been on the outside of official salmon policy—Jim Lichatowich, Willa Nehlsen, and Gordon Reeves. Finally, the joint sponsors were two academic units that also, not long before, would not have recognized common ground on the topic—the colleges of Forest Resources and Ocean and Fishery Sciences at the University of Washington.

As fisheries professionals were surveying their past and trying to chart a new path, they were collectively strengthened by a parallel reform movement within forestry. In the vanguard of that profession was the decidedly activist Association of Forest Service Employees for Environmental Ethics. Founded in 1989 by a disillusioned Forest Service timber-sale planner in Oregon, the organization quickly grew to several thousand members, including many other disillusioned Forest Service employees throughout the country. Members shared a concern over management that emphasized extracting commodities over sustaining resources. These concerns intensified during 1993 after revelations of illegal and improper behavior at the top ranks of the Forest Service.

One congressional report documented more than 180 instances of alleged agency interference or retaliation against law-enforcement officers who were examining agency and timber industry wrongdoings. One Forest Service law officer in Oregon, assigned to the agency's National Timber Theft Task Force, told a congressional committee that the agency had allowed "favored timber companies to steal literally hundreds of millions of dollars worth of old-growth timber." Meanwhile, the agency was accused of knowingly contracting with reforestation companies that employed undocumented workers.

Although the Forest Service seemed to invite disillusionment, the Association of Forest Service Employees for Environmental Ethics was distinguished by its constructive outlook. The association said in its "vision statement" that it "believes that land is a public trust, to be passed with reverence from generation to generation." It continued:

> Humankind has no right to abuse the land. The Forest Service
> and other public agencies must follow the footsteps of Aldo
> Leopold, a pioneer in conservation, and become leaders in the
> quest for a new resource ethic. Together we must work toward an
> ecologically and economically sustainable future.

Given this call to work toward a "sustainable future," members of the organization must have been particularly pleased in November 1993, when the Clinton administration announced the appointment of Jack Ward Thomas as chief of the Forest Service. Thomas, a twenty-seven-year veteran of the agency, was the first wildlife biologist ever named to oversee the National Forests. Most previous chiefs had been foresters who rose through the agency's timber-sales program.

Beginning with the Thomas plan in 1989, Thomas had led all the principal policy studies attempting to resolve the Northwest forest crisis. He personified the emergence of a new conservation ethic within the federal land-management agencies. In accepting the position, he promised to move "ecosystem management" from a concept to a practice. Further, he intended to restore the integrity of the agency. "We will obey the law and we will tell the truth," he said.

Accompanying this impulse for renewal within the resource-management professions were certain governmental policy assessments, which had the potential to support or deflate that impulse. After the release of the FEMAT report, the next important government document, and a major bellwether of salmon policy, was the National Marine Fisheries Service recovery plan for the endangered Snake River salmon. In October 1993, the draft of that plan was published.

Two years in the making, the report underscored a now common theme. "The sole hope for managing a recovery effort is to adopt a comprehensive ecosystem management approach," the recovery team said. No single measure, taken separately, could ensure recovery of the listed Snake River chinook or sockeye.

The seven-member team of independent experts was led by a retired fisheries professor, while the other six included two more biologists, two engineers, an ecologist, and an economist. All but one held doctorates, most had directed research or management programs, most were retired or nearly so; all were considered knowledgeable long-time students of salmon management. As expected, they described changes needed in the "four h's"— harvest, hatcheries, habitat, and hydropower—to recover the dwindling Snake populations. But the most politically controversial element of the team's draft was a new call to put "someone in charge," someone authorized to make decisions to benefit the fish.

"There is no directed authority or accountability to assure effective management of the overall system," the report said. "Among myriad agencies and interests, no one really is in charge. Institutional, jurisdictional, state and federal boundaries make rational overall fisheries management decisions impossible." The agency that should take charge, the team concluded, was the Fisheries Service. It should assemble a staff dedicated to accomplishing the plan. It should establish an "impartial, independent, science-based group" to oversee the plan as it was put into action.

Regarding the "four h's," the team said that hatchery production could be used "judiciously to accelerate recovery of severely weakened stocks," but that hatcheries should be employed with caution. "The highest priority should be given to natural production" of salmon in "all waters supporting the listed stocks." Comprehensive measures, meanwhile, were needed to protect and restore the quality and quantity of spawning, rearing, and migration corridor habitats. Hydropower facilities and operations should be changed to improve survival of juvenile and adult salmon "throughout" the Snake and Columbia Rivers.

Finally, harvest practices would need to be adjusted in order to "maximize passage and survival of listed stocks throughout mixed stock ocean and river fisheries." Among measures the team endorsed was a mandatory buy-back program in the non-Indian gill-net fisheries and in certain ocean fisheries off Oregon and Washington. The team also noted the urgent need to use the Pacific Salmon Treaty to reduce the catch of fall chinook by Canadian fishermen. Canadians were the principal harvesters of Snake River fall chinook.

While the Fisheries Service prepared to review the scientific team's recovery plan, refine, and then implement it, a second group of independent scientists was considering the same set of issues from a still broader perspective. This inquiry embraced recovery of all Northwest wild salmon, not only listed stocks. This scientific group had potentially the greatest influence of any to address the salmon crisis. It was the salmon committee of the National Research Council.

Important as it was, probably no more than a few hundred Northwesterners were even aware of the committee's existence when it began its work. To most Americans outside of government and academia, the National Research Council itself was not well known. Founded in 1916 as the research arm of the National Academy of Sciences, an organization of the most eminent scientists in the United States, the Research Council was designed to provide advice to the government, specifically Congress.

In spite of its comparative obscurity to the general public, in 1993 the Research Council comprised a staff of eleven hundred, which oversaw the activities of some eight hundred separate working committees at any time.

The committees, such as the salmon committee, were made up primarily of academics who served as volunteers. A certain prestige was attached to being asked to serve. The Research Council was known as the scientific brain trust of the government, a source of supposedly impartial, thorough, and clear thinking on any issue.

Clear thinking about the status and needs of wild salmon had been Bill Bakke's motive in asking for the formation of the committee, back in 1991. After the failure of the salmon summit, he and Rick Braun had requested a meeting with Mark Hatfield to propose the idea of what they thought of as a wild salmon "audit." Hatfield, the old college teacher, always liked the idea of collecting advice from the most knowledgeable parties. Getting advice wasn't the same as slavishly following it; everyone knew that. But advice was good to have, and he pushed through an appropriation for more than a half-million dollars for the National Research Council to look into the salmon crisis. The committee was charged with answering the central question of the whole tangled affair. It was to evaluate options "for improving the prospects for the long-term sustainability" of Pacific salmon and sea-run trout. Like Clinton's forest scientists, the salmon committee was also asked to "consider economic and social implications of such changes."

As the committee met through 1993, it sifted through a mountain of testimony and documentation. The seventeen members included natural scientists and social scientists, Northwesterners steeped in the issues, and people from outside the region who knew little about the issues beforehand. The idea behind this composition seemed to be to challenge all of them to think freshly. The challenge of the deadline was formidable enough, given the scope of the task. By summer 1994, the committee was expected to publish its findings.

In the meantime, most of its deliberations were conducted in private, a process intended to ensure the objectivity of its conclusions. The committee's report would be extensively reviewed by peers before it was released. At the end, Congress would receive it, and everyone familiar with the Research Council assumed that the report would receive significant attention.

Hatfield himself said he expected to use the report to guide him in policy decisions.

Studies. Reports. New insights. Maybe new directions for management. *So what?* What would all of this mean for the salmon in the rivers? How would the crisis be solved?

Was the government the key to the solution?

If citizens expected to see an improvement in the long-term prospects for the salmon, it seemed clear that first of all the government agencies whose actions affected the salmon would need to uphold environmental laws. They would also need to ensure that others did, too. Beyond that minimum, a long-term government solution would involve developing a better understanding of what was meant by ecosystem-based management. Thoughtfully and deliberately, the agencies would then need to put that understanding into action.

The Forest Service and the Bureau of Land Management had been chastened enough, one would have thought, about the need for law-abiding behavior. Assuming they had learned that lesson, the federal agencies had more of a start on ecosystem management principles and practices than any others, thanks to the FEMAT report and other agency directives, such as the PACFISH strategy.

The National Marine Fisheries Service knew its fundamental task. The agency needed to not merely follow but lead in the implementation of the Endangered Species Act for the salmon.

For its part, the Northwest Power Planning Council had struggled to craft the beginnings of an ecosystem-based plan that would apply to much of the Columbia and Snake river basins. As long as its enabling legislation stayed the same and the political balance of the council members did not change dramatically, the council could be expected to spend a considerable amount of time just jawboning. It would keep struggling, urging the Bonneville Power Administration, the Corps of Engineers, the Bureau of Reclamation, and all the numerous state and tribal agencies to comply with and support their salmon strategy.

For those who believed that salmon would sink or swim depending on what government did, some further believed that the underlying issue was that no one agency had the authority or the will to "solve the problem." What was needed, according to this way of thinking, was a salmon *super-agency* with sweeping powers, along the lines suggested by the Snake River recovery team. However, of those who believed that the salmon problem was fundamentally a problem of governance, there were probably more who feared the establishment of some salmon superagency than welcomed it. For this majority, neither the available candidates among existing agencies nor the prospects of a new superagency held much appeal. A "salmon czar" might sound appealing, but few would have been comfortable with any individual or organization wielding too much authority in such a complicated issue.

Feeling dictated to by the government had already prompted a backlash to the ESA. As it was, many members of Congress were prepared to weaken environmental provisions of the act when it came up for reauthorization in 1994 or 1995. Giving more dictatorial powers to environmental regulators seemed unlikely to create any better, or lasting, solutions for endangered species.

Government was certainly important to a salmon solution, but underlying and supporting government intervention, some were coming to believe, was the need for something much more basic and much harder to achieve, if the salmon were to persist. It was daunting to think of, but an examination of societal values seemed needed.

Ultimately, whether restoration of the salmon could succeed seemed to depend on the resolve of residents of the Northwest to think hard about the way they saw themselves and the "natural world"—as if the two were so easily separable. Could they modify their expectations of nature to prefer long-term benefits over short-term ones? Could they see themselves as part of nature rather than as its dominator?

The odds seemed formidable against such fundamental changes occurring broadly in American society.

It was hard to make progress on protecting nature in an economy founded on the exploitation of nature.

It was hard to hear the quiet, deliberate voice of shared, community values in a society constantly shouting about individual rights.

It was hard to think about long-term public goals in a culture transfixed by daily personal consumption.

It was hard to worry about some local *fish* when confronted by the demands of an incessantly growing human population, which seemed doomed to compromise the life of the entire planet.

It was hard, finally, to do any of these things without broader public discussion of the public goods that were at stake. Sadly, the opportunities for such discussion were few. There was little public examination of the benefits of salmon or forests or rivers. Few asked about consequences: *What would happen to the Northwest forest environment if all the old trees were indeed cut down? What would happen to the water quality and quantity of rivers if the salmon were gone?*

The majority of people were woefully unprepared to either imagine a diminished future or commit to a rejuvenated one. In a political world in which commitments typically had a life span of two to four years, Northwesterners were nonetheless being confronted with the need to manage natural resources on a hundreds-of-years basis—that is, if they wanted to sustain those resources. Americans had precious little practice in valuing themselves or their environments over such a long time.

If these circumstances posed grave doubts, others encouraged some wild hopes.

Northwesterners might habitually think of themselves as living on a street, in a town, in a county, in a state. But beyond all these social and government compartments, many Northwesterners still cultivated a relationship with the natural world. This was not a coincidence nor the result of some special regional virtue. It seemed, if anything, elicited by nature itself. The Northwest retained more of its original natural character than did most other parts of the nation, and Northwesterners seemed to respond to this quality. It drew people to the area. "Quality of life" values, including contact with a comparatively unspoiled environment, are reasons typically given by immigrants to the region.

So, beyond the mental map of street-city-county-state, if Northwesterners could redraw their conceptual boundaries and come to think of themselves as living in natural watersheds, bigger changes might follow. Out of the realization that everyone in the range of the salmon lives in watersheds, and that actions affecting the watershed ultimately affect everyone in it, might arise a new sense of community. Nurtured, this sense of community might encourage a new ethos of responsibility, both to other people and to the larger ecological system, of which the human community is only a part. Who knows? Restoring watersheds might help restore democratic participation and a regard for place, both at the same time.

As 1994 began, government and private initiatives were under way in each of the Northwest states to involve citizens in watershed restoration efforts. The Northwest Power Planning Council, the Pacific Rivers Council, the states, and the federal agencies implementing the Clinton forest plan all had community-based watershed programs under way. Some principles for these efforts were beginning to emerge.

Watersheds and rivers seemed less likely to improve and salmon less likely to recover if strategies were dictated from the top down and from some centralized authority. Instead, individuals and groups would have to feel that not only were they invited to participate in a planning process, but once they were invested in it that they had significant authority to make decisions within the framework agreed upon. Moreover, everyone who had a stake in the outcome needed to be represented—including, of course, private land owners, who often bore direct costs of environmental improvements. Finally, defining and involving the "stakeholders" needed to be part of perhaps the most important and difficult task of all: finding appropriate means to inform and even educate the public about the true condition of the environment.

Many of the individuals caught up in the crisis of the 1990s—the fisheries managers, the utilities executives, the fishermen, the loggers—could be viewed as prisoners of their histories. Nothing was more important, nor more difficult, than that they should awake from the troubled sleep of those histories.

Such tasks were formidable, to say the least. However, like it or not, the 1990s would be the critical time for personal and societal choice concerning the legacy of the salmon, the forests, and the natural heritage of the Pacific Northwest.

How would Northwesterners and other Americans respond?

Would the fate of the salmon be the all-too-common one suffered by other species throughout the United States and the world from time immemorial—of attrition and, ultimately, extinction before the impositions of their human neighbors?

Or would people act differently?

Would they see that a civilization that destroys its environment is on the path to destroying itself?

Would Northwesterners rediscover that their own fate was in common with that of the salmon, the primordial resident of the place they called home?

Epilogue

We could all just leave for two hundred years and it would be hard to tell
we had been here. But we don't want to leave, and neither do we want to
think of ourselves as despoilers of the land. We need to be able to learn from
what has gone before—if we have made mistakes, admit them and move on.

As inhabitants working to restore natural systems, we will learn to see
the healing processes and to align ourselves with them. It's time now for
human populations to become one of the elements of recovery.

—FREEMAN HOUSE, *ELEMENTS OF RECOVERY*, 1989

A fire in a body of water—this is the image of revolution portrayed in the
world's oldest book, the Chinese *Book of Changes,* or *I Ching.* It seems a fitting
image for revolution to have come from a civilization that was intimate with
the natural world. Revolutionary change involves a conflict of opposites,
which are seen as forces of nature. One force may extinguish the other, but
at the outset the result is not at all certain.

Just so, the outcome of the heated struggle over the land and waters of the
Pacific Northwest could not be discerned in the first months of 1994. A
revolutionary change might well emerge, but a dominant trend was hard to
see amid the sparks and the steam.

Seventy million dollars was appropriated for watershed restoration efforts
during the year as part of the Clinton administration's response to the
Northwest forest crisis. Some Northwest members of Congress praised the
program, and Vice President Gore likened it to the Manhattan Project. But
the timber industry and even some environmental leaders expressed skepti-

cism that the first-year effort would have significant benefits for either displaced timber workers or watersheds.

Ruling on a lawsuit brought by the timber industry, a federal judge said that the Clinton administration violated a federal open-meeting law in preparing the scientific foundation of the plan, the FEMAT report. The industry had complained that it was generally excluded from the report's development. While Judge Thomas Penfield Jackson did not directly overturn the Clinton forest plan, his ruling made it certain that timber interests would appeal it once it was released.

When the plan was presented to Judge William Dwyer, not only timber but also environmental groups indeed filed lawsuits. The plan "has gone an incredible distance politically, but it falls short ecologically," said Andy Kerr. Whatever these legal actions might accomplish, they served to delay resolution of the crisis and to tie up federal timber sales yet again. Most cutting on the public lands that had been proposed for resumption in 1994, albeit at significantly reduced levels, would likely be delayed into 1995 or later.

Meanwhile, cutting on private lands in the region accelerated, as private landowners saw the market opportunity represented by decreased timber supplies and feared the encroachment of endangered species regulations.

Even as the need to protect species continued to affect forestry, the need to protect salmon imposed major constraints on the fishing industry. Setting the most restrictive fishing seasons in history, the Pacific Fishery Management Council banned fishing for coho salmon along the entire West Coast for 1994. Furthermore, all non-Indian ocean fishing for salmon was shut down off northern Oregon and Washington, with only very limited seasons available elsewhere. Commercial and sport fishing interests predicted dire economic consequences, and salmon fishermen requested inclusion in the jobs programs set up under the Clinton forest plan. "Obviously, fishermen have been put out of work by bad timber practices in the past," one fishing industry leader explained.

Environmentalists led by the Oregon Natural Resources Council, meanwhile, prepared to petition for all other remaining anadromous Pacific salmonids south of the Canadian border, including searun cutthroat trout, chum, pink, sockeye, and chinook salmon. The ONRC proposed to complete the petitioning by the end of 1995, citing the Endangered Species Act as "the single best hope" for the fish.

The ESA indeed provided new hope for Columbia River salmon, thanks to a major ruling in March by federal Judge Malcolm Marsh. The judge found that the National Marine Fisheries Service, the Army Corps of Engineers, and the Bureau of Reclamation had violated the law in the 1993 operations of the Federal Columbia River Power System.

Under section 7 of the ESA, the Fisheries Service is obliged to issue biological opinions on the actions of federal agencies that may jeopardize listed species. Marsh rejected the Fisheries Service's 1993 decision that hydrosystem operation presented "no jeopardy" to the fish, calling it "arbitrary and capricious." The agencies knew that operating the dams would kill millions of salmon, he said, but the Fisheries Service decided to support the status quo.

"Instead of looking for what *can* be done to protect the species in jeopardy," the judge said, "NMFS and the action agencies have narrowly focused their attention on what the establishment is capable of handling with minimal disruption." He told the federal agencies they would have to consult with him about the operation of the Columbia power system.

While the Endangered Species Act cooled off one set of antagonists, it further enflamed others. In Congress, legislation aimed at weakening the Endangered Species Act continued to gain support. A bill introduced by Louisiana representative Billy Tauzin addressed the main concern of many developers by promising to compensate private landowners who were "substantially deprived of the economically viable use of property" as a result of the ESA.

Environmentalists argued that such a change in the law was not based on any real conflict between the ESA and property rights, and it would drastically increase the cost of implementing the environmental law. That increased cost, they claimed, was the real purpose of such proposals, which were becoming commonplace in Congress.

"The apparent strategy is very simple," the National Audubon Society commented—"to demand that taxpayers pay financial compensation to prop-

erty owners far more frequently than the Constitution requires, in the hope
that government will be required to abandon or roll back existing regulations
that would otherwise become too expensive."

While the drama over which path to take at the endangered-species
crossroads continued to captivate much of the public's attention, in some
locations individuals and communities were quietly setting a new course for
themselves, apparently embarking on the revolutionary change.

Humboldt County, in northern California, is typical of many coastal counties stretching from the San Francisco Bay Area to Puget Sound; forestry,
fisheries, and farming have traditionally been the foundations of the economy. But the relationships among these traditional interests that Scott
Downie began to forge in Humboldt County were not typical of this broad
coastal region.

Since 1990, Downie, a fisheries supervisor for the state of California, has
been working to develop a relationship between the state and the largest
landowner in the county, Pacific Lumber Company. Pacific Lumber has been
in operation since 1869, harvesting primarily redwood trees on its 350 square
miles of timber lands in the Van Duzen and Eel River watersheds. The major
employer in the area, the company had traditionally managed its lands with
a long-term perspective, but a hostile takeover of the family-owned company
in the 1980s resulted in an acceleration of logging.

Downie saw the need for the company to manage its lands with more
sensitivity to salmon resources. The soils in this part of the coast are extremely prone to erosion, and the quantities of sediment that slide off hillsides following logging or the building of logging roads can and do cause
substantial damage in streams. Sediments can suffocate tiny salmon which
have not yet emerged from the gravel, block entire stream sections from
migrating fish, and cause numerous other problems. As urgent as the needs
were, Downie recognized that regulatory controls could only go part of the
way in achieving his purposes. He determined to strike a relationship which
would be regarded as mutually beneficial.

A stocky outdoorsman with a genial manner, Downie wasn't seen as some government outsider when he approached Pacific Lumber. His stepfather had worked for the company, and Downie has made his living in the county for much of his life as a fisherman, a private fishery consultant, and only more recently as a state employee. People who worked for Pacific Lumber knew Downie, and they were willing to listen to him.

Under an agreement signed by both the company and the state agency in 1992, the two parties promised to work together to enhance the fishery resources on the company's lands. They would start by inventorying the conditions of streams and watersheds there. By 1994, some significant projects had occurred, including the improvement of over thirty miles of fishery habitat and the modification of logging roads so that landslide risks were reduced or eliminated. In 1993 alone, California Fish and Game calculated that more than 5,000 cubic yards of sediments that had been in danger of fouling streams were removed.

Perhaps as significant as the on-the-ground protection and restoration was the new training that company employees received in standard practices such as building, maintaining, and retiring logging roads.

On a tour of some of the project sites on company lands, Downie reflected on the experience.

" 'Resource problems' aren't really resource problems," he said. "They are human problems; I can't emphasize that enough.

"To me, there are three key words in the institution of a watershed program where you have a lot of diverse interests. They are *trust, respect,* and *patience.* It takes a lot of patience to build the trust and respect."

Downie recognized that a primary impediment to improving conditions in watersheds is the fragmentation and mixture of land ownership. A coastal watershed of five or six square miles may have on the order of twenty or thirty landowners, all with different values and goals for their property. The best way to start watershed improvements, he believed, was to have local residents identify their own concerns. On Pacific Lumber land, Downie discovered the seeds of such concern among the 1,200 employees of the company. But he also gained the support and the cooperation of the president of the company.

"Bottom up and top down: That's the ideal combination to get projects going," he said.

Over time, however, he became convinced that "education is the only meaningful way to get long-term change."

He shook his head and smiled. "We'll need to learn to be patient," he said. "We're in this together."

South of the Van Duzen and Eel Rivers along the coast but separated from them by a mountain range, the next major river is the Mattole. The Mattole Valley is the part of California that even the local calls "the lost coast," a kind of Shangri-La, remote and isolated.

In contrast to the Van Duzen with its dominant landowner, the Mattole is more representative of Northwest coast communities with its assortment of property owners, including logging companies, large and small livestock ranches, farmers, and homesteaders. The particular mix in the Mattole may not be typical, however. A substantial number of homesteaders in the valley are self-proclaimed hippies, 1960s-generation back-to-the-landers who found in the Mattole the sweet home for which they had been searching.

For all its current beauties, the 300-square-mile Mattole Valley has been subjected to drastic change in its recent history. More than ninety percent of the original conifer forest of redwoods and Douglas-fir has been logged at least once; much of that activity has occurred in the last fifty years. The 62-mile-long river, whose name meant "clear water" in the dialect of the indigenous people, often runs murky these days as it picks up sediment that has attended road-building. The roads were built not only for logging but for the 1970s and '80s influx of homesteaders.

As on the majority of coastal rivers, the salmon of the Mattole have been seriously harmed by ill-advised practices on the land. Lagoons there once represented an ideal environment in which chinook salmon could find abundant food while they gradually acclimated to a saltwater environment. But the Mattole River lagoon is no longer so hospitable for chinook, as the quantity of water flowing into the protected area has been reduced. Water temperatures overall have risen, while the sediment the river carries chokes the lagoon organisms that the salmon prey upon.

The troubles the salmon face on the Mattole River have their own specific differences, but they are similar in kind to many other places in the Northwest and similar in that the progress toward solutions will require cooperation across a diverse social spectrum.

The challenge seems to have energized the members of the Mattole Restoration Council. With limited technical and professional expertise, like-minded Mattole residents formed the council in 1979, incorporating six years later as a non-profit community based organization. With some funding from government agencies and private foundations, and with a real foundation of volunteer interest and energy, the organization set about restoring the Mattole. The council dedicated itself to "watershed repair and salmonid enhancement, as well as the creation and celebration of a restoration culture."

A typical project was completed in January 1994 on one of the numerous tributaries of the Mattole, the Mattole Canyon Creek. Colum Coyne, a bright-eyed, red-bearded man wearing the kind of rubberized rainsuit that an experienced fisherman would be expected to wear, stood alongside the creek in a springtime rain and pointed to a steep slope a hundred yards away.

The slope had the raw look of a once-forested hillside stripped by a landslide. Small rocks still littered upper parts of the slope. The streambank was chocked with larger rocks and boulders, but Coyne pointed out some green details against the ground. They were small trees, hundreds of them, planted to stabilize the slope and return it to its natural condition. It was just part of a technically varied, three-mile-long project in and alongside the creek, designed to make it inhabitable again for the once-numerous salmon and steelhead.

The landslide occurred after a logging road was put in adjacent to his homestead, Coyne explained. After the trees were cut, the road lay neglected.

"Then you get one hundred inches of rain a year, and you end up with that." He gestured again at the evidence of the landslide.

Coyne had not liked what he had seen, and he had called restoration council staff to find out what could be done. With funding from the state and with the volunteer labor of Coyne and others, a project to stabilize the creek was begun. The fisherman worked for more than a month with his dump truck, picking up rocks, boulders, and stumps, moving gravel around, reshaping the slope and the adjacent creek under the supervision of council staff.

Coyne did not seem particularly fazed that, young and vigorous as he was, he might not live to see the results of his labors.

"Everything starts with a first step," he said. "I hope my kids and grand-kids will be able to see a nice fir forest here. I don't think it will take that long for the salmon to come back. But for the forest to come back and look like it should I'll probably be dead.

"That doesn't bother me," he continued, smiling. "That's just the way it is. It's a good idea to leave things a little better than you found them."

The creek project was not only good for the land, the water, and the fish; it had another value, Coyne believed.

"My neighbors were a bit apprehensive at first about strangers coming on to their property to do this work, but without exception they all see the immediate benefits. Even the people who were a little upset at first about the noise and the heavy machinery have come around and are saying they never saw the creek look so good."

As the rain continued, watering the seedling trees and filling up the creek, Coyne finished his thought.

"It's a good way for people to come together—working to fix things. People are pretty proud of this project.

Lest anyone think that these embryonic examples of watershed restoration refute Woody Allen's quip that California's contribution to American civilization is the right turn on a red light, it should be said that such efforts are not solely California's innovation. Other local projects could be found scattered throughout the Northwest.

In Oregon for example, the Coquille River, a once-prolific salmon river on the rural southern coast, was the site of a decade-old salmon enhancement effort. Led by the marine Extension agent from Oregon State University, the Coquille watershed effort, like that on the Mattole, provided an ongoing forum for citizen-initiated action. In 1994 the state of Oregon recognized the Coquille for major funding under its new Watershed Health Program.

Similarly in Washington, other grassroots efforts could learn from the long-running Chehalis Basin Fisheries Task Force, begun in 1980. The Chehalis River winds through numerous private, state, and tribal lands, in its route from the mountains of southwestern Washington to the city of Aberdeen, where it empties into Gray's Harbor and the Pacific Ocean.

Membership in the task force representing this broad region included recreational, commercial, and tribal fishermen, business and environmental organizations, organized labor, and government agencies. The task force lobbied for the establishment of a federally funded habitat and watershed restoration program, which began in 1990. That same year, the Washington legislature established twelve regional volunteer enhancement groups modeled after the Chehalis Task Force.

The learning that seemed to be emerging from such successful projects was that regulation and the threat of regulation—as necessary as they sometimes were—were not likely to move all people in the needed direction. To reach the goal of restoring streams and watersheds, protecting species, and in sum, preserving the diversity of life, other approaches were needed.

Practitioners and trained observers alike shared a growing recognition of the wisdom of fostering collaboration in developing new land management practices. "A call for collaboration is not a starry-eyed proposal that ignores the current venom and rancor," wrote one team of Oregon researchers in 1993. Collaboration "does not expect the participants to set their self-interest aside.

> Quite the contrary: Participants are expected to clearly voice their interests and energetically work to achieve them. The key is that their efforts are oriented not in opposition to those of their fellow participants, but in concert.

To make collaboration work, those who establish a group need to create "an environment where exploring differences is not hindered, but encouraged," the researchers wrote. When the differences are not openly addressed, they may undermine the process and jeopardize the results.

Just as in addressing local issues, the trend was away from conflict toward collaboration, so in addressing national policies, the trend seemed to be away from regulation toward incentives. The Defenders of Wildlife published a report late in 1993 which signalled an important opening in the thinking of some environmental leaders. The report was titled *Building Economic Incentives into the Endangered Species Act.*

The various environmental professionals who contributed to the report enlarged on the view of Michael Bean, Wildlife Program Chairman of the Environmental Defense Fund, who observed that "strong incentives for conservation on private land must be created. The [Endangered Species] Act relies heavily on penalties to deter harmful conduct and virtually not at all on rewards for beneficial conduct."

The contributors presented several models for introducing incentives into endangered-species protection, including the establishment of altogether new institutions. "Biodiversity Trust Funds" were promoted by several authors as a viable, in fact a necessary, mechanism. Such a trust, funded by both private and public sources and managed by nongovernmental experts, would purchase conservation easements and award grants for conservation activities.

The devil might well be in the details of establishing such a beneficient-seeming institution, and yet few would wish to criticize the impulse to find more widely acceptable approaches to protecting endangered species.

As desperate as the circumstances of the endangered salmon appeared, the efforts of people with differing values and beliefs to seek common ground offered hope.

The fire was still in the stream. But within the prospect of revolutionary change some gradual progress seemed to be occurring.

Twenty five centuries ago, in a time when people were new to the forests and rivers of China, the *I Ching* had established a timeless image for "gradual progress." That image was a tree growing on a mountain.

No doubt fish also grew in the clear stream in the valley below, and in the valley, people talked with—and listened to—each other.

APPENDIX

A Chronology of an Ecosystem Crisis

1805

Lewis and Clark explore the Snake and Columbia Rivers, observing Indians catching large numbers of salmon. Researchers later estimate that, during the predevelopment era, 10 to 16 million Pacific salmon and steelhead trout entered the river system annually to spawn.

1826

Fallen trees prevent explorers with the Hudson's Bay Company from penetrating Oregon coastal rivers to their sources. An abundance of salmon and beaver is observed in the virgin forests.

1855

Treaties between the U.S. government and several Northwest Indian bands and tribes foster European-American settlement of the Northwest; Indians are relegated to reservations. The treaties also reserve to the Indians the right to hunt and fish in their traditional places.

1866

The first salmon cannery in North America is established near the mouth of the Columbia River, not far from Astoria, Oregon. The owners are entrepreneurs from

New England. The Columbia and the Snake River, its largest tributary, are the world's biggest producer of chinook (king) salmon, which is physically the largest and considered by many the choicest of the Pacific salmon. The commercial "harvest" of salmon begins in earnest; nets and traps are the most common fishing methods.

1878

The first salmon hatchery in the Northwest is opened by cannery owners on the Columbia River near Portland, which indicates that salmon are already in decline as a result of intensive fishing.

1883

The lower Columbia River commercial fishery captures 43 million pounds of chinook salmon, the largest catch ever recorded.

1894

The U.S. Fish Commission begins investigations of the "alarming decrease in the salmon catch of the Columbia River."

1896

A militant fishermen's organization leads a strike that turns violent against canneries in Astoria and vicinity over the price paid for salmon. The National Guard is mobilized in Washington and Oregon to break the strike.

1899

The number of fishwheels in use on the Columbia increases to seventy-six. These giant fish-catching devices, which look like ferris wheels with scoops in place of seats, use the river's current to catch enormous numbers of salmon. Individual fishwheels take forty to fifty tons of salmon per year.

1926

The Oregon legislature bans fishwheels; Washington follows suit in 1934. After reaching an all-time high about 1920, the annual catch in the Columbia begins a continuous decline.

1937

As plans to build numerous dams across the Columbia are announced, U.S. Commissioner of Fisheries Frank T. Bell declares that "Contrary to the impression created by certain self-constituted critics . . . we have no reason to believe that the Columbia River salmon are in danger of extinction. The difficulties in the way of their successful migration and spawning have been foreseen and provided for."

1938

Bonneville Dam is constructed on the Columbia 140 miles upriver from the mouth. The dam is originally designed without means to get salmon past it. Arthur Newton Pack, president of the American Nature Association, declares that the dams will doom the Columbia fishing industry, which at the time employs 25,000 people.

1941

Grand Coulee Dam is completed on the Columbia in north-central Washington. The 550-foot-high dam prevents salmon passage altogether, and 1,100 miles of productive salmon habitat are lost. The dam is designed to generate electricity and irrigate a half-million acres.

1948

Construction of federal hatcheries, authorized by the Mitchell Act, begins below Bonneville Dam. The intent of the construction is to compensate for some of the lost salmon production caused by the hydroelectric dams. Paul Needham, Oregon's chief of fisheries, publicly denounces the idea that hatcheries can take the place of natural production.

1955

As timber harvests on federal lands in the Northwest increase dramatically, little attention is paid to the effects of logging on populations of salmon and trout. Likewise, few alarms are raised about the practice of grazing livestock on millions of acres of agricultural and range lands, which degrades salmon streams in the region.

1967

The completion of Hells Canyon Dam, on the Snake River between Oregon and Idaho, prevents salmon migration beyond that point, eliminating more than half of the river's historic spawning area.

1969

The landmark *U.S. v. Oregon* decision confirms the rights of Columbia Basin treaty tribes to a "fair and equitable" share of the salmon harvest. The ruling, the companion to *U.S. v. Washington,* five years later, defines "fair and equitable" as half of all the harvestable salmon destined for the tribes' traditional fishing places. The rulings, based on the 1855 treaties, infuriate many non-Indian fishermen.

1973

Congress enacts the Endangered Species Act.

1978

The National Marine Fisheries Service begins a formal review of the status of some Columbia and Snake River salmon populations. The federal agency, which has responsibility for salmon under the Endangered Species Act, is concerned about declining populations.

1980

One purpose of the new Northwest Electric Power Planning and Conservation Act is to "protect, mitigate, and enhance" salmon runs affected by the hydroelectric development of the Columbia River Basin. The National Marine Fisheries Service puts its salmon petitions on hold.

1982

The Northwest Power Planning Council, established by the Power Act, sets a salmon rebuilding goal. In the fifty years since the construction of the main-stem dams the annual spawning run has plummeted to 2.5 million spawners. The council proposes to double that number.

1983

Fish scientists blame an ocean-warming event known as El Niño as the cause of alarmingly low returns of adult coho salmon to Northwest coastal rivers.

1986

Snake River coho salmon becomes extinct.

1987

January. The U.S. Fish and Wildlife Service receives a petition to protect the northern spotted owl under the Endangered Species Act. The owl, whose population is dwindling, is considered an indicator species of the condition of old-growth evergreen forests in the Pacific Northwest. Timber harvests on federal forest lands in the range of the spotted owl are criticized as excessive by many professional resource managers as well as environmentalists.

December. The U.S. Fish and Wildlife Service announces that the owl does not merit protection under the Endangered Species Act. Environmentalists prepare to appeal the decision.

1989

Only two sockeye salmon return to spawn in Redfish Lake, Idaho. The Shoshone-Bannock Tribes of Idaho prepare a petition to protect Snake River sockeye salmon under the Endangered Species Act. (The petition is filed the following April.)

1990

June. Oregon Trout, a conservation organization, leads petitioners in filing for protection of four Columbia and Snake River salmon populations that are in steep decline. The annual runs of Snake River spring and summer chinook, once the backbone of the fisheries, dropped from 1.5 million fish in the late 1800s, to 125,000 in the 1950s, to 10,000 in the 1980s.

June. The U.S. Fish and Wildlife Service changes its position to list the northern spotted owl as "threatened" under the Endangered Species Act.

October. A "Salmon Summit" is convened by Oregon Senator Mark Hatfield to formulate a regionally determined salmon-recovery program for the Columbia Basin.

October. The Oregon Rivers Council consults with fisheries scientists to develop an environmentally sound recovery strategy for the salmon. The scientists advise concentrating on protecting and restoring salmon ecosystems rather than on individual species at risk.

1991

March. The Salmon Summit concludes without producing a viable recovery plan for salmon.

March. The American Fisheries Society publishes a report of its endangered species committee, "Pacific Salmon at the Crossroads," documenting a widespread regional decline of salmon. The committee calls for a holistic approach to address all causes of the decline.

May. The Northwest Power Planning Council agrees to take up the effort to develop a regionally supported salmon-recovery strategy.

May. A federal judge halts new timber sales in spotted-owl habitat on National Forest lands until the U.S. Forest Service prepares a spotted-owl protection plan.

October. A group of forest scientists (the "Gang of Four") present a report to Congress outlining management options for the owl and old-growth forests. The options include protection of "key watersheds" that provide habitat for imperiled salmon.

November. The National Marine Fisheries Service proposes listing the three petitioned Snake River chinook stocks as "threatened" and says that the petitioned coho may already be extinct.

December. The Fisheries Service lists Snake River sockeye as "endangered."

1992

March. The U.S. Army Corps of Engineers tests the effects of lowering the reservoirs behind two Snake River dams. Such "drawdowns" are widely advocated by salmon biologists as a way of helping salmon.

September. The Northwest Power Planning Council completes its "Salmon Strategy." The plan updates previous council goals and methods; it outlines measures for rebuilding salmon runs with "no net loss of biodiversity."

1993

March. With new federal timber sales still under injunction, timber employment in Oregon slips by 25 percent from 1988 levels, to 51,600 jobs.

April. President Clinton convenes an old-growth-forest conference in Portland in an attempt to resolve issues over management of the forests and dependent species.

July. Clinton announces a management plan for the forests, developed by a large group of scientists. The plan dramatically reduces timber cutting from 1980s levels, which angers the timber industry, but it fails to ensure protection of substantial quantities of old-growth forest and dependent species, which angers environmentalists.

July. Conservation and fishing groups petition for protection of coho salmon in northern California, Oregon, and Washington. Commercial salmon fishing seasons in the Northwest are generally the poorest on record.

October. Senators Gorton of Washington and Packwood of Oregon join in introducing legislation to amend the Endangered Species Act. Their proposal would weaken many environmental provisions of the law and require consideration of economic impacts before a species could be granted protection.

1994

January. Oregon begins $10 million "Watershed Health" program to involve state agencies and local communities in restoring watersheds and salmon populations.

February. Federal resource-management agencies establish plans for $27 million for watershed restoration projects in Washington, Oregon, and northern California during the 1994 fiscal year. Tens of millions of dollars of additional funding is proposed for future years. Much hope is placed in the practice of "adaptive management"—learning from mistakes and making corrections.

March. The spawning runs of some depleted salmon populations are forecast to be terrible. Perhaps only 200 of the threatened Snake River fall chinook, for example, will return to Idaho, down two-thirds from even the year before. Accordingly, salmon fishing seasons are generally the most restrictive ever. Meanwhile, a federal judge rules that the operation of the Columbia River power system constitutes a jeopardy to salmon under the Endangered Species Act, and he requires the river's operators to consult with him. The crisis enters a new stage of litigation and regulation.

May. Unemployment caused by the ban on coastal fishing for coho and most chinook prompts the Clinton administration to declare coastal counties in Washington, Oregon, and California a federal disaster area. The administration promises nearly $16 million in relief. In Oregon, state officials estimate 2,000 fishermen may be eligible.

June. A "salmon war" thretens as U.S. and Canadian negotiations on salmon harvests fail and Canada imposes a $1,500 fee on American commercial fishing boats passing through British Columbian waters. The Canadians are incensed over U.S. demands to reduce the catch of Snake River wild salmon even as Alaskan fishermen resist limiting their catch of Canadian-bred salmon.

August. About 12,000 young sockeye raised in hatcheries are returned to Idaho's Redfish Lake as part of the program to restore the lake's endangered run. Meanwhile, the National Marine Fisheries Service announces the reclassification of Snake River chinook from threatened to endangered. The move signals the worsening condition of what was once the world's largest run of the biggest salmon.

NOTES

1. Denial and Engagement

But if the courage is lacking: Willis H. Rich, "The Future of the Columbia River Salmon Fisheries," *Stanford Ichthyological Bulletin,* 2 (Dec. 1940): 46.

Jedediah Smith: Lewis A. MacArthur, *Oregon Geographic Names,* 5th ed. (Portland, Ore.: Oregon Historical Society Press, 1982), p. 683; and Nathan Douthit, *A Guide to Oregon South Coast History* (Coos Bay, Ore.: River West Books, 1986): passim.

A billion board feet yielded enough lumber: Actually, one board foot of timber on the tree would yield more than that in dimensional lumber—almost twice as much. (Brian Greber, Oregon State University, personal communication, 8/26/93).

Richard the Lion-Hearted: Compact Edition of the Oxford English Dictionary (Oxford University Press: 1971): 2626.

Water falling into a pool creates a standing wave: T. C. Bjornn and D. W. Reiser, "Habitat Requirements of Salmonids in Streams," *Influences of Forest and Rangeland Management on Salmonid Fishes and their Habitats,* W. R. Meehan, ed. (Washington, D.C.: American Fisheries Society, 1991): 87.

More than three times larger: Connecticut is 4,800 sq. mi.; Oregon's national forest lands are 10,152,000 acres = 15,862 sq. mi. That is 3.3. times the size of Connect-icut. Oregon source: Philip L. Jackson and A. Jon Kimerling, *Atlas of the Pacific Northwest* (Corvallis, Ore.: Oregon State University Press, 1993): 105.

Harvests on federal lands exceeded . . . private lands: Oregon Department of Forestry, "50-year summary of timber harvests in Oregon by owner class, 1941–91," *1991 Annual Report* (Salem, Ore.: Oregon Department of Forestry, 1992): n.p.

Ronald Reagan's quip: Originally reported in the *Sacramento Bee,* March 12, 1966, and cited in Mark Green and Gail MacColl, *There He Goes Again: Ronald Reagan's Reign of Error* (New York: Pantheon, 1983): 101.

On the Alsea River: Alexander R. McLeod, "Journal of a Trapping Expedition, Sum-mer 1826," *Peter Skene Ogden's Snake Country Journal, 1826–27,* K. G. Davies, ed. (London: Hudson's Bay Record Society, 1961): 167.

As Sedell continued his studies: James R. Sedell, et al., "What We Know About Large Trees that Fall into Streams and Rivers," in *From the Forest to the Sea,* Chris Maser et al., eds., USDA General Technical Report PNW-GTR-229, 1988.

Reeves drew an important conclusion: G. H. Reeves, "Distribution Patterns of Fish in the Elk River Basin," *COPE Report* (Newport, Ore.: Oregon State University, COPE Program, Summer 1988): 6.

Aldo Leopold had proposed a "land ethic": Aldo Leopold, *A Sand County Almanac* (New York: Oxford, 1949): 224.

When you look closely at the unholy assault: "The Plowboy Interview: Dave Forman," *Mother Earth News* 91 (Jan.–Feb. 1985): 21.

seventeen state and federal agencies: Charles F. Wilkinson and Daniel Keith Con-ner, "The Law of the Pacific Salmon Fishery," *University of Kansas Law Review* 32 (1983): 61.

Energy planning in the region needed to be redefined: See generally Michael C. Blumm, "The Northwest's Hydroelectric Heritage: Prologue to the Pacific Northwest Elec-tric Power Planning and Conservation Act," *Washington Law Review* 58 (1983): 175–244.

more than 1750 percent: Bruce Brown, *Mountain in the Clouds* (New York: Simon and Schuster, 1982): 191, 209.

This vast water power: Cited in Gus Norwood, *Columbia River Power for the People* (Portland, Ore.: Bonneville Power Administration, 1981): 26.

"The Grand Coulee Dam": Words and music by Woody Guthrie; copyright ©1958 (renewed), 1963 (renewed), and 1976 by Ludlow Music, Inc., New York, NY. Used by permission.

eighteen dams: Depending on whether dams on Idaho's Clearwater River and in Canada are also counted, the final tally for the Columbia-Snake Basin can be 19 or more. The most-cited count for the Columbia and Snake main stem is 18. For example, see Northwest Power Planning Council, *1987 Columbia River Basin Fish and Wildlife Program* (Portland, Ore.: NPPC, 1987): 68–69.

greatest producer of hydropower: Kai N. Lee, "The Columbia River Basin: Experimenting with Sustainability," *Environment* 31:6 (July/August 1989): 8.

more than a third of all the salmon habitat: Northwest Power Planning Council, *Strategy for Salmon,* vol. 1 (Portland, Ore.: NPPC, 1992): 9.

"to protect, mitigate, and enhance: Pacific Northwest Electric Power Planning and Conservation Act,* Public Law 96-501, 16 U.S. Code, at 2.(6).

2. Conflict

Living wild species: John D. Dingell, foreword to *The Endangered Species Act: A Guide to Its Protections and Implementation,* by Daniel J. Rohlf (Stanford, Cal.: Stanford Environmental Law Society, 1989): 1.

But no one knew for sure: See, for example, R. L. Burgner, "Some Features of Ocean Migrations and Timing of Pacific Salmon," *Salmonid Ecosystems of the North Pacific,* W. McNeil and D. Himsworth, eds. (Corvallis, Ore.: Oregon State University Press, 1980): passim.

As the American translator: W. H. Fry, trans., *A Complete Treatise on Artificial Fish-Breeding* (New York: D. Appleton and Co., 1854): ix. The titles of the French source works translated and edited by Fry are not cited.

Congress appropriated $15,000: J. L. McHugh, "Trends in fishery research," in *A Century of Fisheries in North America,* Norman G. Benson, ed. (Washington, D.C.: American Fisheries Society, 1970): 27.

Grand Coulee Dam blocked: Columbia Basin Fish and Wildlife Authority, *Review of the*

History, Development, and Management of Anadromous Fish Production Facilities in the Columbia River Basin (Portland, Ore.: CBFWA, Dec. 1988 draft): 11.

construction or modernization of forty hatcheries: Laura Berg, "Where have all the salmon gone?" *Wana Chinook Tymoo:* 1–2 (1993): 16; published by the Columbia River Inter-Tribal Fish Commission.

"If we can't determine: Bill Bakke, "A Sportsman's View of Hatchery Policy," in *Columbia River Salmon and Steelhead,* Ernest Schwiebert, ed. (Washington, D.C.: American Fisheries Society, 1977): 96–97.

"It appears that the ultimate regulation: Bill Bakke, "A Historical Perspective on the Importance of Wild Salmonid Management in the Northwest," in *Proceedings of the Wild Salmon and Trout Conference, March, 11–12, 1983* (Seattle: Washington Environmental Foundation, 1983): 12–13.

Salmonid fishes had inhabited the Northwest: William G. Pearcy, *Ocean Ecology of North Pacific Salmonids* (Seattle: University of Washington, 1992): 6ff. Information about the current species' divergence from their ancestors, at about 5 million years ago, comes from examination of mitochondrial DNA (Douglas Markle, personal communication, 3 May 1994). Markle is an ichthyologist at Oregon State University.

Salmon conservation, Rich had written: Willis H. Rich, "Local Populations and Migration in Relation to the Conservation of Pacific Salmon in the Western States and Alaska," contribution no. 1 (Salem, Ore.: Fish Commission of Oregon, 1939). The article is a reprint from *The Migration and Conservation of Salmon,* Pub. 8 (Lancaster, Pa.: AAAS, 1939): 49ff.

Hatchery fish, moreover, didn't simply replace: Michael L. Goodman, "Preserving the Genetic Diversity of Salmonid Stocks: A Call for Federal Regulation of Hatchery Programs," *Environmental Law* 20 (1990): 123ff.

Bakke requested a formal statement: Bill M. Bakke, writing as Executive Director, Oregon Trout; letter to Don Goddard [*sic*], Oregon Council Member, March 25, 1986.

"The only answer anyone can give: E. O. Wilson, *The Diversity of Life* (Cambridge, MA.: Harvard/Belknap, 1992). Quoted material cited by Charles E. Little, "Books for the Wilderness," in *Wilderness* (Winter 1992): 35.

"The dark side of men: Robert Bly, *Iron John* (New York: Addison-Wesley, 1990): x.

"The extinction of a species: Gary Snyder, *The Practice of the Wild* (San Francisco: North Point, 1990): 179.

The Pacific Yew: Hal Hartzell, Jr., *The Yew Tree* (Eugene, Ore.: Hulogosi, 1991): passim.

"They are potential resources: H.R. 412, 93rd Cong., 1st Sess. 4–5 (1973).

One-third of pharmaceutical prescriptions: Natural Resources Defense Council, "Summary of testimony" of Dr. Thomas Eisner, Director, Cornell Institute for Research and Chemical Ecology, before Merchant Marine and Fisheries Subcommittee, Nov. 9, 1993.

Reeves advocated "integrated management": G. H. Reeves, letter to Sen. Bob Packwood, June 26, 1990, reprinted in *Piscatorial Press* (Sept. 1990): 8–9. The publication is the newsletter of the Oregon chapter, American Fisheries Society.

"They are fighting in the name of: Mark O. Hatfield, *Not Quite So Simple* (New York: Harper, 1968): 155.

"Our material possessions, our wisdom: Mark O. Hatfield, "Can a Christian Be a Politician?" *His,* 28 (October 1967): 4.

"Power and prestige could not be: Mark O. Hatfield, *Between a Rock and a Hard Place* (Waco, Tx.: Word, Inc., 1976): 26.

"contemplation and the preservation of nature": Ibid.: 194.

In a letter to Oregonians: Cited in Mark O. Hatfield, "Process Abused by Certain Individuals and Groups," *Wild Oregon* (Fall 1988): 23.

"The issue will come right down: Paul Koberstein, "Hatfield Cites Crisis in Salmon Runs," *Oregonian,* 1 July 1990: C–1.

"Nothing can stop the growth: Livingston Stone, "A National Salmon Park," *Transactions of the American Fisheries Society* (1892): 152, 160.

"I believe it is especially critical: Ross L. Leffler, "The Program of the U.S. Fish and Wildlife Service for the Anadromous Fishes of the Columbia River," *Bulletin,* Oregon State Game Commission (Oct. 1959): 6–7.

"We don't want that law circumvented": In a telephone conversation with the author (28 March 1994), Jim Jura said that he felt that Bakke misunderstood the BPA's position. Jura said that the BPA did not enter the summit discussions with the intent of "short-circuiting" the Fisheries Service's Endangered Species Act process.

3. Crisis

All right then: D. H. Lawrence, "The Spirit of Place," in *Studies in Classic American Literature* (1923, rpt. New York: Doubleday, 1953): 13.

"Battle on for wild fish: Joan Laatz, "Battle On for Wild Fish, Group Tells NW Summit," *Oregonian,* Nov. 21, 1990: D–1, 12.

"species" also meant: 16 U.S.C. sec. 1532 (16).

Washington's letter: Cited in *Voyages of the "Columbia" to the Northwest Coast, 1787–1790 and 1790–93,* Frederic W. Howay, Ed. (Boston: Massachusetts Historical Society, 1941): 441.

according to fifth mate John Boit: John Boit, *Log of the Second Voyage of the "Columbia,"* Howay, ed., op. cit.: 399.

Lewis and Clark published a first account: Samuel L. Mitchell, *A Discourse on the Character and Services of Thomas Jefferson* (New York: Lyceum of Natural History, 1826): 29. Cited in James P. Ronda, *Astoria and Empire* (Lincoln, Neb.: University of Nebraska Press, 1990): 31.

Astor may well have seen it: Ronda, op. cit.: 31.

The early canning techniques: See generally, Courtland L. Smith, *Salmon Fishers of the Columbia* (Corvallis, Ore.: Oregon State University Press, 1979). Also, R. D. Hume, *Salmon of the Pacific Coast* (n.p., 1893): passim.

The pack increased rapidly: Anthony Netboy, *The Columbia River Salmon and Steelhead Trout: Their Fight for Survival* (Seattle: University of Washington, 1980): 21.

Individual canneries entered into agreements: L. W. Casaday, "Labor Unrest and the Labor Movement in the Salmon Industry of the Pacific Coast" (Ph.D. diss., University of California at Berkeley, 1938): 144–45.

"If the cannery men do not pay: "The Fishermen's Side of the Case," *Daily Astorian,* 3 April 1896: 1.

"There are two ideas of government: Cited in *Harvey Wasserman's History of the United States* (New York: Harper, 1972): 93.

Bouquet of flowers: "Heavy Catch of Royal Chinooks," *Daily Astorian,* 23 June 1896: 1.

"Everybody was happy yesterday: Ibid.

"The vast volume of fresh water": "Fish and fisheries," *Morning Oregonian,* 5 June 1896: 8.

Mont Hawthorne remembered: Martha Ferguson McKeown, *The Trail Led North: Mont Hawthorne's Story* (New York: Macmillan, 1948): 17.

"The town stunk just awful": Ibid.: 13.

Its average annual streamflow: Kai N. Lee, "The Columbia River Basin: Experimenting with Sustainability" *Environment* (July/Aug 1989): 7. Lee cites an average streamflow of 141 million acre-feet, which is probably the amount measured at The Dalles, Ore.

That amount was more than enough: Bonneville Power Administration, et al., *The Columbia River System: The Inside Story* (Portland, Ore.: BPA, 1991): 4.

seven billion gallons: The exact number is 7,368,493,151 gallons per hour. Source: Roger Schiewe, Bonneville Power Administration, memo to author, Feb. 28, 1994. The computation for bathtubs is based on an average bathtub capacity of 35 gallons.

In 1990 . . . the value of exports and imports: The Great Waterway: The Columbia-Snake River System, Marine Publishing, Inc., Seattle, Wash., 1992.

payments were on the order of a half-billion dollars: BPA payments to the Treasury in 1992 were $678 million. Source: "Planning for the Future: BPA's 1993 Rate Case Proposal," *BPA Issue Alert* (Jan. 1993).

On the floor of the Senate: Congressional Record, 21 March 1991: S–3918.

The American Fisheries Society published: Willa Nehlsen, Jack E. Williams, and James A. Lichatowich, "Pacific Salmon at the Crossroads: Stocks at Risk from California, Oregon, Idaho, and Washington," *Fisheries* (March–April 1991): 4–21.

ranches in Oregon, Idaho, Washington: Atlas of the Pacific Northwest: 102. These are state totals for 1987.

The text of the proposed ruling: Federal Register (April 5, 1991): 14055–66.

an opinion piece in the Oregonian: Michael C. Blumm, "Higher BPA fish flow insufficient for salmon," *Oregonian,* 14 March 1991: B–7.

4. Questions of Values

Republicans believed that: Daniel Kemmis, *Community and the Politics of Place* (Norman, Okla.: University of Oklahoma Press, 1990): 15.

In a long valley: Inland Empire Waterways Association, *Yours Is the Land* (Walla Walla, Wash.: Inland Empire W. A., 1952): 12.

Andy Kerr had been snapping: Source: position paper of the Oregon Natural Resources Council, *Threatened and Endangered Columbia River Salmon,* Oct. 15, 1990.

the region's aluminum producers: Letter to the author, July 15, 1993. John Carr noted that "Columbia-based aluminum producers consume about 13 percent of the region's electricity." Andy Kerr's argument for 20 percent specified aluminum producers *in the region,* presumably including ones in northern Washington and Montana.

they paid less than: Jim Lazar, "Electric Power Resource Evaluation for Improved Fish Migration," *Report to Pacific States Marine Fisheries Commission* (Jan. 31, 1991): B–3.

The journalist Richard Neuberger: Richard. L. Neuberger, *Our Promised Land* (1938: reprint, Moscow, Id.: University of Idaho Press, 1989): 92–93.

Kamiakin said: Click Relander, *The Yakimas* (Yakima, Wash.: Yakima Tribal Council, 1955): 14.

Traditionally, among the coast Salish peoples: Pamela T. Amoss, "The Fish God Gave Us: The First Salmon Ceremony Revived," Arctic Anthropolgy 24:1, 1987: 57.

eighteen million pounds: J. A. Craig and R. L. Hacker, "The History and Development of the Fisheries of the Columbia River," *Bulletin of the U.S. Bureau of Fisheries* 32 (1940): 133–216.

Schmitten issued a kind of institutional apology: Schmitten's comments quoted in *Clearing Up* (June 7, 1991): 10.

Bakke had publicly argued the folly: Bill Bakke, "Wild Coho's Decline," *Riverkeeper* (Winter 1991). The remarks were reprinted in Oregon Trout's newsletter.

The council reduced the recommended flows: Michael C. Blumm, "Higher BPA Fish Flow Insufficient for Salmon," *Oregonian,* 14 March 1991: B–7. Also Blumm's "Saving Idaho's Salmon: A History of Failure and a Dubious Future," *Idaho Law Review* 28 (1991–92): 668–713.

"*Politics cannot save:* Daniel J. Rohlf, letter to Northwest Power Planning Council, Aug. 8, 1991.

Al Wright said: Letter to Northwest Power Planning Council, Aug. 9, 1991.

Target 16: Ed Chaney, *Proposed Amendments: Northwest Power Planning Council Columbia River Basin Fish and Wildlife Program* (Eagle, Id.: Northwest Reservation Information Center, 1991): 8.

Sims and Ossiander: C. W. Sims and F. J. Ossiander, "Migration of Juvenile Chinook Salmon and Steelhead in the Snake River, from 1973 to 1979: A Research Summary," a report to the U.S. Army Corps of Engineers. (Portland, Ore.: National Marine Fisheries Service, 1981).

significant errors were found in the report: Cleveland Steward, "An Assessment of Chinook Salmon Smolt Migration Data Used in the Sims and Ossiander Flow-Survival Relationship," draft report, Sept. 8, 1992.

"*a golden era:* Paul Koberstein, "Acerbic Power Council Leader Girds for Salmon Fight," *Oregonian,* 12 Nov. 1991: C–1.

These areas were designed: Jack Ward Thomas, et al., *A Conservation Strategy for the Northern Spotted Owl* (Portland, Ore.: USDA Forest Service, 1991): 30ff.

habitat rehabilitation, no matter how good, was a poor substitute: G. H. Reeves, et al., "Rehabilitating and Modifying Stream Habitats," in *Influences of Forest and Rangeland Management on Salmonid Fishes and their Habitats.* (Washington, D.C.: American Fisheries Society), 1991, Special Publication 19: 519–557.

the generalized deterioration of river systems: Bob Doppelt, et al., *Entering the Watershed* (Eugene, Ore.: Pacific Rivers Council, 1993): viii.

the report began to circulate in Washington: K. Norman Johnson, et al., *Alternatives for Management of Late Successional Forests of the Pacific Northwest,* Report to Congress, Oct. 8.

an agency lawyer had concluded: National Marine Fisheries Service, *Summary of Workshop: Biological Basis for Listing Species or Other Taxa of Salmonids Pursuant to the Endangered Species Act of 1973.* (Seattle: NMFS, 1978): 7. The lawyer was Joan L. MacKenzie, NOAA General Counsel, Seattle.

the Fisheries Service said certain questions: Robin S. Waples, *Definition of "Species" Under the Endangered Species Act: Application to Pacific Salmon.* NOAA Tech. Mem. NMFS F/NWC-194, March 1991: vi.

5. Hope and Dread

at a conference: Gary Snyder, *The Practice of the Wild* (San Francisco: North Point, 1990): 39.

Tree-worship is: Sir James George Frazier, *The Golden Bough* (1922; reprint New York: Macmillan, 1963): 127–8.

The rebuilding program: Bonneville Power Administration, *Fact Sheet No. 4: Snake River Sockeye Salmon Sawtooth Valley Project* (Portland, Ore.: BPA, 1992).

The General Accounting Office reported: General Accounting Office, *Endangered Species Act: Types and Number of Implementing Actions,* (Washington, D.C.: GAO, 1992).

No fish species: Ibid., chart: 38.

The Inspector General: "Agency Fails to Protect Endangered Species," *New York Times News Service,* 25 Oct. 1990.

Woodrow Wilson Bridge: Source for comparison: Michael Bean, Environmental Defense Fund, Washington, D.C. See "Highway Aid up for Area Projects," *Washington Post,* 18 Nov. 1991: B–1, 23.

costs of past actions: See General Accounting Office, *Endangered Species: Past Actions Taken to Assist Columbia River Salmon* (Washington, D.C.: GAO, 1992), GAO/RCED–92–173BR.

Jeaudoin and his companion: Alexander R. McLeod, "Journal of a Trapping Expedition, Summer 1826," *Peter Skene Ogden's Snake Country Journal, 1826–27,* K. G. Davies, ed. (London Hudson's Bay Record Society, 1961): 167.

more than the total annual number: See generally Oregon Department of Fish and Wildlife, *Contribution to Fisheries for Oregon Coastal Coho and Chinook Stocks* (Portland, Ore.: ODFW, Dec. 1992).

some pioneering watershed-improvement work: Examples of such work were rare in those days. Others included efforts in Washington, generally under the terms of a novel state program called the Timber, Fish, and Wildlife Agreement, and particularly on the Chehalis River; and in California on the Mattole River.

a Republican was likely to follow him: One did not; instead Democrat Mike Lowry was elected.

The professors believed: Joel R. Hamilton, Michael Martin, and Ken Casavant, *Lower Snake River Reservoir Drawdown on Barge Transportation: Some Observations* (Corvallis, Ore.: Oregon State University Extension Service 1992).

20 to 30 percent of the natural flows: D. W. Chapman, "Snake River Habitat Issues and Stock Status," transcript of talk to Columbia River Alliance, May 29, 1991.

elephant and rhinoceros remark: Sources and dates of comments are Lujan: *Oregonian,* 28 Oct. 1992: A–1; Jamison: *Oregonian,* 24 Sept. 1992: D–2; Packwood (1): *Oregonian,* 17 May 1992: C–1; Packwood (2): *Oregonian,* 26 Aug. 1992; Bush: Eugene *Register-Guard,* 15 Sept. 1992: A–1; Perot; *Oregonian* 6 July 1992: B–1.

fewer than one percent of development: Paul L. Angermeier and Jack E. Williams, "Conservation of Imperiled Species and Reauthorization of the Endangered Species Act of 1973," *Fisheries* 18 (July 1993): 37.

represented at no charge by the Mountain States Legal: Kathie Durbin, "Lands Coalition Leads Fight for Timber Jobs," *Oregonian,* 27 Jan. 1992: B–1.

the installment "Who's Endangered Next?": portions of this "town hall" program (March 1, 1992) are quoted with the permission of KATU-TV, Portland, Oregon.

much-discussed salmon strategy: Northwest Power Planning Council, *Columbia Basin Fish and Wildlife Program: Strategy for Salmon, Vol. 1* (Portland, Ore.: NPPC, 1992).

"no avoidable . . . losses of genetic diversity": See Larry Riggs, *Principles for Genetic Conservation and Production Quality,* report to Northwest Power Planning Council, March 1990.

The council's call for an 85,000-cubic-feet-per-second flow: In a letter to the author, 4 April 1994, law professor Michael Blumm noted that this figure was approximately what would have been achieved under the 1992 Water Budget. This aspect of the council's 1991 program amendment was "just an effort to make good on its 1982 promises," Blumm pointed out.

a precipitous loss in income: Hans Radtke, *Economic Contribution of Salmon to Oregon's Coastal Communities* (Newport, Ore.: Oregon Coastal Zone Management Association, 1992).

Fifteen inches of precipitation: Philip L. Jackson and A. Jon Kimerling, *Atlas of the Pacific Northwest,* (Corvallis, Ore.: Oregon State University Press, 1993): 52–4.

Chief Joseph: See generally *Northwestern Tribes in Exile: Modoc, Nez Perce, and Palous Removal to the Indian Territory,* Clifford E. Trafzer, ed. (Sacramento: Sierra Oaks, 1987).

seven hundred Indians were awaiting: Confederated Tribes of the Umatilla Indian Reservation, *Umatilla River Subbasin: Salmon and Steelhead Production Plan* (Portland, Ore.: Northwest Power Planning Council, 1990): 43.

a campaign to throw open the Umatilla reservation: Gordon Macnab, *A Century of News and People in the East Oregonian, 1875–1975* (Pendleton, Ore.: East Oregonian Publishing Co., 1975): 77–78.

treaty rights to fish on the Columbia: See generally Fay G. Cohen, *Treaties on Trial* (Seattle: University of Washington Press, 1986).

The hatcheries had helped spur the decline: John Platt and Doug Dompier, "A History of Federal Fish Management in the Columbia and Snake River Basins," *CRITFC News,* July 1990: 9–11.

6. A Common Fate

"There is no final ecological truth: Jack Ward Thomas, "Wildlife in Old-Growth Forests," *Forest Watch* (Jan.–Feb. 1992): 15.

"I have come to believe: Albert Gore, *Earth in the Balance: Ecology and the Human Spirit* (Boston: Houghton Mifflin, 1992).

"Babbitt sounded themes that environmentalists liked: Associated Press, "Interior nominee: Bush mishandled timber crisis" Eugene *Register-Guard,* 20 Jan. 1993: B–2.

more than double the road miles: Interstate highways total 42,795 miles. *World Book Encyclopedia,* 1992 ed., vol. 16: 357.

scientific assessment team's report: Jack Ward Thomas, et al., *Viability Assessments and Management Considerations for Species Associated with Late-Successional and Old-Growth Forests of the Pacific Northwest* (Portland, Ore.: USDA Forest Service, 1993).

"This plan offers: Kathie Durbin, "Clinton Aims to End Logjam, *Oregonian* 2 July 1993: A–1.

"All of the alternatives: U.S. Forest Service and Bureau of Land Management, *Draft Supplemental Environmental Impact Statement on Management of Habitat . . . within the Range of the Northern Spotted Owl* (Portland, Ore.: USDA Forest Service, 1993): S–8.

"We advocate an approach: Jack Ward Thomas, et al., *Forest Ecocsystem Management* (Portland, Ore.: USDA Forest Service, 1993): Appendix V–J.

the boldest recommendation: Ibid.: V–29.

"Not only is he putting: Harry Esteve, "Both sides slam forest plan," *Register-Guard,* 2 July 1993: A–1.

"science must be the cornerstone: Kathie Durbin, "April forest summit raises expectations," *Oregonian,* 11 March 1993: A–1.

"the ratio of common sense: Hatfield's comment cited in "Inadequate forest plan," *Register-Guard,* 2 July 1993: A–12.

more money from political action committees: Western Ancient Forest Campaign and U.S. Public Interest Research Group, *American Taxpayers' Forest Destroyed: Members of Congress Reap the Benefits* (Portland, Ore.: Sept. 1993): 4. Hatfield's PAC contributions in 1990 totaled $87,786, according to the report.

"Ten years ago: Randal O'Toole, *Forest Watch,* April 1992: 3.

"With a $4 trillion debt": Randal O'Toole, "Bringing Home the Bacon: Pork, Congress and the Environment," *Forest Watch* (January 1993): S–4.

Judge Malcolm Marsh scornfully questioned: Marsh's comments quoted in "Court Rules for Columbia River Fishermen in Endangered Species Act Lawsuit," *PCFFA Friday* (16 April 1993): 8. The publication is the newsletter of the Pacific Coast Federation of Fishermen's Associations, based in Sausalito, California.

rates had skyrocketed: K. C. Golden, "New BPA Plan a Ploy to Return to Old Ways" *Oregonian,* 4 Feb. 1994: B–9.

"remove barriers to efficiency: as noted in *BPA Journal,* August 1993.

"The total returns of coho: John Coon, "Coho Salmon Abundance Continues Alarming Decline (Pacific Fishery Management Council) *Council News,* 15 Nov. 1993: 1.

Bottom saw in Marsh: Daniel Bottom, *The Early Fish Culture Movement in America.* Oregon Department of Fish and Wildlife, 1993. Unpublished manuscript.

Williams recommended new goals: Jack E. Williams, "Restoring Watershed Health on Federal Lands," *Trout* (Summer 1993): 18–21.

One Forest Service law officer: Associated Press, "Allegations Prompt Forest Service Reorganization," *Register-Guard,* 17 Nov. 1993: D–4.

The association said in its "vision statement": Association of Forest Service Employees for Environmental Ethics, organizational brochure, 1993.

"Quality of life" values: See, for example, Associated Press, "Quality of Life Draws Newcomers," *Register-Guard,* 25 Jan. 1994: C–4.

Epilogue

We could all just leave: Freeman House, *Elements of Recovery* (Petrolia, Calif.: Mattole Restoration Council, 1989): 2.

"it falls short ecologically: Anonymous, "Environmentalists to Challenge Forest Plan, *Oregonian,* 20 April 1994: B–1.

Instead of looking for what can be done: U.S. Dist. Court, *Idaho Dept. of Fish and Game v. National Marine Fisheries Service,* 28 March 1994: 36.

The apparent strategy is very simple: National Audubon Society, "Property Rights and the Environment," Sept. 1993.

" 'Resource problems' aren't: Downie's comments, and those of Colum Coyne, following, were made to the author during interviews conducted for a videotape produced by Oregon Sea Grant and are used here with permission.

wrote a team of Oregon researchers: Steven E. Daniels, et al. *Managing Ecosystems and Social Conflict,* unpublished report, Oregon State University College of Forestry, 5 March 1993: 10.

"strong incentives for conservation: Michael J. Bean, "Fortify the act," *National Parks* 23, May/June 1993. Cited in Terry L. Anderson and Jody J. Olsen, "Positive Incentives for Saving Endangered Species," in Wendy Hudson, ed. *Building Economic Incentives into the Endangered Species Act* (Washington, D.C.: Defenders of Wildlife, 1993): 109.

Appendix: A Chronology of an Ecosystem Crisis

43 million pounds: Anthony Netboy, *The Columbia River Salmon and Steelhead Trout* (Seattle: University of Washington Press, 1980): 21.

fishwheels take forty to fifty tons: Netboy: 28.

legislature bans fishwheels: Netboy: 26.

"Contrary to the impression: Frank T. Bell, "Guarding the Columbia's Silver Horde," *Nature Magazine,* January 1937: 46.

Arthur Newton Pack . . . declares: Richard L. Neuberger, *Our Promised Land* (1938, rpt. Moscow, Idaho: University of Idaho, 1989): 128.

Grand Coulee Dam: Netboy: 59.

Paul Needham . . . publicly denounces: Netboy: 83.

The annual runs: Snake River Recovery Team, Draft plan: II–10.

INDEX